Hypermasculinities in the Contemporary Novel

Contemporary American Literature
Series Editor: Bob Batchelor

Gatsby: The Cultural History of the Great American Novel, by Bob Batchelor, 2013.
Michael Chabon's America: Magical Words, Secret Worlds, and Sacred Spaces, edited by
  Jesse Kavadlo and Bob Batchelor, 2014.
*Hypermasculinities in the Contemporary Novel: Cormac McCarthy, Toni Morrison, and
  James Baldwin*, by Josef Benson, 2014.

Hypermasculinities in the Contemporary Novel

Cormac McCarthy, Toni Morrison, and James Baldwin

Josef Benson

ROWMAN & LITTLEFIELD
Lanham • Boulder • New York • Toronto • Plymouth, UK

Published by Rowman & Littlefield
4501 Forbes Boulevard, Suite 200, Lanham, Maryland 20706
www.rowman.com

10 Thornbury Road, Plymouth PL6 7PP, United Kingdom

British Library Cataloguing in Publication Information Available

Library of Congress Cataloging-in-Publication Data

Benson, Josef, 1974– author.
Hypermasculinities in the contemporary novel : Cormac McCarthy, Toni Morrison, and James Baldwin / by Josef Benson.
pages cm. – (Contemporary American Literature)
Includes bibliographical references and index.
ISBN 978-1-4422-3760-5 (cloth : alk. paper) – ISBN 978-1-4422-3761-2 (ebook)
1. American fiction–20th century–History and criticism. 2. Masculinity in literature. 3. Men in literature. 4. McCarthy, Cormac, 1933—Criticism and interpretation. 5. Morrison, Toni–Criticism and interpretation. 6. Baldwin, James, 1924–1987–Criticism and interpretation. I. Title.
PS374.M37B46 2014
813'.509353–dc32
2014010281

Printed in the United States of America

For my son, Lazarus Jude Benson, who was present as I wrote, both literally and figuratively.

Contents

Acknowledgments

Writing is a collaborative process. Writing and publishing a book, not unlike life itself, is a downright team effort. With that in mind, I'd like to thank a cadre of folks who've helped me with this book and with life itself. They are the following: Jose Aparicio, Brenda Arnett, Bob Batchelor, Barry Benson, Cory Benson, Mark Benson, Sally Benson, Lawrence Broer, Katy Conard, Lauren Cook, Lee Davidson, Elizabeth Hirsh, Gary Lemons, Carole Reese, Gary Reese, Salvador Torres Martinez, Matt McBride, Jay Mccroy, Susan Mooney, Clancy Parks, Renj Reichert, Stephen Ryan, Phillip Sipiora, and Scott Stormzand.

Introduction

*We can also recognize failure as a way of refusing to acquiesce to dominant
logics of power and discipline and as a form of critique.*

—Judith Halberstam [1]

AMERICAN HYPERMASCULINITIES

African American and white hypermasculinities exist as seductive stereotypes. There remains a certain amount of power and intimidation over other
men in projecting oneself as hypermasculine and hypersexual, but this power
simultaneously diminishes one's humanity and compromises one's intellectual capability in the eyes of others. Further, valuing hypermasculinity and its
attendant qualities primes men and women as agents for mass destruction on
a global scale, possibly leading to the extinction of the human race. Current
American hypermasculinities predicated on violence, recklessness, racism,
sexism, homophobia, and xenophobia have vitiated Americans' notions of
the masculine self, causing widespread destruction. Masculine identity has
devolved into what Donald K. Meisenheimer Jr. calls a "phallicization, a
calcification that makes life itself impossible."[2] Paradoxically, engaging in
any self-preserving act marks the hypermasculine man as a sissy. Marilyn C.
Wesley points out that as of 1978 "the United States was, without even a
close contender, the most violent industrialized nation in the world."[3] This
violence stems from ideologies privileging the sword over the pen, brute
strength over intellect, and men over women.

Hypermasculinities posits a narrative of American hypermasculinity that
courses through Cormac McCarthy's novels *Blood Meridian* (1985) and *All
the Pretty Horses* (1992), as well as Toni Morrison's *Song of Solomon* (1977)
and James Baldwin's *Another Country* (1960). Michael S. Kimmel defines

hypermasculinity as a form of American masculinity based on racism, sexism, and homophobia and marked by violent rapaciousness.[4] Riki Wilchins equates hypermasculinity with "emotional toughness and sexual virility."[5] Charles P. Toombs notes, "super-masculinity" stems from "the dominant culture's superficial and inauthentic definitions of manhood and masculinity," resulting in "a lack of tolerance, respect, or acceptance of difference."[6] I employ the umbrella term "hypermasculinity" in referring to and critiquing a multitude of hypermasculine images in these texts embodied in the frontiersman, the cowboy, and the primarily urban black man. My selected authors explore American masculinities that are frequently excrescent and *hyper*masculine, inviting readings, such as mine, that identify and critique the forces that lead to the hypermasculine performances of the characters as well as the sometimes deadly ramifications of the performances themselves. In part, this study attempts to locate and redefine positive masculinity as *failure* to perpetuate several different hypermasculinities.

One of my central claims is that selected contemporary African American literary texts suggest that some hypermasculine African American men may exist as direct cultural descendants of white frontiersmen and a particular type of southern rural American white man. Hugh Campbell suggests, "masculinity is, in considerable measure, constructed out of rural masculinity. The 'real man' of many currently hegemonic forms of masculinity is . . . a rural man."[7] The archetype of the American cowboy, reflected in many John Wayne characters, has become to many white men *the* image of a quintessential man. As Meisenheimer argues, "Static both personally and racially, cowboy masculinity [hypermasculinity] thus embodies impulses that are, at base, anti-revolutionary. Obviously a deep-seated contradiction exists in a genre— or gender—which promises 'new consciousness' and universal transformation (change) through a totalized stasis (no change at all)."[8] American hypermasculine rural man sprang from the myth of manifest destiny, which suggested Americans had a divine right to all lands west of the Mississippi to the Pacific Ocean. Villainous men, like the judge from McCarthy's novel *Blood Meridian*, imposed an androcentric code of violence and racial purity on the erstwhile palimpsest of the West. For men interested in capitalizing on their white patriarchal privilege, a willingness to wage violence on anyone not white and male develops in *Blood Meridian* as the definition of hypermasculinity the judge oversees as a self-proclaimed suzerain.

Hollywood cinema then appropriated the mythical figure of the cowboy from dime novels and romantic notions of the frontiersman, presenting him as a masculine icon and answer to America's ambivalence about itself after World War II. A sense of disillusionment pervaded the American psyche after the massive technological death caused by the atom bombs and the Jewish Holocaust proved humanity capable of destroying itself. Hollywood capitalized on America's uncertainty, offering a pre–World War II vision of the world rooted in simple, romantic notions of the old West. American boys, like the character John Grady Cole in McCarthy's *All the Pretty Horses*, internalized not only the mythical cowboy figure but also the historically revised West from which he supposedly arose. Toward the end of the nineteenth century, the American South replaced the West as the symbolic space occupied by men who embodied prevailing definitions of hypermasculinity. Consequently, the baser qualities of the frontiersman, including his penchant for violence, sexism, racism, and recklessness, transformed into a (hyper)masculinity embraced by many southern rural American men. The power of this southern rural man depended on his ability to maintain white supremacy in a region where his wealth depended on the systematic oppression and enslavement of African Americans.

As slavery unraveled, the rural man's ability to maintain his power and hypermasculinity proved threatened. In an effort to maintain his white patriarchal privilege in the postbellum South, he constructed the myth of the black rapist as an excuse for the brutal killing of African American men. In creating the myth, this white southern man inadvertently created a figure more hypermasculine than himself, imputing to the black male body all his hidden desires and taboos. Scores of black men subsequently embraced the myth of the black rapist, as well as the baser patriarchal aspects of white southern male power, such as violence, sexism, and materialism. In Morrison's novel *Song of Solomon*, the characters Guitar and Macon Dead II embody violent and materialistic identities that parody whiteness. Guitar and his group, the Seven Days, literally copy white violence enacted on black people by victimizing a white person in the exact manner that a black person was victimized. Macon Dead II exploits his own community as a slumlord, mimicking rigid white capitalists.

A variant of black hypermasculinity became the perfect American hypermasculinity exemplified in the mythical figure of Staggerlee, a black man who shot and killed another black man in cold blood for pilfering his Stetson hat. The Stetson *cowboy* hat evokes the cowboy hypermasculinity from which black hypermasculinity emerged. As Michael K. Johnson notes, "Frontier is an alien word to black America both because blacks were excluded from participation in frontier opportunities and because the role African Americans have played in the history of the American West has been erased. In the wake of the Civil War, movement westward marked the first mass migration by free African Americans."[9] According to Johnson, masking the fact that American frontier masculinity developed among whites *and* blacks initially ensured the exclusion of blacks in definitions of U.S. masculinity. Johnson points out that African American authors such as Nat Love, Oscar Micheaux, and Pauline Hopkins writing about black men on the frontier "often [repeat] problematic elements of the dominant culture's masculine ideal without much critical self-reflection. Thus, an often violent and patriarchal masculine ideal has remained central to the ways these writers have constructed black manhood."[10] Black authors writing about frontier masculinity, rather than signifying upon white frontier masculinity as a means of resistance, merely mimic it. Henry Louis Gates Jr. says of African American literature, "To name our tradition is to rename each of its antecedents, no matter how pale they might seem. To rename is to revise, and to revise is to Signify."[11] According to Gates, these black writers misemploy the black literary tradition of signification, opting for pastiche rather than parody.

Part of the reason some black men quickly embraced the dominant society's hypermasculine notions of self was to redress their thorough emasculation by white America before, during, and after slavery. Black/cowboy hypermasculinity resulted in large part from white oppression, transforming into a version of blackness used to oppress African Americans. Ultimately, black maleness developed into the very essence of American masculinity by which large numbers of men measure one another. Cornel West points out, "white youth . . . [imitate] and [emulate] black male styles of walking, talking, dressing and gesticulating . . . One irony of our present moment is that just as young black men are murdered, maimed and imprisoned in record numbers, their styles have become disproportionately influential in shaping popular culture."[12] While blackness predicated on violence, homophobia, sexism, and materialism may operate for some as revolutionary redress for hundreds of years of emasculation by whites, it is still the primary justification for white supremacy. This long evolution of African American masculinity has not gone unnoticed by many in the black community; as bell hooks writes,

> Older black males often understand that embracing the cowboy masculinity of patriarchy dooms black men (they've seen the bodies fall down and not get up). They know cowboy culture makes black men kill or be killed by younger black men who are more seduced by the politics of being a gangsta, whether a gangsta academic or a gangsta rapper or a gangsta pimp. It is a seductive invitation to embrace death as the only logic of black male existence.[13]

The American cowboy and the urban African American male function as the two most powerful referents of U.S. hypermasculinity. For the African American male, living up to white notions of cowboy hypermasculinity has resulted in new paradigms of hypermasculinity predicated on blackness, eclipsing the cowboy and functioning as the standard of American masculinity for both blacks and whites. Unfortunately, this new regard for black hypermasculinity, cherished by many black men, resulted in men like Eldridge Cleaver, the minister of information for the Black Panther Party, fulminating against James Baldwin that "Negro homosexuals . . . are outraged because in their sickness they are unable to have a baby by a white man."[14] For the African American man who embraces the status of masculine icon, black homosexuality poses a terrible threat. Cleaver attempted to feminize James Baldwin in order to distance himself from any behavior he felt jeopardized the masculine gains of African American males during the Black Power and Civil Rights Movements. Cleaver and other black militants failed to realize that images of black/cowboy hypermasculinity actually limit black men, reducing them to their bodies and marginalizing them as hyper-sexual fearsome beasts. Further, the privileging of hypermasculinity in the black community alienates black homosexuals, causing men like the charac-ter Rufus Scott in Baldwin's *Another Country* to reject their homosexual desire in favor of an ever more hypermasculine persona, a process that leads to suicide in Scott's case.

U.S. frontier-cowboy-black hypermasculine attributes have grown so un-viable, so egregious in the contemporary world, that some novelistic charac-ters who fail to perpetuate these hypermasculinities can be perceived as more heroic than those who succeed. This reading extends previous critiques of American masculinity and literature by critics such as Leslie A. Fiedler, who argues, "The typical male protagonist of our fiction has been a man on the run, harried into the forest and out to sea, down the river or into combat—anywhere to avoid . . . the confrontation of a man and a woman which leads to the fall to sex, marriage, and responsibility."[15] Fiedler's critique of male flight in early-twentieth-century American literature focuses on flight from heterosexuality, which he sees as a flaw in U.S. literature. My critique of male flight in contemporary U.S. literature focuses on flight from family, community, and the possibility of a feminine masculinity. I champion the possibility of new images of alternative masculine sexualities but critique masculinities predicated on sexism and the eradication of the feminine with-in.

IRONIC FAILED HEROISM

Hypermasculinities argues that some protagonists in postwar American liter-ature fail heroically to perpetuate hypermasculinities endemic to their iden-tities—cowboys in the mid-nineteenth-century American West and mid-twentieth-century Texas, as well as black men in the mid-twentieth-century American Midwest, South, and New York City. The selected protagonists—the kid (Cormac McCarthy, *Blood Meridian*), John Grady Cole (Cormac McCarthy, *All the Pretty Horses*), Milkman Dead (Toni Morrison, *Song of Solomon*), and Rufus Scott (James Baldwin, *Another Country*)—fail to per-petuate hypermasculinity, proving themselves heroic since their failure illus-trates its destructiveness. The heroic failure of these protagonists reflects a continuation of the modernist trend of anti-heroism in American literature. Jesse Matz writes,

Characters in modern novels are not heroes: they are rarely singled out for their superior traits, and they rarely achieve much. If anything, they are worse than normal . . . In the larger scheme of things, there is a long and steep descent from the epic heroes of myth and legend to the *anti-heroes* of modern fiction. The former were far better than average, superior to their environments, and destined for triumph; the latter are weak, disaffected, and passive, undone by circumstance, and lucky to make it through at all.[16]

While modern and contemporary anti-heroes prove decidedly weaker than preceding epic heroes, the former two groups accomplish greater feats of social critique in their failings. In other words, the lack of heroic traits in many modern and contemporary heroes points to the ills of society at large and illuminates a reality hostile to traditional heroism. Matz further notes, "In a way, all modern characters are anti-heroes, because no modern character can connect perfectly to society as a whole . . . Instead, alienation became definitive; character came to be something defined in terms of opposition to society."[17] In this sense, to be heroic in the modern or contemporary world would mean affirming an unjust world. Consequently, for those characters under examination here, failure emerges as a preferred fate from the reader's point of view. For the anti-heroes in this study, failure equals social progression, since hypermasculine success would perpetuate destructive behavior. The anti-hero confronts a society's very moral fabric, questioning its values and failing as the novel's manifestation of protest. Most often the protagonist's failure to live up to a society's demands results from an unconscious choice that causes the character's demise. In this sense, as Stephanie S. Halldorson notes, "the reader and the heroic character are equal in their creation of the hero."[18] The reader supersedes the characters, and even the author, in having the power to locate heroism. The heroism of these characters may exist unknown and unintended by the author and unknown to the characters themselves. Halldorson further points out, "The non-hero or reader is integral to the concept of hero because through listening and incorporation of the narrative it is the non-hero who differentiates between what is heroic and what is not."[19] Because the power to designate heroism lies with the reader, a sense of unintended or ironic heroism may emerge from the narrative through a character possessing no traditionally heroic qualities other than his or her existence within an oppressive society that he or she rejects. Matz writes, "Characters became more isolated, alienated, detached . . . Almost just by being, they were rebels, fighting the system, and they took on the glamour and power always associated with people who do so."[20] These new anti-heroic characters transformed into human beings perhaps more like the readers who have the power to deem them heroic. Halldorson notes, "Readers have the same impulse to do heroic acts as the hero of the fiction but being unable to complete such acts they content themselves that under the same circumstances . . . they would have done the same actions."[21] Often the inability to act heroically stems not from a lack of a superpower such as X-ray vision or great strength but rather from suspicions of prevailing notions of heroism; consequently, non-action or rejection or even self-negation becomes the heroic act with which readers sympathize. The existence of anti-heroes as social criticism ultimately benefits readers most: "Is this not how we create ourselves? Is it through heroic narratives, gone to the brink of destruction only to return with the fictional—even arbitrary—narrative to give community identity to those who will never make such a journey?"[22] Literature provides a sense of shared experience and has the power to effect social change precisely because readers have the power, even the obligation, to vicariously live through the lives of the protagonists, sharing in their success and, more importantly, their failure.

For Eldridge Cleaver, a leading voice in the Black Power Movement, the paradigmatic shift of the American hero reflects the feelings of marginalized populations who have been outraged for centuries by American white power structures:

> What has suddenly happened is that the white race has lost its heroes. Worse, its heroes have been revealed as villains and its greatest heroes as the arch-villains. The new generation of whites, appalled by the sanguine and despicable record carved over the face of the globe by their race in the last five hundred years, are rejecting the panoply of white heroes, whose heroism consisted in erecting the inglorious edifice of colonialism and imperialism; heroes whose careers rested on a system of foreign and domestic exploitation, rooted in the myth of white supremacy and the manifest destiny of the white race.[23]

Cleaver recognizes America's power to identify its own heroes and, like Matz, heralds a shifting cultural landscape where the predatory heroes of old signify obsolete and mistaken values. He also locates the origination of society's ills in the American western frontier: "They recoil in shame from the spectacle of cowboys and pioneers—their heroic forefathers whose exploits filled earlier generations with pride—galloping across a movie screen shooting down Indians like Coke bottles."[24] And also, "The great white statesmen whom school children are taught to revere are revealed as the architects of systems of human exploitation and slavery."[25] Although Cleaver points out the origination of America's hypocrisy and associates it with frontier masculinity, unfortunately he ultimately does nothing to correct the issue and instead embraces his own form of black hypermasculinity, which in turn has become an archetype of American hypermasculinity, even besting southern rural American hypermasculinity.

The ironic failed heroism of the protagonists studied here provides the most important link among the four novels. In each case the protagonist evinces either complete ignorance or, at best, a mere sliver of awareness of his heroic failure to perpetuate destructive hypermasculine behavior in his historic American setting—the 1850s American West, 1950s Texas and Mexico, the 1950s American Midwest and South, and 1950s New York City, respectively.

Blood Meridian revises the nineteenth-century notion of manifest destiny and the gold rush as perhaps not an era of renewal, rebirth, and progress but rather of lawlessness, violence, and moral depravity. Not only is the hypermasculinity of the lawmakers and lawbreakers shrouded in violence shown to be faulty and destructive but so too the whole notion of America as a Garden of Eden. The novel explores how white Americans settled the West by robbing and murdering Native Americans and Mexicans. In *Blood Meridian*, the ineffectual kid fails heroically to construct a masculinity and an identity outside of the textual order of the judge, a sort of hypermasculine suzerain of the western frontier; the kid repudiates the judge's notions that a man must embrace war as his God in order to dance the dance of masculinity. Reading the kid as ironically heroic in his failure indicts the hypermasculine philosophies of the judge and calls into question the violence the book seems to espouse. In no way is the kid a classic hero. Rather, his heroism exists as a direct critique of the judge's destructive philosophies and the hypermasculine order as an emerging system in the West. The judge's unyielding hypermasculine law provides a space where a weak, ineffectual character like the kid can be ironically heroic in his meager rebellion. The kid fails, but not before casting a modest light in the text on the judge and his philosophies.

All the Pretty Horses addresses both an American context and a Mexican one. John Grady's desire to live in Mexico is a reaction to America's newfound postwar industrialization and feminist social changes that threaten his cowboy hypermasculinity. In Mexico, he initially finds a country less developed and consequently less threatening to his manhood. Eventually, he and Rawlins experience a culture of deadly Mexican hypermasculinity that dwarfs their own. John Grady fails to actualize his cowboy fantasy but proves heroic in exposing the danger and destructiveness of the fantasy. He abolishes viable notions of the modern cowboy as a positive figure and thereby erases himself. Like the disappearing figure of the mythic cowboy, at the end of the novel he vanishes into the countryside a failure. But unlike the mythic cowboy, he assumes the role of heroic failure because his narrative contributes to the relinquishment of a destructive male myth.

Song of Solomon takes place both in the North and the South, Ohio and Virginia, during Reconstruction and the Civil Rights and Black Liberation Movements. These eras provide sources of African American hypermasculinities, to wit, materialism, violence, and flight. These sources of black hypermasculinities reflect a preoccupation with white patriarchal power denied African American men since slavery. In *Song of Solomon*, Milkman Dead functions as a black man who has the opportunity to break free from choking black hypermasculinities passed down to him from his father, his oldest friend, and his grandfather. In the end, he fails and arguably flies to Africa, leaving his family and his only hope at real freedom, his aunt Pilate, to die. His figural flying back to Africa may be redemptive in the sense of repeating his great-grandfather Solomon's flight out of oppression, but the fact that he continues a cycle of male flight, or male escape, at the expense of his family and cultural guide renders him a failure. Morrison's final critique of hypermasculinity, specifically male flight, positions Pilate as the failed hero and shifts the emphasis of the novel to the women who represent victims of kinship systems and the incest taboo. The incest in the novel functions as a metaphor for Pilate's philosophy that black identity ought to come from black culture, a notion I refer to as cultural incest. Pilate's positioning as the failed hero of the novel not only helps critique black hypermasculinities but also provides an alternative African American identity based on nonnormative sexualities, oral tradition, and black culture derived from African American history. This alternative black identity, in part based on sexual variance, dovetails with Darieck Scott and other critics' call for a definition of blackness predicated on the repudiation of patriarchal heteronormative whiteness.

Another Country takes place in New York City during the 1940s and 1950s, detailing the plight of an urban African American man struggling to reconcile conflicting sexual identities. Just before the Civil Rights and Black Liberation Movements, Rufus Scott fails to construct a version of self outside of the dominant definition of black masculinity that in the actual contemporary world Norman Mailer described as psychopathic. I argue that in the novel Rufus's death proves heroic as an indictment of the violent pressures of this particular urban black masculinity.

The authors in this study in some cases ruin the lives of their protagonists in order to show that success might be a worse fate, that a repositioning of sexual values and gender is necessary. Deeming the failures of contemporary hypermasculine American characters "heroic" dismantles particular U.S. hypermasculinities, exposing them as unviable constructs in dire need of reevaluation.

AESTHETICS AS CRITIQUE

Many of the aesthetic features of the novels in this study shed light on and often critique notions of hypermasculinity. For instance, in *Blood Meridian* narratological choices and recurring imagery emphasize the judge's destructive power. *All the Pretty Horses* relies on mythical cowboy tropes and conventions to first affirm cowboy masculinity only to ultimately undermine it. The shift in thematic focal points from flight to orality in *Song of Solomon* highlights Morrison's critique of black masculinities as destructive forces for black women. In *Another Country*, the sex scenes, functioning as sites of racial and sexual intersection, reveal how several of the characters contribute to Rufus's deadly hypermasculine identity.

Blood Meridian stresses the power of frontier hypermasculinity by employing an unobtrusive third-person narrator who seems overwhelmed by the awesome presence of the hypermasculine judge; the latter's text-making abilities and verbal virtuosity allow him to hijack the text and emerge as its most dominant force. The lack of textual assertiveness by the narrator clears a path for the judge to dominate the text, forcing the reader to interact with the judge's philosophies and, like the kid, either embrace or reject him. Further, *Blood Meridian*'s recurring images of mutilated children and defiled Christian icons operate as symbols of potential threats to the judge that are destroyed. Images of filial conflicts litter the text, suggesting that the American Southwest during the mid-nineteenth century extirpates family structures and renders young boys and men vulnerable to paternal men such as the judge. The destruction of Christian images and icons, namely that of God the Father and Christ the Son, reflects the judge's philosophy of war and hypermasculinity. The motifs, images, and symbols that threaten the judge's philosophy come under attack.

Much of the style of *All the Pretty Horses*, including its dialogue, slapstick comedy, and physical descriptions of the characters, originates in large part from dime novels and Hollywood Westerns that glorify cowboy hypermasculinity by creating consummate heroes who clearly subscribe to it. The lack of a referent based firmly in reality renders the characters in *All the Pretty Horses* ciphers or nonentities subject to erasure, exposing cowboy hypermasculinity as a destructive social construction rather than a fixed reality. Fantasy and comedic humor, such as slapstick and curt dialogue, work as aesthetic conventions the novel has appropriated from the Western genre. The fantasy, humor, and dialogue position *All the Pretty Horses* among mid-twentieth-century Western narratives and contribute to John Grady's fantasy. Grady, Rawlins, and Blevins give up their adolescent American discourse for a simulacrum of cowboy discourse based on a hypermasculine cowboy myth. With a tenuous grasp on their own identities, the boys must tread lightly lest they inadvertently fall victim to the Mexican power structures capable of erasing people's existences. Mexico has grown into a country of lost identities wherein men try so desperately to live up to a version of hypermasculinity that they lose sight of their own humanity, rendering themselves pawns in violent games of power and materialism.

Song of Solomon employs images and tropes of flight in order to frame an ethical dilemma haunting black families since slavery, namely whether hypermasculine male flight equals freedom or failure. The book suggests oral storytelling as an alternative to flight, through which one might access the past in order to preserve the future. Flight and orality reflect the general focal movement from men to women. Milkman's discovery of Solomon's "heroic" flight or suicide, though bittersweet in that Solomon escaped slavery, emerges as a critique of the male penchant for escaping responsibility through selfish notions of freedom. By contrast, Pilate Dead represents an alternative construction of freedom predicated on cultural healing and communal storytelling that by novel's end Milkman regards as Pilate's way of flying without ever leaving the ground. Elemental to Pilate's being and philosophy of life, the spoken word replaces the written word as the privileged means of cultural sharing and healing. Orality, or communal storytelling of a shared cultural history, replaces flight and the written word as a positive vehicle for blackness, including notions of black masculinity.

In *Another Country*, the sex scenes between Rufus and Leona, Vivaldo and Ida, and Vivaldo and Eric reveal how race informs these characters' sexuality. For instance, during sex with Ida, an African American woman, Vivaldo, an Italian American, imagines himself at first as the groom in an arranged marriage on his wedding night, deflowering a young virgin, and then as some sort of white explorer conquering a savage, untouched land. Later, Vivaldo's sexual experience with Eric confirms Vivaldo's interest in Rufus and that he has invested his homosexual desire in a black body that he simultaneously fears and needs to remain in the closet. Vivaldo's sexual obsession with black bodies exposes his investment in hypersexualized blackness as a means to maintain his white supremacy.

The literary tropes of failure these novelists utilize suggest new strategic possibilities for reenvisioning U.S. masculinity as white heteronormative patriarchal failure. For example, Darieck Scott, bell hooks, and Riki Wilchins argue that African Americans might contribute to a revision and overhaul of U.S. masculinity by employing their history of oppression as a platform for a new vision of sexuality and gender based in part on that very oppression. In this sense, blackness would signify sexual and cultural rebirth rather than a parody of white domination. The very failure of African Americans in measuring up to destructive notions of white masculinities might exist as a new definition of blackness and masculinity for all Americans. Since some black (hyper)masculinities have emerged as defining images of American masculinity, their revision would have far-reaching effects for all Americans.

At heart, this study is an exploration of the tangled images of American hypermasculinities in the selected novels. Much of this work has found its way to scholars of American literature, African Americanists, Queer theorists, and gender theorists, as well as college students of mine; these generous and sometimes incredulous minds continue to be my audience. I want to offer up a way out, a way to, as Wilchins suggests, "nuke the discourse . . . completely undermine it"[26] by championing failure as a healthier strategy than U.S. hegemonic masculine success. I speak from the point of view of a scholar who spent eight years in graduate school studying these issues, and a human being who has never felt comfortable with identity labels, to the point that I reject most of them anyway, however futile that effort might be. As Wilchins further notes, "Identity politics may have permanent problems. Because the concept of identity that underlies it—of *being* one's race or sex or sexual orientation—is itself seriously flawed."[27] I do not wish to speak from any particular gendered, racial, or sexual subject position but rather from the point of view of someone who is constructively angry and perhaps a little scared. In these selected novels, McCarthy, Morrison, and Baldwin offer fictional protagonists who would seriously benefit from more elastic definitions of U.S. masculinity. In delivering this deceptively simple message to the reader, perhaps unwittingly, these characters are martyred by the authors.

NOTES

1. Judith Halberstam, *The Queer Art of Failure* (Durham: Duke University Press, 2011), 88.
2. Donald K. Meisenheimer Jr., "Machining the Man: From Neurasthenia to Psychasthenia in SF and the Genre Western," *Science Fiction Studies* 24, no. 3 (1997): 441–58.
3. Marilyn C. Wesley, *Violent Adventure* (Charlottesville: Virginia University Press, 2003), 1.
4. Michael S. Kimmel, "Masculinity as Homophobia: Fear, Shame, and Silence in the Construction of Gender Identity," in *Feminism and Masculinities*, ed. Peter F. Murphy (Oxford: Oxford University Press, 2004), 191–92.
5. Riki Wilchins, *Queer Theory, Gender Theory: An Instant Primer* (Los Angeles: Alyson, 2004), 114.
6. Charles P. Toombs, "Black-Gay Man Chaos in *Another Country*," in *Re-viewing James Baldwin: Things Not Seen*, ed. D. Quentin Miller (Philadelphia: Temple University Press, 2000), 109–10.
7. Hugh Campbell, "Masculinity and Rural Life: An Introduction," in *Country Boys: Masculinity and Rural Life*, ed. Hugh Campbell, Michael Mayersfeld Bell, and Margaret Finney (University Park: Pennsylvania State University Press, 2006), 19.
8. Meisenheimer, "Machining the Man," 446.
9. Michael K. Johnson, *Black Masculinity and the Frontier Myth in American Literature* (Norman: University of Oklahoma Press, 2002), 74.
10. Johnson, *Black Masculinity*, 242.
11. Henry Louis Gates Jr., *The Signifying Monkey* (Oxford: Oxford University Press, 1988), xxiii.
12. Cornel West, *The Cornel West Reader* (New York: Basic Books, 1999), 518. Adam Gopnik notes, "For a great many poor people in America, particularly poor black men, prison is a destination that braids through an ordinary life, much as high school and college do for rich white ones." Gopnik further argues that as a result, a sort of U.S. prison hypermasculinity has quietly spread across the country across racial lines: "Wealthy white teen-agers in baggy jeans and laceless shoes and multiple tattoos show, unconsciously, the reality of incarceration that acts as a hidden foundation for the country." Adam Gopnik, "The Caging of America," *The New Yorker*, Jan. 30, 2012, 72–73.
13. bell hooks, *We Real Cool: Black Men and Masculinity* (New York: Routledge, 2004), 156.
14. Eldridge Cleaver, "Notes on a Native Son," in *James Baldwin: A Collection of Critical Essays*, ed. Kenneth Kinnamon (Englewood Cliffs: Spectrum, 1974), 70.
15. Leslie A. Fiedler, *Love and Death in the American Novel* (New York: Stein and Day, 1966), 26.

16. Jesse Matz, *The Modern Novel: A Short Introduction* (Malden: Blackwell, 2004), 45.

17. Matz, *The Modern Novel*, 47.

18. Stephanie S. Halldorson, *The Hero in Contemporary American Fiction* (New York: Palgrave, 2007), xi.

19. Halldorson, *The Hero in Contemporary American Fiction*, 5.

20. Matz, *The Modern Novel*, 47–48.

21. Halldorson, *The Hero in Contemporary American Fiction*, 6.

22. Halldorson, *The Hero in Contemporary American Fiction*, 180.

23. Eldridge Cleaver, *Soul on Ice* (New York: Delta, 1968), 90–91.

24. Cleaver, *Soul on Ice*, 91.

25. Cleaver, *Soul on Ice*, 92.

26. Wilchins, *Queer Theory, Gender Theory*, 97.

27. Wilchins, *Queer Theory, Gender Theory*, 124.

Chapter One

An Ironic Contention

The Heroic Failure of the Kid in Blood Meridian

In its depiction of life on the frontier, *Blood Meridian* constructs a virulent form of hypermasculinity born out of the lawlessness, violence, and racism prevalent in the mid-nineteenth-century American Southwest (1833–1878).[1] The events in the novel unfold during a time when western expansion predicated on American exceptionalism and entitlement created a rugged and violent frontier where women were scarce and masculinity manifested in violence and a belief that any ethnicity other than white had no claim to the land or to life. The deep-seated racial divide among the Apaches, Comanches, Mexicans, and Americans, as well as other American Indian tribes, created a hotbed of violence where competing ethnicities fought unrelentingly for land, respect, and wealth.[2] Laws in place in the developed and civilized East have little power in the underdeveloped Wild West. Human beings and their families live in a state of vulnerability. Power, mostly held by the roving male gangs, evolves into the ability and willingness to wage war against anyone not male, white, and willing to worship war. This power develops into a specific yet not all-encompassing definition of hypermasculinity, resulting in warfare marked by culturally contrived symbols of emasculation, such as the sodomizing of corpses and the wounded and the cutting away of genitalia.

The judge,[3] the antagonist, evolves into the authority and judge of the extreme gender code and acts as a metaphorical father to the kid, the protagonist, and to the whole Glanton gang of scalp hunters.[4] Language plays a defining role in the novel in that the judge wields language like a weapon to promote, justify, and, punish those who do not abide by his philosophies. The judge's voice reigns supreme in a text full of competing voices, including those of the narrator and the kid. His speeches, philosophies, and wit gradually overwhelm the deadpan unobtrusive voice of the third-person narrator and the illiterate kid. The judge reveals himself as the leader, role model, and arbiter of the flourishing hypermasculinity present in the novel. He provides the explanations and moral reasoning for the heinous acts he and the entire gang commit, so much so that the ability to create language, to name the natural world, develops into another component of this particular brand of hypermasculinity, one that prevents the kid from openly and successfully defying him. The judge's verbal virtuosity overwhelms the indifferent narrator, who never morally comments on the events of the novel. The narrator seems to invite the reader to make his or her own judgments and to assign meaning to the text, thus situating her or him as a culpable participant in the carnage. Further, the kid, an illiterate, has very little to say throughout the text. The kid exists as a symbol of hypermasculine lack. He, like the rest of the children and men in the novel who cannot live up to the judge's definition of masculinity, dies a violent death.

Further, a plethora of images of dead children, mostly sons, symbolizes the judge's rigid code in that children are weak and helpless, unable to live up to the code's standards. Domesticity and child rearing pose a feminizing threat to men, potentially compromising their place within the code; therefore children become symbols of weakness and threats to the judge's philosophy of war.

The novel's images of Christ and Christianity appear as destroyed or grotesque, suggesting that the most lasting paradigm of a positive relationship between father and son, God the Father and Christ, functions as an obsolete idea and broken image. Also, due to the fact that Christian law, Christ's teachings, contradicts the law the judge attempts to legislate, the former appears futile and broken. The judge's narrative influence marks these artifacts and iconography as meaningless and constructed by a desperate humanity. The judge must overturn the notion of God the Father in order to take his place as the true metaphorical father.

In an ironic reading, the ineffectual kid fails heroically to construct a masculine identity outside of the textual order of the judge even though the kid ultimately repudiates the judge's notions that a man must embrace war as his God in order to dance the dance of masculinity. Reading the kid as ironically heroic in his failure dismantles the philosophies of the judge and calls into question the violence the book seems to espouse. In no way is the kid a classic hero. Rather, his heroism exists as an indirect indictment of the judge's destructive philosophies. The judge's unyielding law provides a space where a weak, ineffectual character like the kid can be heroic. The kid does fail, but not before casting a light in the text on the judge. Others disagree with the judge, such as the ex-priest, but only the kid rebels openly and attempts to construct an identity outside of the judge's pale. The kid never fully accepts the judge's philosophy of absolute warfare. For the judge, "war is god."[5] If a man does not fully commit to this new religion, the judge defines him as something less than a man. Toward the end of the novel, the judge equates masculinity to a dance: "Only that man who has offered up himself entire to the blood of war . . . only that man can dance."[6] The kid accepts the fact that he cannot dance and that in the eyes of the judge he exists as something less than a man. Suspiciously, and perhaps speciously,[7] the judge invites the kid to shoot him, to take his place as the metaphorical father or the "suzerain" of the amoral order he thinks he helms. Almost from the very beginning of their relationship the kid seeks to distance himself from the judge as much as he can without sacrificing his position in the Glanton gang. He never outright rebels, but throughout his service he executes little rebellions against the judge and the gang, mostly by evincing hints of compassion and traces of a moral center, such as his refusal to execute an injured fellow gang member and drawing an arrow from Brown's leg when no one else will. The judge ultimately acknowledges these small rebellions and accuses the kid of mutiny and breaking "with the body of which [he] [was] pledged a part and [poisoning] it in all its enterprise."[8] In a final showdown, the judge arguably rapes and kills the kid, destroying him like the other children and sub-men in the novel, but not before the kid casts an illuminating pall on the judge and the gang's philosophy of war and masculinity. The unlikely nature of the kid's heroism makes it ironic in that the kid by all accounts projects a paltry figure. His eventual rebellion against the judge proves meager at best.

THE ORIGINS OF AMERICAN FRONTIER HYPERMASCULINITIES

McCarthy's *Blood Meridian* can be looked at as what Sara Spurgeon calls "one of our most pervasive national fantasies—the winning of the West and the building of the American character through frontier experiences."[9] This national fantasy suggests that the winning of the West defines the American character as tough, adventurous, resourceful, and exceptional, thus exemplifying American entitlement. America, according to this notion, has a God-given claim to any land west of the Mississippi all the way to the Pacific Ocean. "Here is the bloody tie," Spurgeon points out, "binding the West's mythic past to its troubled present, here in this mythic dance is the violent birth of a national symbolic that has made heroes out of scalphunters and Indian killers."[10] McCarthy paints an entirely different story than the national fantasy, one that suggests that the winning of the West relied on a philosophy of violence and racism that disavowed any moral law, human law, or governmental law. Marilyn C. Wesley agrees: "*Blood Meridian* . . . exposes . . . violence as a ruinous basis for both personal manhood and communal integrity."[11] Violence, which the judge insists defines the fundamental law of masculinity, fails to turn the kid into a man and mutilates any attempt at harmony in the novel. On the contrary, violence simply breeds more violence and causes competing factions to respond with ever more gruesome atrocities.

Blood Meridian shatters the utopian idea of America as a Garden of Eden. The judge has the words *"Et in Arcadia Ego"*[12] inscribed on his gun, which Spurgeon translates as "even in Arcadia am I [Death]."[13] *Et in Arcadia Ego* references how the great American democratic experiment has always relied and will always rely on death and bloodshed. The judge's inscription mocks the idea of America as a Garden of Eden and positions him as a living contradiction to the master narrative of manifest destiny. Robert L. Jarrett points out, "The ideology of Manifest Destiny held that one race, the Anglo-Saxon, combined with the political form of republican government, comprised an elect nation that held the true title to the American landscape."[14] The notion of manifest destiny then created a frontier of lawlessness where men like Captain White in the novel justified the mass murder of Native Americans and Mexicans by suggesting that America and Americans were "dealing with a people manifestly incapable of governing themselves. And do you know what happens to people who cannot govern themselves? That's right. Others come in to govern for them."[15] Captain White and other American groups feel justified in acquiring land by force since in their minds the aboriginals are unsophisticated and unable to control themselves. Captain White presents a paternal case for violence and theft, as though he, like the judge, acts as an oppressive but necessary father.

HYPERMASCULINITIES ON THE FRONTIER

McCarthy's Southwest exists not as a land of pure lawlessness but rather as a land where lawlessness breeds a destructive version of androcentrism. Androcentrism emerges as a code of behavior that holds that only masculinity predicated on violence and racial purity has the power to control. Wallace Stegner describes this new law in a new land as having the "blind ethics of an essentially false, imperfectly formed, excessively masculine society."[16] This hypermasculine society influences the warfare found in the novel, in that the warfare exists as an extension of and a testament to the hypermasculinity of the warring parties. The novel is replete with war scenes that generally exceed the usual Western narrative's heroic boundaries. For instance, the narrative depicts a gory yet detailed account of a clash between Anglo-Americans and Native Americans. The Comanches attack Captain White and his gang, including the kid, eventually "gutting the strange white torsos and holding up great handfuls of viscera, genitals . . . and some . . . fell upon the dying and sodomized them with loud cries to their fellows."[17] The Comanches gut the torsos in order to feminize their white enemies. The bloody crotches of the white soldiers symbolize menstruation. The Comanches sodomize the dying and the wounded in order to emasculate their assailants. The Comanches realize that emasculating the white men, who make such a decisive claim to the land and want to kill them, results in a humiliating and dispiriting defeat. Further, the Comanches realize that like their tribe, the white men value masculinity perhaps above all else. Emasculating a white soldier while engaged in warfare resonates deeply because warfare testifies to one's masculinity; warfare equals one's masculinity. Suffering sodomy at the hands of the Comanches *during* warfare then translates into the most severe insult available to the Comanches; they eroticize power and turn warfare into a sexual conquest. This warfare of perceived emasculation is based on destructive and fraudulent notions of heteronormative, sexist, and homophobic hypermasculinities the Native Americans share with their white oppressors. Consequently, the Native Americans enact symbolic warfare that affirms the very white patriarchal privilege that oppresses them.

One can find ubiquitous evidence of gendered warfare in the novel. For example, just before the Glanton gang slaughters the Gileños in chapter twelve, they happen upon a group of "dead argonauts[18] . . . Some by their beards were men but yet wore strange menstrual wounds between their legs and no man's parts for these had been cut away and hung dark and strange from out their grinning mouths."[19] Homosexual imagery makes an appearance as a taboo form of sexuality, suggesting weakness. Someone, likely one or more of the Comanches, has inserted genitalia into the mouths of the argonaut corpses in an attempt to simulate fellatio. The beards of the men contrasting with the genitalia hanging from their grinning mouths function as a reference to a homosexual act. This works to emasculate the men and to scare away any travelers who happen upon the corpses. Sexualized warfare conveys the idea that out on the frontier one's masculinity is on the line. One's very masculinity becomes the stake, and clearly these men appear to have lost. Patrick W. Shaw rightly observes, "With such dismemberment, the Indians feminize their enemy and force him to pantomime the one sex act that is abhorrent to the white man's frontier culture."[20] Clearly, the "Indians" *know* that white frontier culture finds images of male-on-male fellatio revolting. The Native Americans observe the hypermasculine performance of the white men and deduce that compromising this would prove an effective technique of warfare. The Native Americans witness what Adam Parkes describes as the "performativity of American selfhood" through masculinity.[21] The Native Americans understand that Americanness and masculinity have a symbiotic relationship, and compromising the latter undermines the former. American entitlement proves no more fixed and natural than the performed hypermasculinity of all the warring parties. In a narrative twist, we find out a few lines later that the men who enact the brutality on the argonauts are "white men who preyed on travelers in that wilderness and disguised their work to be that of the savages."[22] Startlingly, what we have here Baudrillard would say "is a question of substituting the signs of the real for the real" or a "liquidation of all referentials."[23] The simulation of the manner of the emasculating violence implies that the masculinity and therefore the American exceptionalism that the imagery is supposed to undermine also function as signifier. The *appearance* of masculinity does not ensure it or define one as a "real man" and likewise the *appearance* of emasculation does not mean the men have lost something real besides their lives. The white men violently rob and kill and attempt to present the violence as that of the "savages" by copying their manner of warfare, namely the emasculating mutilation of the white men. Parkes notes, "In *Blood Meridian*, the concept of American nationhood turns out to be no more fixed or stable than the notions of racial and sexual identity on which it depends."[24] To the Comanches and others, hypermasculinity exists as a salient definition of Americanism, and this sexual identity appears performed and therefore constructed and mutable.

Regarding gender performance, Judith Butler writes, "Gender is in no way a stable identity or locus of agency from which various acts proceed; rather, it is an identity tenuously constituted in time—an identity instituted through a *stylized repetition of acts*."[25] Applying these notions to *Blood Meridian*, one can say that in the same way that gender exists as unstable, so too does the American identity that emerges from its performance. The hypermasculinities that emerge and thrive in the West are also not fixed, and yet when we apply Butler's dictum that "those who fail to do their gender right are regularly punished,"[26] we realize that American identity relies on abidance by an unstable law.

In *Blood Meridian* a hyperbolic masculine code emerges that allows America's manifest destiny to materialize. As Jay Ellis suggests, "Most of McCarthy's fifth novel describes a space devoid of law and morality, testing the reader with the severity of its violence."[27] Consequently, this space, devoid of law and morality, grows vulnerable to laws enacted through violence. As Jacques Derrida points out, "Force without justice is condemned. It is necessary then to combine justice and force; and for this end make what is just strong, or what is strong just."[28] Force and strength cause the fluidity and mutability of the law, but a law must also be just for it to be good. The law can be changed if the lawmakers and judges prove strong enough to uphold the change, indeed prove willing to punish lawbreakers with violence. As Derrida further argues, the dialectic between violence and the law points to "violence as the exercise of the law and law as the exercise of violence. Violence is not exterior to the order of law."[29] The American Southwest of *Blood Meridian* exists in a lawless state of violence, warfare, and racism that becomes vulnerable to new unjust laws predicated on violent hypermasculin-ities that ensure the winning of the West. Within this paradigm, the judge functions as the upholder of the unjust law. He provides the force and vio-lence necessary to create and maintain the law. The hypermasculine perfor-mances the judge demands of his gang, along with their devotion to his religion of violence, hold only because the judge proves willing to punish transgressors. The strength of the code rests on the degree of punishment doled out to those who do not abide by it. In other words, the strength of law depends largely on the violence that ensures it.

The fact that Glanton and the judge employ a black man and Delaware Native Americans in their gang does not alter or contradict the gang's racist and violent code. The existence of Black Jackson and the Delawares simply illuminates the idea that race functions more as an abstract political designa-tion to advance white interests than a fixed reality. Black Jackson and the Delawares, by taking part in the violence against other races, in effect be-come white; they assimilate themselves into the white fray by stripping themselves of their own identities and adopting the ethos of the oppressor.[30]

When the kid first lays eyes on the gang, their beastly performance[31] thunders spectacularly:

> They saw one day a pack of viciouslooking humans mounted on unshod indian ponies riding half drunk through the streets, bearded, barbarous, clad in the skins of animals stitched up with thews and armed with weapons of every description, revolvers of enormous weight and bowieknives the size of clay-mores and short twobarreled rifles with bores you could stick your thumbs in and the trappings of their horses fashioned out of human skin and their bridles woven up from human hair and decorated with human teeth and the riders wearing scapulars or necklaces of dried and blackened ears . . . foremost among them, outsized and childlike with his naked face, rode the judge.[32]

The regalia of the gang evince the very standards by which the kid, and anyone else who might either join the gang or get in the way of the gang, will be judged. Further, foremost among them rides the judge, a testament to his role as de facto leader. The bowie knives and two-barreled rifles link the phallus with the hypermasculine narrative Kaja Silverman defines as the "dominant fiction" of patriarchy and phallic privilege.[33] These phallic im-ages signify the power of the Glanton gang. The human hair and human teeth represent those individuals who have been sentenced by the judge for their lack as well as trophies from scalping parties. One can exist before the law as an enemy, an innocent bystander, or a fellow gang member. One is then already always before the law and therefore before the judge who sustains the law by his willingness to enact violence to uphold it.

Even though the kid proves an ironic hero in his fairly weak repudiation of the judge and the judge's philosophy of war, his fate illustrates that the law of the Southwest in the novel functions as a hypermasculine law. As Robert L. Jarrett points out, "The kid undertakes the American masculine romance of lighting out for the territory."[34] He sets out alone to find himself and his manhood by running away from his drunken father at fourteen and finding a job on a flatboat. McCarthy writes, "He lives in a room above a courtyard behind a tavern and he comes down at night like some fairybook beast to fight with the sailors. He is not big but he has big wrists, big hands."[35] From the very beginning of the novel the kid attempts to prove his masculinity by engaging in violence.

The kid's eventual failure to live up to the judge's unjust and exaggerated standards of hypermasculinity renders the kid less than a man in the judge's eyes. Only that man can dance, says the judge, who has "seen horror in the round and learned at last that it speaks to his inmost heart."[36] The kid does not buy into the judge's philosophy and refuses to perform his masculinity, to dance before the judge. The judge asks the kid, "What man would not be a dancer if he could . . . It's a great thing, the dance."[37] The judge's ability to dance might also suggest his confidence in his rapacious male sexuality. The kid, on the other hand, is uneasy about his own sexuality, succumbing to violent homosexual panic every time someone mistakes him for a homosexual. The kid's insecurity about his sexuality prevents him from dancing or acting in any way other than strictly masculine.

The kid's inability to perform sexually with a prostitute further reflects his failure to perform his masculinity correctly. As Ellis points out, "McCarthy . . . shows us the kid's failure sexually. The kid's inability to perform with the prostitute . . . makes it clear that in place of the judge's dance, the kid has no alternative procreative power. In this sense, he is still 'the kid' in relation to the judge as father."[38] Before this encounter, the kid is "taken for a male whore and set up drinks and then shown to the rear of the premises. He left his patron senseless in a mudroom where there was no light."[39] Rather than politely refusing, the kid reacts violently due to his lack of confidence in his own masculinity. His masculine quest fails because he does not perform his gender consistently at the exaggerated level of the judge. He is ultimately judged less than a man by the judge himself, and total emasculation and death result as his punishment. The kid's life ends in the arms of the judge, his metaphorical father: "The judge was seated upon the closet. He was naked and he rose up smiling and gathered him in his arms against his immense and terrible flesh and shot the wooden barlatch home behind him."[40] Shaw argues that perhaps not only does the judge rape and kill the kid, but that the kid might be a "willing participant."[41] He contends that "no other act could offend their [the witnesses'] masculine sensibilities so thoroughly as to cause the shock they display."[42] It seems unlikely that the kid *allows* the judge to enter him anally, largely because of the kid's ultimate lack of courage in constructing a truly progressive masculinity, but the fact that the judge is naked does suggest that the judge rapes and kills him. [43]

It remains unclear whether or not the judge ever *really* intends for the kid to replace him. Despite repeated opportunities, the kid does not kill the judge, to the outrage of Tobin the ex-priest: "You'll get no second chance lad. Do it. He is naked. He is unarmed. God's blood, do you think you'll best him any other way?"[44] Tobin functions as the kid's counsel, but counsel that has already given in to the judge. Ellis admits, "I have never been sure that the judge is serious in his characterization of the kid as a potential disciple, a son who might truly follow in his footsteps."[45] The judge exemplifies a trickster figure throughout the novel, and perhaps only after the kid rebels against the gang and emerges as a threat to the judge does the judge beseech the kid, "Don't you know that I'd have loved you like a son."[46] This particular line rings ironic in that the judge kills just about every symbolic son he has in the novel, including the "halfbreed" and the kid. The imbecile is the only character the judge protects and nurtures like a son, one who would have no way of usurping the power of his father.

On several occasions the judge mocks, tricks, and teases the men in his outfit, further suggesting that he never intends for the kid to kill him. The judge at one point, holding up a rock, tells Glanton's men that God "speaks in stones and trees, the bones of things . . . And these are his words." After he says this, "the squatters in their rags nodded among themselves and were soon reckoning him correct . . . [H]e laughed at them for fools."[47] The judge appears fully aware that in a world where humans impose an artificial order on the universe, the idea that words equal things rings ridiculous. Further, he proves a master at sleight of hand as well as sleight of word. He performs a coin trick in order to illustrate his point that humanity creates whatever order exists in the universe: "He flung it and it cut an arc through the firelight and was gone in the darkness beyond . . . The coin returned back out of the night and crossed the fire with a faint high droning."[48] The judge often says the opposite of what he means and enjoys toying with the gang, including the kid.

In an earlier scene, the judge admits, "it is the death of the father to which the son is entitled and to which he is heir, more so than his goods."[49] Notwithstanding, the judge appears to have no desire to relinquish his role as metaphorical father, for the last words before the epilogue, after he has raped and killed the kid, read, "He says that he will never die."[50] One could argue the judge means that a patriarchal system ruled by a male suzerain will forever dominate the world; but given the arrogant, supernatural quality of the judge it seems clear that he means that he will never die.

THE JUDGE AS NARRATIVE FORCE

Despite the trickster nature of the judge, he appears very serious about language and textuality. The judge's text-making abilities and verbal virtuosity allow him to hijack the text and emerge as its most dominant force. Joshua J. Masters asserts, "As suzerain, as an overlord or hegemonic force who commands all other forms of power, the judge has *complete* textual control, and thus the power to strip things naked in the act of naming" (emphasis mine).[51] Masters overstates the judge's control over the text but not entirely. As a character, the judge cannot have complete textual control. Only the actual author has complete control; and critics such as John Barthes argue that readers provide meaning to the text. The novel employs a third-person limited-omniscient narrator who reports events as they happen without offering much moral assessment. The narrator follows the exploits of many of the characters and only sometimes conveys the thoughts of the kid. George Guillemin notes, "Nowhere in the novel does the narrative voice devote itself to the question of ethics, not even by pointing out the conspicuous absence of moral positions."[52] The absence of moral positions activates the reader's potential for ethical thought and allows us to condemn (or agree with) the judge. Perhaps Guillemin means that there are no moral positions conveyed with any force that contradict the judge. Consequently, only the judge's moral positions remain on the page. As Masters asserts, "We find only the judge's voice, for he provides the coherence, the order, *the meaning* that defines the scalp hunter's pilgrimage west."[53] The lack of textual assertiveness by the narrator clears a path for the judge to dominate the text. Though other voices exist in the text, such as Tobin's and Toadvine's, the judge's clearly emerges as the strongest. As Barcley Owens suggests, "In the second half of the novel, the judge patiently explains the philosophy behind what we are witnessing. As the judge's rhetoric increasingly intrudes upon the primary narrative, he takes on the metafictional quality of an author-figure."[54]

The kid cannot read or write and so has difficulty rebelling against the judge. Guillemin notes, "The kid remains mostly silent and talks only in random, monosyllabic utterances hardly enough to sustain a dialogue. It is the narrator who speaks for, but not through the kid, while the judge (the monstrous child) monopolizes the novel's monologues."[55] The judge appears to value language and textuality nearly as much as he values violence. He intuits that what power men do have over the world lies in language and the ability to name the natural world. He says at one point, "Whatever in creation exists without my knowledge exists without my consent."[56] The reason we might take the judge seriously here, instead of attributing this to another one of his games, lies in the fact that he painstakingly takes the time to sketch and document everything of interest to him. After naming the thing, the judge often destroys it, whether a "footpiece from a suit of armor hammered out in a shop in Toledo three centuries before" or "flint or potsherd or tool of bone."[57] He appears to want to usurp God and to squash and belittle any religion or belief system that threatens his authority and his philosophy of violence. Masters contends,

> The kid finally lacks the Adamic capacity to name and create, and his illiteracy . . . functions as a defining feature: he lacks the judge's textual capabilities. The judge claims that language and the knowledge necessary to apply it are the keys to creating and preserving power; thus, the kid's lack of that text-making ability engenders his failure and leads to his death.[58]

Masters suggests that the judge sees himself as God, naming and creating the unusual things that he encounters. The kid, on the other hand, lacks the power to rival God in this dystopia and therefore fails to eventually stand up to the judge.

IMAGES OF DEAD CHILDREN

If we believe that *Blood Meridian* contains the metaphorical dynamic of a father rejecting a son for not living up to particular standards of various frontier hypermasculinities, then we might accept that many of the images of dead babies and dead fathers evince this metaphor. Images of filial conflicts litter the text, suggesting that the American Southwest during the mid-nineteenth century extirpates family structures and renders young boys and men vulnerable to older men such as the judge. The repeating images throughout the text of dead babies and men brutalizing children operate as a synecdoche for the central conflict between the kid and the judge. Because the kid will not devote himself to the philosophy of the judge, he and other children like him must die brutal deaths. As Ellis notes, "The kid's resistance to the judge's arguments for war, then, constitute the betrayal of a father by a son."[59] In *Blood Meridian*, the judge's character symbolizes a suzerain of all fathers, and the kid is the metaphorical son, and thus the shortcomings of the kid symbolize the shortcomings of children in general.

Even though the judge says he would have "loved you [the kid] like a son"[60] and at one point—just before he kills him—refers to the kid as "son,"[61] it remains unclear whether the judge really would have loved him like a son or whether the judge merely enjoys playing the trickster. When asked how one ought to raise a son, the judge quips, "At a young age . . . they should be put in a pit with wild dogs."[62] Further, children often go missing and wind up raped and/or dead when the judge is around.[63]

The conflict between fathers and sons takes center stage and not always in favor of the fathers. At the outset of the narrative, not long after the kid escapes his own drunken father and just before he meets the judge, "he sees a

parricide hanged in a crossroads hamlet and the man's friends run forward
and pull his legs and he hangs dead from his rope while urine darkens his
trousers."[64] The image resonates in that it appears at the beginning of the
novel and exists as the only example of a father perhaps killed by a son. The
image sets up the battleground between fathers and sons and leads us beyond
the real into the metaphorical realm of the judge and the kid. The rest of the
children and babies, including the adult kid, representing hypermasculine
lack and the enervating institution of domesticity, die gruesome deaths at the
hands of the men and fathers: "By and by they came to a bush that was hung
with dead babies";[65] "In the doorway there lay a dead child with two buz-
zards sitting on it";[66] "One of the Delawares emerged from the smoke with a
naked infant dangling in each hand and squatted at the ring of midden stones
and swung them by the heels each in turn and bashed their heads against the
stones so that the brains burst forth through the fontanel in a bloody spew."[67]
The men hunt the children down instead of leaving them vulnerable to the
elements, suggesting that the evil, hypermasculine force in *Blood Meridian*
exists a shade darker than typical naturalistic force.

CHRISTIAN IMAGERY

The destruction of Christian images and icons, namely that of God the Father
and Christ the Son, reflects the judge's philosophy of war. The judge's philosophy informs much of the novel, and the motifs, images, and symbols that
threaten the philosophy come under attack. The judge's ideas seem to antici-
pate Friedrich Nietzsche's notion that "the morality of pity which spread
wider and wider, and whose grip infected even philosophers with its disease,
was the most sinister symptom of our modern European civilization."[68] For
Nietzsche, Judeo-Christianity turned morality on its head, championing
weakness and failure while condemning strength and power. The judge appears to want to reverse the reversal and, like Nietzsche, names Christianity
as an insidious force that weakens humanity. Further, the judge and his
teachings provide a close replica of Nietzsche's notions of the overman.
Nietzsche writes, "*I teach you the overman*. Man is something that shall be
overcome . . . The overman *shall* be the meaning of the earth . . . *remain
faithful to the earth* . . . [D]o not believe those who speak to you of other-
wordly hopes! . . . Once the sin against God was the greatest sin; but God
died, and these sinners died with him."[69] The judge, who obsessively and
deftly sketches into a notebook many forms of rock, animal, and artifact that
intrigue him or that he has never seen before, privileges the corporeal over
the celestial. The first time the judge appears in the text he accuses a preacher
of bestiality and pedophilia, and he later announces to several men at a bar, "I
never laid eyes on the man before today. Never even heard of him."[70] The

men in the bar highly admire the judge's power to render a man of the cloth a heathen in the eyes of the people. The judge realizes that Christianity and its principles may pose a threat to his law and so it is in his best interest to denounce it whenever possible. Further, by slandering the preacher the judge appears to overcome man's otherworldly hopes, positioning the judge as the true overman.

To further defile the institution of Christianity, the judge employs an ex-priest in his gang. The judge mocks the ex-priest even though the man performs violent acts against the enemy right along with the gang. When the judge says, "Moral law is an invention of mankind,"[71] echoing Nietzsche, and asks the ex-priest if he agrees with him, the ex-priest says, "I'll not secondsay you in your notions . . . Dont ask it." The judge then replies, "Ah Priest . . . What could I ask of you that you've not already given."[72] To the judge, the fact that the ex-priest engages in violent warfare and seems to embrace his philosophy of war supports the judge's power and philosophy and the weakness of Christianity; for if of all things he convinces an *ex-priest*, everyone else should fall in line easily.

In order to subvert the belief system of Christianity, which poses a threat to the judge's immorality, on at least three occasions a church or place of worship has degenerated into a place of slaughter rather than a sanctuary for believers: "In the room was a wooden table with a few clay pots and along the back wall lay the remains of several bodies, one a child . . . a carved stone Virgin held in her arms a headless child."[73] The images in *Blood Meridian* serve the purpose of the judge, further advancing the idea that the judge has a profound textual influence over the novel. These gruesome, striking images suggest that previous laws of morality have broken down and given way to laws overseen by the judge. Religious asylums exist as false refuges for the weak instead of places of healing: "The stone floor was heaped with the scalped and naked and partly eaten bodies of some forty souls who'd barricaded themselves in this house of God against the heathen . . . and a dead Christ in a glass bier lay broken in the chancel floor."[74] Places of worship are shorn of their power: "Many of the people had been running toward the church where they knelt clutching the altar and from this refuge they were dragged howling one by one and one by one they were slain and scalped in the chancel floor."[75] The judge feels threatened by Christianity and its attendant icons and so even in the judge's absence the novel presents the vestiges of Christianity in ruin. One could argue that perhaps the judge functions as a mouthpiece for McCarthy himself, who once wrote, "There's no such thing as life . . . without bloodshed . . . I think the notion that the species can be improved in some way, that everyone could live in harmony, is a really dangerous idea. Those who are afflicted with this notion are the first ones to give up their souls, their freedom. Your desire that it be that way will enslave you and make your life vacuous."[76] McCarthy means that notions of peace enslave humanity and cost them their souls. Implicitly, he means that war is natural to humanity, a notion the judge believes in wholeheartedly. [77]

THE KID AS IRONIC HERO

Ultimately, the hypermasculinity of the judge wins out, trumping and rendering silly any notions of love and compassion. That the kid makes an attempt to construct a masculine identity, however flimsy and misdirected, outside of the judge's textual influence, though, cannot be ignored. As Masters points out, "The only character who threatens to usurp the judge's textual order is the kid. His lack of absolute faith in the gang's warfare indicates a moral possibility existing outside the judge's ego." [78] The kid's lack of absolute faith and construction of an alternative moral possibility, as well as an alternative definition of masculinity, position him as a failed ironic hero. An ironically heroic reading of the kid employs Linda Hutcheon's "concept of irony as 'counterdiscourse' . . . a 'mode of combat' . . . 'a *negative* passion, to displace and annihilate a dominant depiction of the world.'" [79] The dominant depiction of the world is as one of hypermasculine patriarchy, and the kid as failed hero provides a counterdiscourse that critiques the philosophies of the judge. Hutcheon further asserts, "Irony has been seen as 'serious play,' as both a rhetorical strategy and a political method . . . that deconstructs and decenters patriarchal discourses. Operating almost as a form of guerilla warfare, irony is said to work to change how people interpret." [80] Irony works as an interpretive mode, not a writerly mode. It makes no difference whether McCarthy intended for *Blood Meridian* to be ironic; intention would lessen the power of an ironic reading.

Even though the kid participates in the violence of the gang early on, he eventually repudiates the judge and gang, once again striking out on his own to forge a new identity outside the shadow of a father. Unlike the ex-priest or the other gang members, the kid sustains his dissent and does not acquiesce to the judge's power.

The second entry for "irony" in *The Oxford English Dictionary* reads, "A condition of affairs or events of a character opposite to what was, or might naturally be, expected; a contradictory outcome of events as if in mockery of the promise and fitness of things." [81] One might not expect the kid to emerge as a heroic figure in *Blood Meridian*, given the fact that through most of the novel he engages in violent acts just like the consummate villains in the Glanton gang do. For instance, early in the novel, without much reason except to help Toadvine exact revenge on a man, "the kid stepped . . . into the room and turned and kicked the man in the face." [82] Also, later in the novel, when the kid is jailed for taking part in White's outfit and children are mocking him, "he picked one [a rock] from the dust the size of an egg and with it dropped a small child cleanly from the wall with no sound other than the muted thud of its own landing on the far side."[83] Though the narrator does not show the kid taking part in the violence against the Apaches and Comanches, it is implied that he does. The kid does not function as an obvious hero in the tradition of classic cowboy-and-Indian tales. His rejection of the judge's hypermasculinity and philosophy of war signals his emergence as an ironic hero. The kid's ironic heroism proves "a contradictory outcome of events as if in mockery of the promise and fitness of things."[84] The idea that the lowly, illiterate kid could emerge as a hero reflects the ridiculous, excrescent nature of the judge and his ideas. Intellect, the capacity for violence, and the belief that war is God are not ingredients for heroism and success; they are ingredients for villainy and degradation. The kid's weakness proves to be the defining characteristic of his heroism. One does not need to be a demigod to be a hero. In this case, one needs only to reject the destructive philosophies of the judge, even if the rejection proves limp and unsuccessful, and even if the kid's alternative masculinity is itself normative and problematic.

Victor Brombert describes the literary ancient hero as "divine,"[85] the hero of the Middle Ages as a "love-hero," the romantic hero as a "bourgeois . . . rebel,"[86] and the modern hero as a "hero of consciousness," one who feels "torn between the desire to act and the conviction that action is absurd."[87] Further, he argues that the concept of the hero is a "shrinking . . . ideal" and often takes on an "ironic quality."[88] "Ultimately," he writes, "the hero tends to disappear altogether."[89] None of these definitions apply to the kid; he harbors no divine blood (though the judge might), he does not seek out love, at least in the heroic sense, he does not count himself as a member of the bourgeois, and arguably his brand of heroism proves unconscious rather than conscious. The kid's brand of heroism may not register as heroic at all by these definitions, but one has to admit that even a shadow, a wisp, or a suggestion of the good or the redemptive in a novel like *Blood Meridian*, which "alienated," and continues to alienate, many "mainstream critics . . . with its relentless brutality,"[90] must be addressed. The kid's brand of heroism results from what the text permits. Neither the narrator nor McCarthy equip the kid with the necessary faculties to stage a full rebellion against the judge. The kid represents the hope that in every man there does not live an instinct for violence, racism, and destruction, that in some there exists an instinct for salvation and compassion and healing, even though that person might not recognize it as such. The kid's rejection of the judge as a father suggests that not every man aspires to usurp the father in order to dominate women and the other through violence and oppression. The kid fails to kill the judge, even though, as Spurgeon notes, to do so would have only been right and proper . . . as well as within the relationship of father and son, because, as the judge has said at the Anasazi ruins, it is the death of the father to which the son is entitled. When the kid will neither shoot him nor join him, the judge charges, "There's a flawed place in the fabric of your heart . . . You alone were mutinous. You alone reserved in your soul some corner of clemency."[91]

Because the kid does not even attempt to kill the judge, the judge realizes that the kid has rejected his philosophy and considers himself outside of the judge's control. Spurgeon further points out that after the kid refuses to kill the judge "he becomes a guide for other travelers passing through the wilderness . . . [and] he begins to carry a bible, a book already made defunct by the judge as a false book and symbol of . . . empty moral laws."[92]

Even before this point in the novel, as Jarrett points out, "[the kid] has demonstrated his good intentions . . . aiding Brown in drawing an arrow through his leg . . . Given the charge of killing two of the wounded . . . the kid leaves them to the 'mercies' of the pursuing Elias and the [Apaches],"[93] even though Elias and the Apaches will surely torture and murder the men. After the kid and Tate get separated from the gang and make their way to "the high country,"[94] which Ellis defines as "a place more humane,"[95] the kid encounters "a lone tree burning on the desert."[96] He finds warmth and sleeps next to the fiery branches among all manner of creatures "deadly to man,"[97] "all bound in a precarious truce before this torch whose brightness had set back the stars in their sockets."[98] This representation of harmonious life once again symbolizes the fact that not all manner of life harbors an inclination toward violence. Perhaps within all life there exists a capacity for violence, but not everyone has to succumb to that capacity.

Though the kid's illiteracy prevents him from utilizing the rhetoric necessary to confront the judge, he succeeds in avoiding the vortex of the judge's philosophy. As Masters points out, "Because the kid has preserved a capacity for judgment, mercy, and morality, he has preserved some portion of himself outside of the judge's textual domain."[99] The other gang members, by accepting the judge as their de facto leader, after he saves them from the Apaches by fashioning gunpowder out of saltpetre, charcoal, sulphur, and urine, surrender their autonomy and their will to challenge much the judge says or does. The Glanton gang grows into one expression, one force, a force created by the judge, like the gunpowder the gang uses to massacre the Apaches. Only the kid denies the judge. Toadvine and the ex-priest at times express their distaste for some of the judge's acts, but at no point do they act upon their feelings. Only the kid has the courage to break away from the gang (albeit after the gang has been decimated and one of its leaders is dead) and construct his own identity outside the law of the judge. The judge says to the kid, "You came forward . . . to take part in a work. But you were a witness against yourself. You sat in judgement on your own deeds. You put your own allowances before the judgements of history and you broke with the body of which you were pledged a part and poisoned it in all its enterprise."[100] The judge feels that the kid's weakness stems from his moral uncertainty, which runs contrary to the judge's certainty that progress results from bloodshed.

By rejecting the judge's law of hypermasculinity predicated on violence and racism the kid lays a foundation for an alternative definition of masculinity marked by compassion and humaneness even more profound since it appears in a land devoid of civilized law. The climax of the kid's new definition takes place when he attempts to confess his sins to a dead Native American penitent woman: "He told her that he was an American and that he was a long way from the country of his birth and that he had no family and that he had traveled much and seen many things and had been at war and endured hardships. He told her that he would convey her to a safe place . . . or she would surely die."[101] Had the old woman not "been dead in that place for years,"[102] no doubt the kid would have unburdened himself even more, but as it turns out, he confesses too late. The kid identifying himself as an American suggests that he might have apologized to all Native Americans for his country as well.[103]

The fact that he confesses to a fossil indicates the profundity of what the kid has been up against. His repudiation enacts a little narrative of hope compared to the judge's master narrative of war as God, but his little narrative nonetheless proves ironically heroic because it provides the only alternative to the hypermasculinity defined by the judge.

In *Blood Meridian*, the heteroglossia, which Mikhail Bakhtin defines as "authorial speech, the speeches of narrators, inserted genres, and the speech of characters,"[104] allows for the judge to have a driving influence on the text of the novel. One might say the philosophies of the judge, as well as the hypermasculinity the judge imposes on the American Southwest, heavily influence not only the events of the text but also its symbols and narrative drive. The judge muscles out the third-person, unassuming narrator in order to engender a form of hypermasculinity necessary to achieve the historical aims of the United States. By fulfilling his duty as a metaphorical father, the judge attempts to breed all manner of men who live up to his corrosive standards. When he says at the end of the novel that "he will never die,"[105] he means that the white and violent patriarchy that he helms will never die, or perhaps, and amounting to the same thing, due to his supernatural qualities, he really means *he* will never die. The judge crushes any potential threat to his power, including Christianity and anyone who does not live up to the standards of hypermasculinity required for American progress, including children.

The kid represents an answer to the judge, a possibility outside of the judge's textual power. Even though the kid fails to fully stand up to the judge, or enact a truly progressive version of masculinity, he provides a voice of dissent. The kid proves ill equipped to confront the judge. His illiteracy and weak mind prove no match for the judge's God-like ability to create. Nonetheless, without the kid, *Blood Meridian* exists as a text that espouses violence and vindicates the judge and his religion of war. The fact that the third-person narrator does not morally comment on the events situates the reader in a precarious position. McCarthy's engaging writing, particularly during the most gruesome scenes, allows for reader complicity in the bloodshed. The kid provides a fragment of hope for humanity. Even though he proves weak and acts far too late and fails to stage any sort of lasting rebellion against the judge, his dissent, his suggestion of a possible masculinity outside of the judge's pall, proves heroic, if only ironically.

NOTES

1. Michael S. Kimmel notes that some hypermasculinities emerge from both "sexism and racism" and "the fear . . . that others might perceive us as homosexual." By othering women, who "threaten emasculation by representing the home," and other races or sexualities, men ensure that "manhood is only possible for a distinct minority," namely white American males. Kimmel further states, "By the middle of the [nineteenth] century . . . Native Americans were cast as foolish and naïve children, so they could be infantilized as the 'Red Children of the Great White Father' and therefore excluded from full manhood." In other words, hypermasculinities in some cases depend more on what one is not rather than what one is. Ironically, in order to further emasculate non-Americans, including Native Americans, white America defined them as "hypermasculine, as sexually aggressive, violent rapacious beasts, against whom 'civilized' men must take a decisive stand and thereby rescue civilization." Michael S. Kimmel, "Masculinity as Homophobia: Fear, Shame, and Silence in the Construction of Gender Identity," in *Feminism and Masculinities*, ed. Peter F. Murphy (Oxford: Oxford University Press, 2004), 191–92. In *Blood Meridian*, the judge and the entire Glanton gang, while defining themselves as the opposite of women and non-whites, are very much hypermasculine rapacious monsters. Both the Glanton gang and the Native Americans fit Kimmel's definition of hypermasculinity.

2. Joseph F. Park writes, "Much of the enmity that existed between Arizona and Sonora in the decade following the Gadsden Purchase in 1853 arose from the failure of the United States to comply fully with Article XI of the Treaty of Guadalupe Hidalgo in 1848, which pledged prevention of Apache raiding across the border." Park goes on to write that "after the Mexican War, Apache depredations increased," resulting in a series of bloody battles between Mexicans and Apaches. Joseph F. Park, "The Apaches in Mexico-American Relations, 1848–1861," in *U.S.-Mexico Borderlands: Historical and Contemporary Perspectives*, ed. Oscar J. Martinez (Wilmington: Jaguar, 1996), 50. The arrival of Anglo-Americans in the area only fueled the racial hostility. The United States made the same mistakes with the Apaches as Mexico, negotiating meaningless treaties with a people of whom it was wholly ignorant.

3. Perhaps the most important historical source for *Blood Meridian* is *My Confession: Recollections of a Rogue*, by Samuel Chamberlain. Along with detailing the Glanton gang's scalp-hunting enterprise, Chamberlain's book provides the only known historical record of the historical figure Judge Holden. Chamberlain, who rode with the Glanton gang, tells how Holden "stood six foot six in his moccasins, had a large fleshy frame, a dull-tallow colored face destitute of hair and expression . . . His desires were blood and women . . . And before we left

Fronteras a little girl of ten years was found in the chaperal, foully violated and murdered, the mark of a huge hand on her little throat pointed out him as the ravisher . . . He was by far the most educated man in northern Mexico. He conversed with all in their own language, spoke in several Indian lingos, at a fandango would take the Harp or Guitar from the hands of the musicians, and charm all with his wonderful performance, out waltz any Poblana of the ball, 'plum centre' with rifle or revolver, a daring horseman, acquainted with the nature of all the strange plants and their botanical names." Samuel Chamberlain, *My Confession: Recollections of a Rogue* (Austin: Texas State Historical Association, 1996), 306, 309. Along with the judge, Tobin, Glanton, Shelby, *et alii* can be found in Chamberlain's text, described very close to how McCarthy describes them in *Blood Meridian*.

4. *Blood Meridian* follows the kid and his tenuous relationship with the Glanton gang of scalp hunters led by John Joel Glanton and Judge Holden, a gang that historically became active in the "lucrative market in Apache scalps." Gary Anderson notes that "[the] scalp market had been activated by Mexican authorities who began to advertise rewards for Apache scalps in the 1830s." The market was cornered by, among others, Benjamin Leaton, a man who in 1849 notified authorities that "Major Michael Chevallie and John Glanton had organized more than one hundred armed men to raid into Chihuahua, stealing for the most part but also hunting Apaches for money." Chevallie and Glanton were in the army together but soon wore out their usefulness due to their murdering rampages. Anderson asserts that "the governor of Chihuahua had offered Chevallie and Glanton $150 for an Apache scalp and $200 for a captive." Gary Clayton Anderson, *The Conquest of Texas: Ethnic Cleansing in the Promised Land, 1820–1875* (Norman: University of Oklahoma Press, 2005), 232–33.

5. Cormac McCarthy, *Blood Meridian* (New York: Vintage, 1992), 249.

6. McCarthy, *Blood Meridian*, 331.

7. The judge is, among other things, a magician, illusionist, con artist, and trickster. It is plausible that he views the kid as a threat and only then invites the kid to shoot him. Further, it is hard to believe that the judge might accept the kid as a sort of son. Likely, the judge wishes to fool the kid into thinking they are allies in order to more easily kill him.

8. McCarthy, *Blood Meridian*, 307.

9. Sara Spurgeon, "The Sacred Hunter and the Eucharist of the Wilderness: Mythic Reconstructions in *Blood Meridian*," in *Cormac McCarthy: New Directions*, ed. James D. Lilley (Albuquerque: University of New Mexico Press, 2002), 75.

10. Spurgeon, "The Sacred Hunter," 98.

11. Marilyn C. Wesley, *Violent Adventure* (Charlottesville: Virginia University Press, 2003), 70.

12. McCarthy, *Blood Meridian*, 125.

13. Spurgeon, "The Sacred Hunter," 84.

14. Robert L. Jarrett, *Cormac McCarthy* (New York: Twayne, 1997), 70.

15. McCarthy, *Blood Meridian*, 34.

16. Wallace Stegner, "Walter Clark's Frontier," in *Walter Van Tilburg Clark: Critiques*, ed. Charlton Laird (Reno: University of Nevada Press, 1983), 61.

17. McCarthy, *Blood Meridian*, 54.

18. McCarthy employs the term "argonauts," which in Greek myth refers to the men who sailed with Jason on his adventure to recover the Golden Fleece. The ship the men sailed on was built by "Argus" and "Athena," and "they called it the *Argo*, in honor of its builder"; thus the men who sailed on it were known as the Argonauts. Carl Fischer, *The Myth and Legend of Greece* (Dayton: Pflaum, 1968), 150. Like Faulkner in *Absalom, Absalom!* (Clytemnestra, Jason, Theophilus), McCarthy uses Greek names and terms to create a sense of myth in the text. By utilizing mythic language, the author can create a sense of established legend as well as a sense that the events are interpretable. Jason's quest for the Golden Fleece was a fool's errand, a suicide mission, undertaken to prove his masculinity and worthiness of the throne of Iolcus. Unlike Jason's Argonauts, who emerge unscathed, McCarthy's argonauts are gruesomely emasculated, suggesting that perhaps McCarthy uses the myth ironically to distinguish harsh reality from romanticized myth.

19. McCarthy, *Blood Meridian*, 152–53.

20. Patrick W. Shaw, "The Kid's Fate, the Judge's Guilt: Ramifications of Closure in Cormac McCarthy's *Blood Meridian*," *The Southern Literary Journal* 30, no. 1 (Fall 1997): 102–119.

21. Adam Parkes, "History, Bloodshed, and the Spectacle of American Identity in *Blood Meridian*," in *Cormac McCarthy: New Directions*, ed. James D. Lilley (Albuquerque: University of New Mexico Press, 2002), 107.

22. McCarthy, *Blood Meridian*, 153.

23. Jean Baudrillard, *Simulacra and Simulation*, trans. Sheila Faria (Glaser: University of Michigan Press, 2010), 2.

24. Parkes, "History, Bloodshed, and the Spectacle of American Identity," 117.

25. Judith Butler, "Performative Acts and Gender Constitution," in *Literary Theory: An Anthology*, ed. Julie Rivkin and Michael Ryan (Malden: Blackwell, 2004), 900.

26. Butler, "Performative Acts," 903.

27. Jay Ellis, *No Place for Home: Spatial Constraint and Character Flight in the Novels of Cormac McCarthy* (New York: Routledge, 2006), 169.

28. Jacques Derrida, *Acts of Religion*, ed. Gil Anidjar (New York: Routledge, 2002), 238.

29. Derrida, *Acts of Religion*, 268.

30. On two separate occasions Black Jackson kills a white man for his racist comments seemingly with Glanton and the judge's blessing. When another man named Jackson does not want Black Jackson eating at the same fire as he, Black Jackson "[steps] forward and with a single stroke [swaps] off [white Jackson's] head." Later in the novel, when a white restaurant owner named Owens will not serve Black Jackson, Brown gives Owens a gun and tells him to shoot Black Jackson. Black Jackson responds by nonchalantly shooting Owens: "The big pistol jumped and a double handful of Owens's brains went out the back of his skull." McCarthy, *Blood Meridian*, 107, 236. These events suggest that as long as Black Jackson acts violently enough and subscribes to the philosophies of the judge, his race does not matter.

31. Kaja Silverman defines another form of "hyperbolic masculinity," a visual form marked by "'macho' clothing (denim, leather, and the ubiquitous key rings)," which some American homosexuals, "over the course of the [nineteen] seventies," appropriated for themselves as markers of a new macho homosexuality. Further, "by taking the signs of masculinity and eroticising them in a blatantly homosexual context, much mischief is done to the security with which 'men' are defined in society." Kaja Silverman, *Male Subjectivity at the Margins* (New York: Routledge, 1992), 345. The Glanton gang mark themselves as hypermasculine by their appearance, dress, and gruesome accessories. Human and animal skins equal denim and leather, and guns and knives echo key rings. The signifying American homosexual one hundred years later destabilizes the visible hypermasculinity of the Glanton gang and illustrates that masculinity in general is a fluid notion.

32. McCarthy, *Blood Meridian*, 78–79.

33. Silverman, *Male Subjectivity at the Margins*, 42.

34. Jarrett, *Cormac McCarthy*, 64.

35. McCarthy, *Blood Meridian*, 3–4.

36. McCarthy, *Blood Meridian*, 331.

37. McCarthy, *Blood Meridian*, 327.

38. Ellis, *No Place for Home*, 165.

39. McCarthy, *Blood Meridian*, 311.

40. McCarthy, *Blood Meridian*, 333.

41. Shaw, "The Kid's Fate, the Judge's Guilt," 117.

42. Shaw, "The Kid's Fate, the Judge's Guilt," 118.

43. On several occasions the judge is shown naked. In chapter nine, just before he likely kills and possibly rapes a "half-breed" boy, he is reported "naked atop the walls . . . striding the perimeter up there and declaiming in the old epic mode." In chapter eighteen, the judge happens on the drowning idiot "stark naked himself," saving him, suggesting a metaphorical birth. After the Yumas slaughter most of the Glanton gang, the kid finds the judge and the idiot in the desert, "both of them naked." Lastly, after the judge rapes and murders the kid, he returns to the bar with the dancing bear and dances naked, "bowing to the ladies, huge and pale and hairless." McCarthy, *Blood Meridian*, 118, 259, 281, 335. The judge's open nakedness further

evidences his exaggerated hypermasculinity, as though he bares his phallus every chance he gets in order to evince his power. Further, the judge's nakedness does not *prove* that he raped the kid. Given that the judge has a penchant for male rape, and that male rape has been shown to be an emasculating act on the frontier, it is likely that the judge has raped and killed the kid. It is also possible that the judge may have partially eaten him or enacted some other atrocity. McCarthy leaves it to our imaginations.

44. McCarthy, *Blood Meridian*, 285.

45. Ellis, *No Place for Home*, 152.

46. McCarthy, *Blood Meridian*, 306.

47. McCarthy, *Blood Meridian*, 116.

48. McCarthy, *Blood Meridian*, 246.

49. McCarthy, *Blood Meridian*, 145.

50. McCarthy, *Blood Meridian*, 335.

51. Joshua J. Masters, "'Witness to the Uttermost Edge of the World': Judge Holden's Textual Enterprise in Cormac McCarthy's *Blood Meridian*," *Critique: Studies in Contemporary Fiction* 40, no. 1 (Fall 1998): 33.

52. George Guillemin, "'See the Child': The Melancholy Subtext of *Blood Meridian*," in *Cormac McCarthy: New Directions*, ed. James D. Lilley (Albuquerque: University of New Mexico Press, 2002), 240.

53. Masters, "'Witness to the Uttermost Edge of the World,'" 25.

54. Barcley Owens, *Cormac McCarthy's Western Novels* (Tucson: University of Arizona Press, 2000), 50.

55. Guillemin, "'See the Child,'" 255.

56. McCarthy, *Blood Meridian*, 198.

57. McCarthy, *Blood Meridian*, 140.

58. Masters, "'Witness to the Uttermost Edge of the World,'" 35.

59. Ellis, *No Place for Home*, 156.

60. McCarthy, *Blood Meridian*, 306.

61. McCarthy, *Blood Meridian*, 327.

62. McCarthy, *Blood Meridian*, 146.

63. After the gang meets a group of Mexicans and a "half-breed" boy in an abandoned mining town, the boy is soon found with "his neck . . . broken and his head [hanging] straight down and it flopped over strangely when they let him onto the ground." Just before this the judge is shown "picking his teeth with a thorn as if he had just eaten." On another occasion, after the gang arrives at a Mexican village, a "girl was missing and parties of citizens had turned out to search the mineshafts. After a while Glanton slept and the judge rose and went out." McCarthy, *Blood Meridian*, 118–19, 191. The judge's pedophilia further reflects his power lust and likens him to a Nietzschean overman poet who defines his morality as he goes along rather than subscribing to moral laws already in place.

64. McCarthy, *Blood Meridian*, 5.

65. McCarthy, *Blood Meridian*, 57.

66. McCarthy, *Blood Meridian*, 61.

67. McCarthy, *Blood Meridian*, 156.

68. Friedrich Nietzsche, *On the Genealogy of Morals*, trans. Horace B. Samuel (New York: Barnes and Noble, 2006), xxi.

69. Friedrich Nietzsche, *Thus Spoke Zarathustra*, in *The Portable Nietzsche*, ed. and trans. Walter Kaufman (New York: Penguin, 1982), 124–25.

70. McCarthy, *Blood Meridian*, 8.

71. McCarthy, *Blood Meridian*, 250.

72. McCarthy, *Blood Meridian*, 251.

73. McCarthy, *Blood Meridian*, 26–27.

74. McCarthy, *Blood Meridian*, 60.

75. McCarthy, *Blood Meridian*, 181.

76. Richard B. Woodward, "Cormac McCarthy's Venomous Fiction," *The New York Times Magazine*, Apr. 19, 1992, 36.

77. Linda Hutcheon argues, "the final responsibility for deciding whether irony actually happens in an utterance or not (and what the ironic meaning is) rests, in the end, solely with the interpreter." Further, she notes, "irony would then be a function of reading . . . in the broad sense of the word, or, at the very least, irony would 'complete itself in the reading' . . . It would not be something intrinsic to the text, but rather something that results from the act of construing carried out by the interpreter who works within a context of interpretive assumptions." Linda Hutcheon, *Irony's Edge: The Theory and Politics of Irony* (New York: Routledge, 1994), 45, 122. I am not overly interested in implicating McCarthy, or pinpointing his intent. This quote might lead one to believe he is sympathetic to some of the judge's views, and therefore in some ways allows the judge to, in a sense, take over the text. Authors sometimes admit that characters are that powerful, such as Toni Morrison, who said that Pilate, a female character in *Song of Solomon* (the focus of a later chapter), had to be silenced: "I had to do that, otherwise she was going to overwhelm everybody. She got terribly interesting; characters can do that for a little bit. I had to take it back. It's my book; it's not called Pilate." Quoted in Elissa Schappell, "Toni Morrison: The Art of Fiction," in *Toni Morrison's* Song of Solomon: *A Casebook*, ed. Jan Furman (Oxford: Oxford University Press, 2003), 251. Perhaps McCarthy ought to have titled *Blood Meridian* "The Judge." Likely, McCarthy did not intend the kid to be the hero of the text, and this lack of intention, frankly, creates a space for my reading.

78. Masters, "'Witness to the Uttermost Edge of the World,'" 33.

79. Hutcheon, *Irony's Edge*, 30.

80. Hutcheon, *Irony's Edge*, 32.

81. *The Oxford English Dictionary*, 2nd ed., s.v. "irony."

82. McCarthy, *Blood Meridian*, 13.

83. McCarthy, *Blood Meridian*, 71.

84. *The Oxford English Dictionary*, 2nd ed., s.v. "irony."

85. Victor Brombert, ed., *The Hero in Literature* (Greenwich: Fawcett, 1969), 11.

86. Brombert, *The Hero in Literature*, 19.

87. Brombert, *The Hero in Literature*, 21.

88. Brombert, *The Hero in Literature*, 20.

89. Brombert, *The Hero in Literature*, 20.

90. Rick Wallach, "Twenty-Five Years of *Blood Meridian*," *Southwestern American Literature* 36, no. 3 (Summer 2011): 5.

91. Spurgeon, "The Sacred Hunter," 96.

92. Spurgeon, "The Sacred Hunter," 96.

93. Jarrett, *Cormac McCarthy*, 85.

94. McCarthy, *Blood Meridian*, 210.

95. Ellis, *No Place for Home*, 159.

96. McCarthy, *Blood Meridian*, 215.

97. McCarthy, *Blood Meridian*, 215.

98. McCarthy, *Blood Meridian*, 215.

99. Masters, "'Witness to the Uttermost Edge of the World,'" 34.

100. McCarthy, *Blood Meridian*, 307.

101. McCarthy, *Blood Meridian*, 315.

102. McCarthy, *Blood Meridian*, 315.

103. Lydia R. Cooper argues, "*Blood Meridian*'s narrative refuses its characters any redemption by insisting that they neither acknowledge their sins nor recognize their need for forgiveness." She never acknowledges the scene with the penitent woman because allowing the kid any sort of redemptive quality would contradict her thesis that "*Blood Meridian* possesses no confessional qualities because no character is granted an interior world." Lydia R. Cooper, *No More Heroes: Narrative Perspective and Morality in Cormac McCarthy* (Baton Rouge: Louisiana State University Press, 2011), 53, 73. For a character to have an interior world, according to Cooper, his or her thoughts must be textually revealed via a third-person limited or first-person perspective. The kid's rejection of the judge and moral inclinations, especially toward the end of the novel, are no less significant simply because of the perspective in which they are revealed.

104. Mikhail Bakhtin, "Discourse in the Novel," in *Literary Theory: An Anthology*, ed. Julie Rivkin and Michael Ryan (Malden: Blackwell, 2004), 674.

105. McCarthy, *Blood Meridian*, 335.

Chapter Two

A Hero by Default

John Grady Cole as Hypermasculine Heroic Failure in
All the Pretty Horses

I wish things were simple like they used to be, when cowboys rode horses and were heroes to me. My mother was a lady and my dad was a man, and I wish things were simple again.

—Merle Haggard [1]

In Cormac McCarthy's *All the Pretty Horses* the ruthless, hypermasculine frontiersman of *Blood Meridian* has evolved over a period of one hundred years (1849–1949) into the restless, domesticated hypermasculine cowboy who is suspicious of the social gains of women and ignorantly nostalgic for the days before barbed wire industrialization. John Grady Cole, the sixteen-year-old protagonist of *All the Pretty Horses*, aspires to embody a cowboy code of behavior, stemming from a strict tough-guy rural hypermasculinity defined by intense self-reliance and recklessness. Ultimately, his failure to do so renders him ironically heroic since success would perpetuate the reckless myth of the hypermasculine cowboy hero. In large part, John Grady's notion of cowboy hypermasculinity rests in fiction and cinema, where Western writers like Owen Wister and directors like George Stevens created the popular culture Hollywood cowboy, itself based mostly on an abstract notion of the frontiersman. [2] *All the Pretty Horses* simultaneously affirms and undermines these early manifestations of the cowboy by appropriating comic and dialogic conventions endemic to the Western genre. [3]

For John Grady Cole and Lacey Rawlins, [4] Mexico stands in for an imaginary western space where the two boys can realize their desires to actualize living, breathing cowboys. In Mexico truth exists as an elastic, fabricated notion, manipulated by those in power with personal agendas. The elasticity of truth in Mexico as controlled by government apparatuses endangers the boys, since their shaky identities stem not from the bedrock of reality but from the myth of popular culture.

In Texas, John Grady responds to what he views as white male victimhood by destructively attempting to prove himself capable of embodying an elusively heroic cowboy hypermasculinity predicated on masochism, violence, and sexism.[5] His desire to flee a country increasingly incompatible with his brand of cowboy hypermasculinity drives him and his friend Rawlins into Mexico, a country that has not yet fully industrialized or embraced the relative gender equality threatening his manhood. Rawlins and John Grady imagine Mexico as a frontier similar to the one in which their cowboy fantasy lies.

John Grady and Rawlins illustrate that cowboy and rural hypermasculinities may evince one's closeted homosexuality more than one's heterosexuality. The relationship between Rawlins and John Grady suggests a closeted homosexual dynamic incompatible with their U.S. cowboy hypermasculinity before they ever go to Mexico, but their inability to act on it because of their strict cowboy code further fragments and enfeebles their Mexican cowboy identities.

After playing the role of *chingados* (fucked ones), John Grady and Rawlins return to the United States, vaguely realizing the destructiveness of the cowboy hypermasculinity they covet. In revealing its pernicious nature, John Grady inadvertently renders himself obsolete. Josef Früchtl describes the modern popular culture hero as "an individual [who] sacrifices himself for the sake of the universal, but . . . the universal does not reward him for his heroic deed."[6] John Grady fails to actualize his cowboy fantasy but proves ironically heroic in exposing the danger and destructiveness of the fantasy. Früchtl further identifies modern popular culture heroes as "heroes [who] only seemingly die at the hands of their enemies; it is far truer to say that through their glorious deeds they do away with themselves . . . They are secret agents of their own abolition."[7] John Grady abolishes any viable notion of the modern cowboy as a positive figure and thereby erases himself. Like the disappearing figure of the mythic cowboy, at the end of the novel John Grady vanishes into the countryside a failure, but unlike the mythic cowboy, he assumes the role of ironic heroic failure because his narrative contributes to the relinquishment of a destructive male myth.

BLOOD MERIDIAN AND *ALL THE PRETTY HORSES*

McCarthy's *All the Pretty Horses* images the possible fate of the descendants of the wild killer frontiersmen of *Blood Meridian.* The frontiersman has evolved into a man without a frontier, a hunter without prey, an anachronism lost in an industrial, capitalistic world where male privilege, while still pervasive, for the first time exists in a threatened, vulnerable state. As Sara Spurgeon points out, "The figure of the hunter engaged in holy communication with nature has, by the end of *Blood Meridian*, been replaced with that of the cowboy digging postholes, preparing to string barbed wire across the tamed body of the wilderness in order to populate with cattle what he so mercilessly emptied of buffalo."[8] The epilogue of *Blood Meridian* portrays *"a man progressing over the plain by means of holes which he is making in the ground."*[9] The holes that will be filled with barbed wire fence posts herald a disappearing frontier, circumscribing the buffalo and the wandering, marauding bands of hunters ubiquitous in *Blood Meridian*.

At the outset of *All the Pretty Horses*, set exactly one hundred years later, John Grady pensively witnesses a train's headlamp "creating out of the night the endless fenceline down the dead straight right of way and sucking it back again wire and post mile on mile into the darkness."[10] These same barbed wire fences render the hunter of *Blood Meridian* immobile and prevent John Grady from realizing his dream of riding unfettered across the frontier in search of a cowboy heroicism no longer viable on the American landscape.

John Grady's naiveté emerges as an early theme in *All the Pretty Horses*, illustrated by his ignorance of what has gone on before. He idealizes a violent and destructive past where the sixteen-year-old boy might not survive twenty-four hours. Still, he continues to lament the fact that he will never witness "the past where the painted ponies and the riders of that lost nation came down out of the north with their faces chalked and their long hair plaited and each armed for war which was their life and the women and children and women with children at their breasts all of them pledged in blood and redeemable in blood only."[11] Never mind that many of these same Comanches would regard him and his family as enemies and spare him and his no quarter. He seems to overlook the idea that the blood the Native Americans wish to redeem themselves in is his. John Grady's romanticization of the warring "cowboys and Indians" provides the central contrast between *Blood Meridian* and *All the Pretty Horses*, highlighting the former as hyperreal and the latter as Hollywoodized simulacrum. Though *All the Pretty Horses* was far "more commercially successful than . . . *Blood Meridian*,"[12] both novels offer devastating critiques of U.S. hypermasculinities. Many critics and readers failed to see any redemption in *Blood Meridian* and conversely failed to grasp in *All the Pretty Horses* the devastating critique of the very genre they celebrated.

COWBOY HYPERMASCULINITIES

John Grady's version of cowboy hypermasculinity equates American rural masculinity. As Hugh Campbell suggests, "Masculinity is, in considerable measure, constructed out of rural masculinity. The 'real man' of many currently hegemonic forms of masculinity is, as we noted, a rural man."[13] Many of John Grady's actions abide by a code of rural masculinity often causing great harm to him and others. The recklessness and devil-may-care attitude in part stem from the insecurities of white men, resulting from the political gains of women and other minorities. The white males respond by throwing themselves in harm's way in order to more thoroughly prove their own manhood. Campbell further defines hypermasculine rural men as

> more likely to start drinking at a young age than their urban counterparts, and . . . more likely to drive while drunk . . . They also take more risks, perhaps in part because of a tough-guy vision of masculinity, which leads to poor health behavior like refusing to use sun-block lotion. Rural men have smaller social networks, seek help for medical issues (especially health issues) more slowly than urban men, and are more susceptible to suicide. With fewer resources and job prospects and less education and political power, rural men are perhaps more easily seduced by "hypermasculine" behavior.[14]

The lack of strong male role models who do not subscribe to a rural hypermasculine code functions as another aspect of rural hypermasculinity afflicting John Grady. The insular nature of rural America exposes John Grady to very few men who do not live up to these destructive male codes. Indeed, "his [John Grady's] grandfather was the oldest of eight boys and the only one to live past the age of twenty-five. They were drowned, shot, kicked by horses. They perished in fires. They seemed to fear only dying in bed."[15] His forefathers, including his grandfather who seems to have escaped death only by chance, represent to John Grady "real men" he can only hope and wish to emulate. By selling the family farm, John Grady's mother denies him his birthright to the land. John Grady's father, a gambler traumatized by his time spent in a Japanese prisoner camp, offers John Grady a cautionary narrative that he ignores. His father smokes, even though he likely has lung cancer, and brags about big pots he has won gambling: "I won twenty-six thousand dollars in twenty-two hours of play. There was four thousand dollars in the last pot, three of us in. Two boys from Houston. I won the hand with three natural queens."[16] John Grady's mother provides the stronger role model for John Grady, but because of his upbringing, which has taught him that women exist as mere attendants to men, he cannot recognize her worth. Campbell notes, "Common images of a stereotypical masculinity may tell us little about any actual man, but they point to a sociologically significant feature of the imagined real man: in many important and resonant instances, he is a *rural* man."[17] Like the cowboy of yore John Grady emulates, the rural man exists as a vanishing, precarious figure. The rural man often lives a tragic life because to die young equals living up to the hypermasculinity required of a rural man. Contrarily, a rural man who lives in security and takes care of himself may be considered a sissy. McCarthy, from the outset, presents readers with a traditionally rural character in John Grady, whose very rurality contributes to his demise.

THE TENUOUSNESS OF IDENTITIES BASED ON MYTH

John Grady's notions of the cowboy, particularly the accoutrements and visual markers such as hats and boots, stem in large part from cultural images created by Western novels and, later, the Hollywood Western. The mid-twentieth century, the setting of the novel, Gleeson-White points out, was "also the era of the Golden Age of the Hollywood Western and the rise of the television Western, reflecting . . . a more pervasive *national* nostalgia."[18] The Western genre fed American people hungry for the simpler times before World War II, where plots predicated on clear-cut good guys and bad guys played out and reaffirmed the superiority of white America. Postwar disillusionment and the emasculating, enervating effects of war created a need for images of masculinity embodied in the self-sufficient loner cowboys thought to inhabit the western frontier one hundred years earlier.[19] John Cant writes, "The initial vehicle of this mythicization was the dime novel. The cinema created a genre of its own from the literary source."[20]

McCarthy's original intent that *All the Pretty Horses* be a film explains why in large measure the novel borrows many of the conventions of the Western film. Edwin T. Arnold notes, "The Border Trilogy had its genesis in a screenplay entitled 'Cities of the Plain' that McCarthy wrote in the early 1980s . . . After unsuccessful attempts to place the screenplay, McCarthy recast the material in novel form."[21] Much more than *Blood Meridian, All the Pretty Horses* relies on dialogue, comedic elements, and visual markers to create context and pace. Gleeson-White observes,

> *All the Pretty Horses* uncovers the conventions of the genre by explicitly citing classic Western *styles*: stock images of the Hollywood cowboy, as well as allusions to the literary and cinematic tradition of the outlaw and to the Wild West Show. The novel is thus self-reflexive; it self-consciously enacts the process by which all Western narratives depend upon "icons" to become the most compelling and comprehensive of American grand narratives.[22]

Audiences identified cowboys of the early Western novels and films by their hats and boots; similarly, these accoutrements signify the all-important markers of identity for John Grady, Rawlins, and Jimmy Blevins. After the Mexi-

can captain, Raul, arrests Blevins, Raul strips the cowboy markers that identify Blevins as a cowboy prior to shooting him: "The boot had fallen to the
ground. Wait, said Blevins. I need to get my boot."[23] Without his boots, he
loses his powers and bandit identity, rendering him a mere child. Likewise,
John Grady and Rawlins appear vulnerable without their hats, which function
more like costumes, especially after they witness the murder of one of their
gang: "He [John Grady] almost reached to pull down the front of his hatbrim
but then he remembered that they had no hats anymore and he turned and
climbed up on the bed of the truck and sat waiting to be chained. Blevins's
boot was still lying in the grass. One of the guards bent and picked it up and
pitched it into the weeds."[24] The irreverent treatment of the boys' costumes
suggests that the boys must face an involuntary change of identity from
cowboys to young, vulnerable Americans.

John Grady, Rawlins, and Blevins attempt to construct an identity from a
heap of mythical images. The entire mythology of the frontier exists in the
minds of nostalgic cowboys exaggerating what life was like in the imaginary
nineteenth-century West. In the first chapter of the novel John Grady's
grandfather demonstrates a clear understanding of the difference between
myth and reality:

> On the wall opposite above the sideboard was an oilpainting of horses . . .
> They'd been copied out of a book . . . no such horse ever was that he had seen
> and he'd once asked his grandfather what kind of horses they were and his
> grandfather looked up from his plate at the painting as if he'd never seen it
> before and he said those are picturebook horses and went on eating.[25]

It is unfortunate that John Grady's grandfather does not discern his grand-
son's existential dilemma and elaborate on the difference between the mythology and reality surrounding frontier life. Perhaps the grandfather is not
fully aware of the difference himself and because of his land, which always
afforded him a space to actualize his cowboy hypermasculinity, never fully
needed to know the difference. Gleeson-White contends, "Not only is this
fantasy represented as a painting, but it is a mere *copy* of a picture of horses
that in fact never existed. Although the space of the West, symbolized by the
horses, is so displaced—it enters the narrative as a copy of a copy of the
unreal—John Grady Cole determines to live out everything the horses represent."[26] The problem, Jean Baudrillard notes, with continually mistaking
fantasy for reality is that eventually there exists a "liquidation of referentials,"[27] meaning an absence of reality. The reality of the frontier disappears
in favor of its simulacrum that glosses over much of the gruesome violence
and romanticizes the hypermasculinity that prevails. John Grady, all too
willingly, gives up his reality in favor of a fantasy, and in so doing he renders
himself vulnerable.

Fantasy, comedic humor, such as slapstick, and curt dialogue work as aesthetic conventions the novel appropriates. These aesthetic conventions position *All the Pretty Horses* among early Western narratives and contribute to John Grady's fantasy. Früchtl notes that the mythology underlying the Western is "essentially a comic mythology. With its humor, the Western literature of the nineteenth and early twentieth centuries understood this consistently better than movies did, and the old ballads of the West were always familiar with it."[28] On several occasions in the novel the narrative fords rather shallow comedic moments in order to reach the tragic moments. In chapter one, after John Grady and Rawlins meet up with Blevins and determine that his horse and his gun likely belong to another man and suspect trouble will soon arrive, the three boys are offered a meal and a place to sleep in a ranch just inside of Mexico. A few pages later a man offers to *buy* Blevins, but before the trouble arises the novel takes a shallow turn:

> Rawlins was showing two little girls how he could pull his finger off and put it back on again when Blevins crossed his utensils in the plate before him and wiped his mouth on his sleeve and leaned back from the table. There was no back to the bench and Blevins flailed wildly for a moment and then crashed to the floor behind him, kicking the table underneath and rattling the dishes and almost pulling over the bench with Rawlins and John Grady.[29]

Blevins's pratfall operates on two levels. First, after his fall two girls laugh at him; embarrassed and stubborn, he leaves, refusing the room and board and showing the immaturity and impulsiveness that will later cement his doom. Besides building his character, the scene is meant to be comedic, providing the reader with a breather and preparing him or her for the tragic events that follow. Blevins's explanation to John Grady and Rawlins of his fear of lightning is perhaps the most humorous passage of the novel, offering levity, character development, and plot movement:

> My grandaddy was killed in a minebucket in West Virginia it run down in the hole a hunnerd and eighty feet to get him . . . They had to wet down the bucket to cool it fore they could get him out of it . . . It fried em like bacon . . . Great uncle on my mother's side . . . got killed on a horse and it never singed a hair on that horse and it killed him graveyard dead they had to cut his belt off him where it welded the buckle shut and I got a cousin aint but four years oldern me was struck down in his own yard comin from the barn and it paralyzed him all down one side and melted the fillins in his teeth and soldered his jaw shut . . . Another cousin on my daddy's side it got him it set his hair on fire. The change in his pocket burned through and fell out on the ground an set the grass alight. I done been struck twice how come me to be deaf in this one ear.[30]

Blevins's fear, though real and understandable, reminds us of his adolescence, a far cry from the hypermasculine cowboy he attempts to enact. His fear eventually relieves him of his horse and gun, launches the narrative, causes his death, and results in John Grady's and Rawlins's incarceration and near-death. Blevins's colorful dialogue and the absurdity of an entire family prone to lightning strikes echo Faulkner's dark humor in novels such as *As I Lay Dying*, further situating *All the Pretty Horses* as a parodic text. Wade Hall believes that "in *All the Pretty Horses*, when Jimmy Blevins joins John Grady Cole and Lacey Rawlins in Mexico, the balance is tilted toward comic bravado and bloodshed. Their swaggering dialogue mocks the grownup boasting of renegades and desperados, and they play boyish games with the finality of adults."[31] Accompanying their comic willingness to prove their hypermasculinity, frequently ending in disaster, is their verbal aping of mythic cowboys drawn right out of dime novels and Western films.

The curt, affected dialogue, mostly among the boys, distinguishes *All the Pretty Horses* from many of McCarthy's other novels, including *Blood Meridian*. Cant points out, "The relation between the text and the culture of the cinema is also discernible. The prose is sparer and more economical than before. There are few of the complex 'run on' sentences and lengthy rhetorical passages of the kind that occur in *Suttree* and *Blood Meridian*."[32] In a dramatization, dialogue functions as the most important aspect of the narrative. Dialogue must move the story and build character. In *All the Pretty Horses*, dialogue works in those ways and shows the boys' desire to act like cultural cowboys. Philip A. Snyder contends, "This figure [the cowboy] typifies the notions that in the West actions speak louder than words and that the truth distinguishes itself from the lie essentially by behavioral evidence, in short, we expect cowboys to reflect the strong silent stereotype of the western hero."[33] The boys try to resemble men of few words, for "in Westerns talking is for politicians and women."[34] Often, the boys break their code of silence with one another, as when Blevins details the origins of his fear of lightning. Rawlins often gets chatty when nervous, but John Grady almost never does. John Grady's curt dialogue can also result in irony—for instance, toward the end of the novel, when the judge asks him if he "[got] the girl in a family way" and he responds, "No sir. I was in love with her."[35] Clearly, he could have impregnated her regardless of whether or not he was in love with her. Barkley Owens points out, "The understated, ungrammatical lingo of the cowboys also leads to moments of wry comic repartee."[36] Sometimes the boys' dialogue reflects their youth and thus rings comic, but most of the time, particularly concerning John Grady, it strictly adheres to the cowboy code of brevity. In chapter one, when he hitchhikes to San Antonio to see his mother act in a play, the man who gives him his first ride tells him, "You dont talk much, do you? . . . Not a whole lot. That's a good trait to have."[37] In Texas and rural America, "talk is cheap" and endemic to politicians or men who make their living indoors. John Grady and other rural men privilege action over talk. When he and Mary Catherine part for the last time, she tells him, "What if it is just talk? Everything's talk isnt it?" To which John Grady replies, "Not everything."[38] To him, Mary Catherine has already left him for the boy with the car regardless of what she says. He has already planned to leave for Mexico as revenge for his treatment by Mary Catherine and his mother. His action, leaving the United States, in his mind speaks louder than anything he might say.

Not only do John Grady, Rawlins, and Blevins mimic a myth drawn out of popular culture, but they also seek an imaginary space in which to actualize their dream identities, causing them to nearly disappear into their fantasy. For the boys, Mexico exists as their West. Donald K. Meisenheimer Jr. holds, "the American West has always offered a mythic space in which people can make themselves anew, importing one assemblage of organs, processes, and behaviors and plugging into landscape discourses to machine themselves new bodies, link themselves to new assemblages."[39] The boys attempt to avail themselves of new hypermasculine cowboy hard-bodies by appropriating the lingo of the frontier and the persona that goes with it. The American West of the cowboy imagination, like the cowboy himself, emerges as an amalgamation of some fact but mostly fantasy. The West may not have anything to do with the western United States. In the novel Mexico supplants the western United States as a frontier untainted by too much modern industrial development and feminist social change. Andrew Blair Spencer asserts, "In McCarthy's novel, this search for new frontiers takes John Grady and Lacey to Mexico, to a ranch where their boyhood fantasies about the West and about the American frontier can come true. It is only in this mythical place that these fantasies can become reality."[40] Once the boys cross the border into Mexico, only initially do their fantasies turn into a reality. Gleeson-White writes,

> Mexico becomes a substitute for the unscouted Territory of the Old West, a supposedly empty—yet nonetheless dangerous—space upon which Manifest Destiny could make its "scouring" mark, and it is thus the antithesis of the heavily fenced modern West. It is a mythic space outside of an American history driven by progress, from the frontier settlement to metropolitan modernity.[41]

The boys do not realize that by giving up their American identities tied to their families, respective ages, and places in American society, they give up themselves. By riding "back in history by riding south,"[42] and locating their version of the West, the boys enter a world of their own creation. Because their inchoate Mexican identities exist untethered to their former lives, their creation is a vulnerable one.

McCarthy signifies the otherworldliness of Mexico for John Grady by blurring the timeline between John Grady's crossing into Mexico and his return to Texas.[43] Once in Mexico the boys gain a fantasyland where they can enact their cowboy dreams at the expense of reality. There, they can both escape their adolescence and adopt a cowboy guise that preserves the idealism of their youth.

Once in Mexico, John Grady and the boys encounter two types of people: those who attempt to take advantage of the fact that the boys exist in a fantasyland where the truth of their existence is vulnerable, and those who attempt to explain to the boys that they need to hold on to their truth. Linda Townley Woodson observes,

> In Mexico . . . he [John Grady] encounters teachers who try to make him understand that the truth depends upon the world of discourse in which it is spoken . . . They seem to understand . . . that truth has been controlled, selected, organised and redistributed through history like a system of exclusion, a historical, modifiable, and institutionally constraining system.[44]

John Grady, Rawlins, and Blevins give up their adolescent American discourse for a simulacrum of cowboy discourse based on a hypermasculine cowboy myth. They do not know that this discourse has no purchase with the various Mexicans they encounter. The truth in Mexico has already had a long history of manipulation by those in power. John Grady and his gang, with their tenuous grasp on their own identities, must tread lightly in case they inadvertently fall victim to the Mexican power structures capable of erasing people's existences. Blevins dies largely because his identity is the one most shrouded in mystery and susceptible to erasure. Jimmy Blevins likely appropriated his own name from a radio preacher popular in the area: "What's your name? said John Grady. Jimmy Blevins. Bullshit, said Rawlins. Jimmy Blevins is on the radio. That's another Jimmy Blevins."[45] Nothing in Blevins's life ties him to his own existence; consequently, once the boys break the law in Mexico, exposing their shaky identities, Blevins has no power. In Mexico those in power have the ability to erase people, like the government in George Orwell's *1984*. After the captain murders Blevins and John Grady exacts his revenge on the captain, John Grady attempts to find the Blevins family in order to return Blevins's horse, or at least find its real owner. For John Grady, finding the Blevins family, or the real owner of Blevins's horse, will restore Blevins's identity. John Grady realizes that no Jimmy Blevins exists. Like himself, Blevins has willfully assumed the identity of a figment of his own imagination and in the process liquidated his own referent. Cant suggests, "McCarthy makes it clear that we do not discover the truth of Blevins, neither his name nor his horse, because we cannot always find the truth, even of the world of material possessions and human identity."[46] The truth is hard to find, especially when one purposefully masks it to begin with. When John Grady finally locates the real Jimmy Blevins, a radio preacher broadcasting a disembodied voice and conveying a message about an arguably made-up individual in Christ, John Grady realizes he will never find out the truth about his young friend murdered right in front of him.

John Grady and Rawlins nearly experience the same fate as Blevins when they find their truth, their existence, in the hands of the captain, an evil man seemingly used to misplacing the identities of people he kills or has killed. He tells John Grady,

> You have the opportunity to tell the truth here. Here. In three days you will go to Saltillo and then you will not have this opportunity. It will be gone. Then the truth will be in other hands. You see. We can make the truth here. Or we can lose it. But when you leave here it will be too late. Too late for truth. Then you will be in the hands of other parties. Who can say what the truth will be then? At that time?[47]

The captain wishes to hear a *truth* from John Grady that will justify his incarceration. He wants John Grady and Rawlins to admit that they are bandits, robbers, and bad men. When John Grady refuses to give up his real identity, the captain tells him, "You stay here you going to die. Then come other problems. Papers is lost. Peoples cannot be found. Some peoples come here to look for some man but he is no here. No one can find these papers."[48] The captain senses the precarious situation of the young men and feels free to construct any sort of identity he sees fit, one that will render the young men even more vulnerable to Mexican authorities. When John Grady argues to Pérez, the de facto leader of the prison, that they have committed no crimes and do not deserve punishment, he responds, "You think there are no crimes without owners? It is not a matter of finding. It is only a matter of choosing. Like picking the proper suit in a store."[49] Pérez understands more than John Grady that Mexican authorities have the power to alter one's identity and history with the arbitrary ease of choosing a suit. Mexico has grown into a country of lost identities, a country where men try so desperately to live up to a version of hypermasculinity that they lose sight of their own human truth and human dignity, rendering themselves pawns in violent games of power and materialism.

AN AMERICA WITH NO ROOM FOR A COWBOY

All the Pretty Horses, set in Texas and Mexico in 1949, unfolds in an ever more industrialized United States in the process of granting more rights to previously disenfranchised and marginalized people such as women. These two aspects of modern life more than anything else threaten the hypermasculinity of the rural male embodied in the character John Grady Cole. The constant industrial reminders on the frontier, such as barbed wire fences and the sounds of the nearby highway, concern and alienate John Grady, causing him to grow more and more disenchanted with his native country. Gleeson-White notes, "he [John Grady] inhabits a modernized West, in the form of a post-war Texas in the process of transition from a predominantly agricultural- to an industry-based society and economy."[50] A cowboy requires a prairie, preferably a frontier uninhabited and unspoiled by development. He needs open land in order to embody the image in his mind of the lone rider galloping into the sunset, driving livestock or buffalo. In chapter one, when Rawlins and John Grady camp out on the land—something they seem to do often—"they [can] hear the trucks out on the highway and they [can] see the lights of the town reflected off the desert fifteen miles to the north."[51] The sounds of industry and the winking lights of technology and development interrupt the boys' playacting, exposing their anachronistic identities.

The final insult to John Grady, and a personal reminder that the modern world no longer has room for a cowboy, comes when his girlfriend, Mary Catherine, breaks up with him for a boy with a car. Rawlins tells him, "I don't know what you expect. Him two years oldern you. Got his own car and everthing."[52] For John Grady, Mary Catherine has chosen the car over the horse, the gearhead over the cowboy, the contemporary man over the frontiersman. These early events in the novel provide the impetus for John Grady and Rawlins to abscond to Mexico in search of a frontier unfettered by modern industry, where a cowboy can roam and maintain his privileged position as independent man. Cant suggests, "the trilogy may be read as a comment on the twentieth century consequences of those nineteenth century events, of the failure of modernity to take root in Mexico and of the deeply troubling consequences of its all too profound success in the United States."[53] Once Rawlins and John Grady begin their journey to Mexico, John Grady seems resigned to the fact that his identity as a cowboy is no longer viable in America: "Rawlins led the horses through and then [raised] the wires back and beat the staples into the posts and put the catspaw back in his saddlebag and [mounted] up to ride on. How the hell do they expect a man to ride a horse in this country? said Rawlins. They don't, said John Grady."[54] John Grady feels as though the partitioning off of land with barbed wire directly compromises his ability to actualize his obsessive dream of embodying a cowboy. The barbed wire cuts off the open range and migration of buffalo and signals the capitalist appropriation of land, squeezing the frontiersman and the Native American into less fecund spaces.

Besides the newly modernized technological United States, John Grady's identity and cowboy hypermasculinity in the novel become threatened by the women in his life. Jay Ellis argues,

Mrs. Cole, nee Grady, has divorced from John Grady's father, a troubled
veteran of World War II who survived a Japanese prisoner of war camp. It is
notable that throughout the *Trilogy*, her son is never referred to as "John," but
rather as "John Grady." Of course, in Texas it is common for people to be
referred to by both their first and middle name, but by calling his main character "John Grady," the narrator reminds us that his mother's blood runs stronger
than his father's. In a patriarchal culture, John Grady's strongest heritage is
matrilineal: his mother is the exception in a long line of ranching men. [55]

After her father's death, John Grady's mother sells the ranch against John
Grady's wishes. Her lawyer tells him, "Son not everbody thinks that life on a
cattle ranch in west Texas is the second best thing to dyin and going to
heaven."[56] John Grady has no backup plan. Without the ranch he realizes he
cannot continue his life as a cowboy. When he approaches his mother and
suggests he run the ranch, his mother emasculates him by saying, "You cant
run a ranch . . . You're being ridiculous. You have to go to school."[57] John
Grady cannot understand how a woman, even his mother, has the right to sell
the ranch. He feels that by selling the ranch his mother commits a betrayal of
her father, of himself, and perhaps of the entire patriarchal social order. Nell
Sullivan finds, "a merely cursory reading of Cormac McCarthy's novels
reveals an unmistakable ambivalence about women, even an outright misogyny, manifested in the objectification of women . . . as absence in much of
All the Pretty Horses."[58] Few women populate the text of *All the Pretty
Horses*, and the ones that do, like Mrs. Cole and Mary Catherine, beset John
Grady's actualization of a cowboy, assuming the roles of emasculating villains. Sullivan further concludes, "*All the Pretty Horses* begins with John
Grady Cole's betrayal by the two most important women in his life, his
mother and his girlfriend."[59] His mother's betrayal of the family climaxes
after John Grady travels to San Antonio unbeknownst to his mother to watch
her perform in a play. After the play, John Grady follows her to a hotel like a
spying father, surreptitiously observing her as "she came through the lobby
bout nine oclock. She was on the arm of a man in a suit and a topcoat and
they went out the door and got into a cab."[60] Moments later John Grady asks
the hotel clerk, "Have you got a Mrs Cole registered . . . No, he said. No
Cole."[61] John Grady assumes his mother has begun an affair with a strange
man and never speaks with her again. He seems to disavow any notion that
his mother may have a right to her own life. He apparently never considers
that his mother has a right to follow her dreams of acting and perhaps remar-
rying or finding love.

His second betrayal by a woman, further alienating his cowboy hypermasculinity and driving him away from the country of his birth, comes at the
hands of his girlfriend, Mary Catherine. When he admits to his father that he
has broken up with his girlfriend and that he does not know who initiated the
breakup, his father remarks, "That means she quit you."[62] John Grady does

not argue. He sees Mary Catherine one last time, suggesting that the breakup partially provides the impetus behind his exile to Mexico: "I thought we could be friends. He nodded. It's all right. I aint goin to be around here all that much longer."[63] He wants Mary Catherine to know that he does not need her and might have left regardless. After they shake hands and part, he mentally notes, "He'd never shaken hands with a woman before."[64] He feels that a man only shakes hands with another man, not a woman.

John Grady responds to the women in his life by playing the role of white male victim and consequently redoubling his efforts to prove his ability to succeed. David Savran says of American men in the 1950s and 1960s, "The remarkable increase in prosperity of white households relative to black ones, and of men relative to women . . . has by no means prevented white men from identifying themselves as the victims of the slender and precarious gains made by these groups."[65] John Grady's redoubled efforts to prove his manhood in response to emasculation by women and the subsequent guilt cause him to engage in masochistic behavior even after he reaches Mexico. Savran further states, "Concealed under a veneer of righteous indignation, willfulness, anger, grief, or guilt, and repudiated by the would-be heroic male subject, reflexive sadomasochism has become the primary libidinal logic of the white male as victim."[66] John Grady's sadomasochism culminates in his abduction and torture of the Mexican captain, Raul, responsible for Blevins's murder. John Grady receives a bullet wound during the abduction, eventually treating it by cauterizing it with the barrel of his gun, to the dismay of the captain: "When next he dragged the pistol from the coals the end of the barrel glowed at a dull red heat and he laid it on the rocks and picked it up quickly by the grips in the wet shirt and jammed the redhot barrel ash and all down into the hole in his leg."[67] John Grady penetrates himself with his gun, underscoring his desire to masochistically prove his manhood and punish himself for his hypermasculinity.

MEXICAN CONTEXT

Mexico's apparent lack of industrial development attracts John Grady; its wilderness offers a place for him to actualize his cowboy dreams. Once over the border he and Rawlins converse: "There aint no electricity here . . . I doubt there's ever even been a car in here. I dont know where it would come from."[68] The lack of cars symbolizes Mexican freedom from American materialism and modernity. In Mexico, the horse maintains its rightful place as the preferred means of transportation. Contrasting the industrial development with the poverty of Mexico, Duena Alfonsa tells John Grady, "In the towns you'd see them trying to sell things which had no value. A bolt fallen from a truck picked up in the road or some wornout part of a machine that no one could even know the use of . . . The industrial world was to them a thing unimaginable and those who inhabited it wholly alien to them."[69] Rather than understanding that he may never penetrate the culture of Mexico completely, that his Americanness prevents him from doing so, John Grady feels drawn to the Mexican landscape's lack of development; it acts as a sign that the frontier remains a viable space where he can assume the role of hypermasculine frontiersman. Spurgeon comments,

> John Grady clings to the values of a myth that hides the true nature of the world. He refuses or is unable to recognize that the falseness of the sacred cowboy is equivalent to the broken bits of machinery the peasants gather from the roads. The peasant's faith in a myth, in this case their belief in the value of all things associated with the industrialized world coupled with a profound ignorance of the true nature of that world, strengthens but also dooms them.[70]

The ignorance of the peasants and their belief that anything industrial has value strengthen them by giving them a false hope that they can one day access the industrial world. Similarly, John Grady's belief in the viability of a cowboy persona drives him forward and keeps his hopes alive. These beliefs rooted in myth can only sustain so long before reality creeps in and shatters them.

In Mexico he observes a country that has not experienced the same modern advancements, evidenced in part by the lack of social gains by women. John Grady realizes this slowly, even though the contrast in gender equality between the two countries is greater than the technological differences. Martha I. Chew Sanchez maintains that in Mexico, "women are trained from a very early age to be cautious about not opening up their legs, since that posture is a sign of making themselves available for sex. At the same time, the girls are encouraged to dress, pose, and behave in a manner attractive to men by showing their bodies. Girls are trained to dress and to see themselves as the object of men's gaze and eroticism."[71] While these oppressive social mores exist in the United States, though less intensely, in Mexico they inform just about every nook and cranny of the culture.

John Grady's ignorance of Mexican social norms, especially when it comes to young women of established families, manifests the first time he sees Alejandra Rocha, the ranch owner's daughter, away from the ranch where he works. The ranch's name, "Hacienda de Nuestra Senora de la Purisima Conception,"[72] translated as the "Ranch of Our Lady of the Immaculate Conception,"[73] evokes images and values of the Virgin Mary, such as carnal purity and holiness, suggesting that the hacendado, Don Héctor Rocha y Villareal, cherishes his daughter's chastity above all else. Sanchez further reports,

Dances are an important site to meet partners. The spaces where dances occur
are very much regulated by the roles the community assigns to each sex . . .
Young couples have to demonstrate to the community that they are not engaging in any sexual activity out of wedlock and that young girls will remain
virgin until married. Parents of young women prohibit the practice of allowing
boyfriends to visit their unmarried daughters at home for fear of being perceived as too sexually permissive.[74]

John Grady recklessly refuses to adhere to Mexican customs. Instead, "at the
band's intermission they [John Grady and Alejandra] made their way to the
refreshment stand and he bought two lemonades in paper cones and they
went out and walked in the night air."[75] This act jeopardizes the reputation of
Alejandra, embarrasses Rocha, and threatens the jobs and safety of John
Grady and Rawlins. John Grady receives a warning for his actions when
Alejandra's aunt Alfonsa tells him, "You must understand. This is another
country. Here a woman's reputation is all she has . . . There is no forgiveness.
For women. A man may lose his honor and regain it again. But a woman
cannot."[76] Even though Mexico's differences from America attract John Grady, he refuses to acknowledge Mexican customs and propriety. In order to
succeed in Mexico, he must relax his aggressiveness and try to understand
the culture rather than perceiving the lack of industry and strict gender codes
as license to wield his cowboy hypermasculinity like a rope. Molly McBride
contends, "In his refusal to acknowledge the cultural law of female chastity
and the very real consequences for a woman who does not adhere to this law,
he is guilty of negating a national reality."[77] John Grady's central flaw stems
from allowing his cowboy fantasy to cloud reality. His desire to replace
Rocha as the patriarch at the Hacienda with Alejandra as his attentive wife
vitiates his judgment and endangers him and Rawlins.[78] McBride observes,
"John Grady's mistake lies in his assumption that it is possible to substitute
one set of rules for another, to impose his American mentality with all its
codes and regulations on the Mexican culture."[79] John Grady ignores at least
two warnings by Rocha and Alfonsa, spoken while playing billiards and
chess with each individually. The games symbolize the fact that John Grady's actions exist on a "court," or in an environment, not his own. When one
plays a game in the environment of one's adversary, one must abide by the
house rules. John Grady ignores Mexico's house rules. Rocha, while shooting billiards with John Grady, points out the table's flaws: "I asked Carlos if
he could make the table more level. The last time we played it was quite
crooked. We will see what has been done. Just take the corner there. I will
show you."[80] John Grady plays on Rocha's imperfect home table, granting
him an advantage. The table represents Rocha's Mexico and the imperfections he has grown reliant on and comfortable with. Conversely, Rocha's
home court advantage exposes John Grady's vulnerable position as outsider.

John Grady feels more suited to a country where his mother would not have the right to sell the family farm and his old girlfriend Mary Catherine would not so easily have broken up with him for an older boy with a car. John Grady fails to understand that the cowboy hypermasculinity he wishes to embody pales in comparison to the Mexican hypermasculinities that preside over such social functions as the *coleadero*.[81] Gloria Anzaldua reveals the oppressive state of the Mexican woman and the harsh gender roles women must abide by when she says, "If a woman doesn't renounce herself in favor of the male, she is selfish. If a woman remains a *virgin* until she marries, she is a good woman."[82] By spending time with Alejandra away from her elders, John Grady casts doubt on Alejandra's virginity and ipso facto her goodness as a human being. The two begin a passionate love affair, and for this John Grady encounters a version of Mexican hypermasculinity dwarfing his own in intensity and brutality. Anzaldua further claims that the Mexican "woman has been silenced, gagged, caged, bound into servitude with marriage, bludgeoned for 300 years, sterilized and castrated in the twentieth century. For 300 years she has been a slave, a force of cheap labor, colonized."[83] John Grady and his mythic cowboy masculinity pale in comparison to the Mexican male tyranny that has existed for three hundred years.

Mexican machismo, the cultural entrenchment of many forms of Mexican hypermasculinities, confronts and dismantles John Grady's mythic cowboy hypermasculine desires. He cannot handle himself in a country where hypermasculinities function as a way of life, illustrating that his desires are destructive at best. John Grady's failure to operate successfully in Mexico, a country synonymous with machismo, renders him and Rawlins vulnerable and *chingados*. Robert McKee Irwin holds that "by the time of the Mexican revolution, Mexico came to mean machismo and machismo came to mean Mexico."[84] John Grady and Rawlins are eventually jailed in the Castelar prison and forced to perform a series of tests in order to determine whether they have *cojones*. Irwin further contends that Mexican "manhood is often achieved through certain competitive or ritual acts; men who do not perform these acts properly are seen as immature at best, or, more often, effeminate."[85] Just as Rocha's billiards table has imperfections that give the owner an advantage, John Grady and Rawlins are subjected to masculinity tests impossible to overcome for outsiders ignorant of Mexican culture. They are sent to a hellish prison, symbolizing the very apex of violent hypermasculinity:

> The prison was no more than a small walled village and within it occurred a
> constant seethe of barter and exchange in everything from radios and blankets
> down to matches and buttons and shoenails and within this bartering ran a
> constant struggle for status and position. Underpinning all of it like the fiscal
> standard in commercial societies lay a bedrock of depravity and violence

where in an egalitarian absolute every man was judged by a single standard and that was his readiness to kill. [86]

The prison functions as a dream realized for John Grady and Rawlins, a place devoid of women, where violent hypermasculinity runs wild and unchecked and a man's worth depends on his willingness to kill. The de facto leader of the prison tells John Grady, "The world wants to know if you have cojones. If you are brave."[87] In the prison, bravery means death; having cojones equals possessing the willingness to die for no reason. A willingness to kill in the Castelar prison necessarily implies a willingness to also die. Ironically, in a prison where life and death seem to be predicated on violent hypermasculinity, "only after Duena Alfonsa buys their freedom can they leave."[88] Without the help of Alejandra's aunt, John Grady and Rawlins would have died in the Mexican prison. That the boys are rescued by a woman in a country where machismo rules proves ironic. Despite John Grady's repudiation of strong women throughout the novel, in the end one saves him.

HOMOSEXUALITY

Ironically, the rural hypermasculine code of the United States creates a space conducive to homosexual desire. This is ironic because hypermasculine men stereotypically do not harbor same-sex desire. This stereotype stems more from limited definitions of masculinity than it does from reality. Heterosexual men do not own the rights to masculinity. On the contrary, perhaps the more hypermasculine a man appears, the more likely he might possess gay longings. A man's hypermasculinity may manifest as overcompensation for his closeted homosexual desire. Alfred Kinsey's book *Sexual Behavior in the Human Male*[89] offers evidence that rural space and culture may facilitate homosexuality. Quoting the Kinsey report, Campbell points out,

> The boy on the isolated farm has few companions except his brothers, the boys on an adjacent farm or two, visiting male cousins, and the somewhat older farm hand. His mother may see to it that he does not spend much time with his sisters, and the moral codes of the rural community may impose considerable limitations upon the association of boys and girls under other circumstances. Moreover, farm activities call for masculine capacities, and associations with girls are rated sissy by most of the boys in such a community. [90]

The exclusion of women is the strongest characteristic of rural hypermasculinity and perhaps most forms of hypermasculinity. Many rural men associate women with weakness, domesticity, and emotion, all attributes they wish to avoid; but in order for one to engage in a heterosexual relationship both sexes must interact. Campbell goes on to note, "These archetypal 'farm boys' get their teenage kicks off each other (and, as the report notes, farm animals) because girls are not available to them."[91] Essentially, by defining rural masculinity in part as a space absent of women or as flight from the feminine, rural hypermasculine gender codes and social mores create spaces conducive to same-sex desire. The hypermasculine rural adolescent engaging in homosexuality often evolves into a hypermasculine adult who engages in homosexual activity. As Campbell further reveals,

> There is a fair amount of sexual contact among the older males in Western rural areas. It is a type of homosexuality which was probably common among pioneers and outdoor men in general. Today it is found among ranchmen, cattle men, prospectors, lumbermen, and farming groups in general—among groups that are virile, physically active.[92]

Without women around, men look to other men to relieve their sex drive. Hypermasculine men often raise prospective hypermasculine men to privilege and value maleness over femininity; homosexual behavior results as an extension of this valuation. One must not discount those men who likely emerge from the womb with homosexual desire. For them, regardless of the circumstances of their upbringing, same-sex desire exists as an inevitability. The problem arises when hypermasculine gay rural men evolve into homophobic, racist, and sexist closeted hypermasculine men because they cannot reconcile their desire with their strict masculinity.

In *All the Pretty Horses* there are strong indicators that John Grady and Rawlins, particularly Rawlins, harbor homosexual desire for one another. Sullivan relates, "One of the most striking patterns to emerge is the narrative expulsion or containment of women."[93] John Grady's experience with American women functions as one of the main impetuses for his rejection of the United States. Rawlins vehemently supports John Grady's repudiation of women. When John Grady and Mary Catherine break up, Rawlins tells John Grady, "She aint worth it. None of em are."[94] When John Grady shows a desire for Alejandra, Rawlins warns, "I've told you before but I dont reckon you'll listen now any more than you done then . . . I just figure you must enjoy cryin yourself to sleep at night . . . This one of course she probably dates guys got their own airplanes let alone cars."[95] Rawlins worships John Grady and regards him as the quintessential cowboy and therefore the perfect man. After riding for some time with Blevins, Rawlins tells him, "There's a lot of good riders. But there's just one that's the best. And he [John Grady] happens to be settin right yonder."[96] For the boys and their rural cowboy code, the ability to ride a horse is tantamount to sexual prowess among urban men. Rawlins bestows the crown of alpha male on John Grady by admitting that he rides the best. Sullivan argues, "This homoerotic longing is evident in the verbal and nonverbal expressions of jealousy so prevalent in the trilogy. Lacey is jealous not only of Alejandra, but of Blevins, as is evident when he advocates leaving Blevins behind."[97] Rawlins seems to prefer to have John Grady all to himself and appears most content when the two boys interact alone.

Many rural hypermasculine men in creating their sense of self reject what they deem feminine. Recklessly adventurous and accepting violence as a way of life, the rural man may suppress in himself anything others homosocially might consider feminine. Consequently, these rural men eventually come to value hypermasculinity, laying a foundation for homosexuality in a generally homophobic space. The third-person narrator of *All the Pretty Horses* says of John Grady, "What he loved in horses was what he loved in men, the blood and the heat of the blood that ran them. All his reverence and all his fondness and all the leanings of his life were for the ardenthearted and they would always be so and never be otherwise."[98] If a man his whole life equates passion with masculinity, it follows that he may eventually prefer the company of men and the activities endemic to men. Relegating women to a liminal domesticated space creates a sexist and homophobic environment conducive to male homosexuality.

In the text, on several occasions, the boys strip naked as a sort of tacit act of homosexual exhibition, further suggesting the quotidian nature of exposing themselves to one another. Not long after John Grady and Rawlins meet up with Blevins, "they crossed the river under a white quartermoon naked and pale and thin atop their horses . . . and dressed only in their hats they led the horses out onto the gravel spit and loosed the girthstraps and mounted and put the horses into the water with their naked heels."[99] After the three boys have ridden together for some time and eaten lunch, John Grady "tied up the cloth and stood and began to strip out of his clothes and he walked out naked through the grass past the horses and waded out into the water and sat in it to his waist."[100] Never do the boys say a word about each other's nakedness, something that homophobic urban boys would certainly do to make clear their heterosexuality.[101] Perhaps they sense the incongruence of their desire and shroud it in silence so as to protect it and themselves.

Once the boys enter Mexico, the transparency of their fraudulent cowboy hypermasculinity renders them vulnerable to men who acquire their masculinity by exposing chingados. Irwin maintains, "by the 1940s and 50s . . . homophobia became the guiding principle in Mexican culture . . . The idea was to use male-male relations to *chingar* as much as possible to achieve an ever more pronounced masculinity, without becoming tainted with homosexuality, as only the *chingado* was made homosexual by homosexual contact."[102] Homosexual contact among men did not necessarily signify homosexuality. Only the chingado in the sexual dynamic bore the mark of a homosexual. Determining the chingar and the chingado often had nothing to do with homosexual physical contact. Any sort of confrontation, competition, or comparison between men where there existed a winner and loser resulted in a chingar and chingado, not unlike the African American pastime of playing the dozens. [103] The assailability of masculinity among men in Mexican society stems from the oppression of women and strict gender codes. Irwin goes on to note, "Women are seen as open, penetrable beings, and their femininity is a sign of weakness, while men are closed beings who show their power over others by penetrating them. Men must never allow themselves to crack and must flaunt their power by fucking others over, in one way or another." [104] Cultural warfare often exists as the natural state of men in Mexico and the determining factor in a Mexican man's self-worth; consequently, "masculinity is frequently put to the test among men. Contests of wit, authority, or brute force produce symbolic relations of sexual penetration, in which the loser cracks, gets fucked, and is feminized by the winner, who, in this way, enhances his masculinity." [105] In a society as sensitive to fraudulent hypermasculinities as Mexico, where men strut around on the lookout for other men who might bolster their own masculinity, the boys present themselves as easy targets. After Blevins loses his gun, his horse, and most of his clothing, the boys encounter a group of Mexican wax peddlers who assume the half-naked Blevins to be a sort of sex slave for John Grady and Rawlins:

> Blevins sat with his bare legs stretched out before him but they looked so white and exposed lying there on the ground that he seemed ashamed and he tried to tuck them up under him and to cover his knees with the tails of the borrowed shirt he wore . . . The workers had for the most part finished their meal and they were leaning back smoking cigarettes and belching quietly. [106]

To the Mexican men, Blevins represents an obvious chingado. Consequently, "the man in the vest studied John Grady and he looked across the clearing at Blevins. Then he asked John Grady if he wished to sell the boy . . . The man offered that he would trade for him in wax." [107] After John Grady declines the sale, the boys' relationship confuses the Mexican men. If Blevins, John Grady, and Rawlins are equals, then Blevins's obvious femininity feminizes John Grady and Rawlins as well.

The most obvious example of the boys' vulnerability to Mexican hypermasculinities occurs after their arrest, when the captain seemingly rapes Rawlins. As Jay Ellis argues, "Torture in the shower is clearly indicated. That it involves some form of rape is strongly implied." [108] The captain begins his interrogation of Rawlins by saying to him, "You must co-porate . . . Then you dont have no troubles. Turn around. Put down your pants." [109] The text does not reveal what happens next, but later "they let Rawlins go just inside the door and he slid to the floor and sat for a moment and then bent slowly forward and to one side and lay holding himself." [110] Rawlins bending forward suggests, among other possibilities, that the captain may have anally raped him. After John Grady's interrogation, Rawlins asks him, "You didnt get to go to the shower room? . . . He keeps a white coat back there on a hook. He takes it down and puts it on and ties it around his waist with a string."[111] John Grady avoids rape because the captain senses his role of chingar to Rawlins's chingado. He intuits that John Grady may not submit as easily as Rawlins. The fantasyland of John Grady and Rawlins becomes a nightmarish hyper-gendered culture where any chink in one's hypermasculine armor results in violent unmasking. The boys would have been better off engaging one another sexually at home instead of trying to prove their hypermasculinity in a country where men often prey on other men's perceived fragmented masculinity.

FAILED HEROISM

John Grady's failure to embody a hypermasculine cowboy hero capable of saving Blevins, winning the hand of Alejandra, and returning to the United States a triumphant man renders him ironically heroic since his failure casts a destructive light on frontier/cowboy hypermasculinity itself.[112] Unlike the kid in *Blood Meridian*, who in chapter one I argue is an ironic failed hero by virtue of being an unlikely hero full of rather unheroic traits, John Grady possesses some heroic qualities, namely the wisdom to realize, if vaguely, that his actions in Mexico, hypermasculine actions befitting a cowboy hero, are destructive. Further, he at times resembles a mythic hero in his singular ability with horses. Kevin Alexander Boon argues, "Despite the postmodern emphasis on heterogeneity that characterizes much of the 70s, 80s, and 90s, the hero figure is primarily a male figure; thus the hero figure is part of the metanarrative of masculinity, defining, as it does, idealized man."[113] The cowboy hypermasculinity John Grady aspires to also equates his idea of an idealized man, a man who Boon suggests "largely defines the masculinity to which many western men aspire and just as thoroughly defines their inevitable failure."[114] Their inevitable failure stems from the idea that "in seeking manhood at its fullest, they must pursue heroic status, but the achievement of that status can only be chimera and requires alienation and abject solitude. Thus they either seek the impossible or abandon their cultural status as men."[115] Like Boon's notion of the hero, hypermasculinity requires men to alienate women, to embrace violence and recklessness with no regard for self-preservation: "This is the paradox of contemporary American men: they either embrace the mythic figuration of the hero, which they inevitably fail to embody . . . or they reject the mythic figuration of the hero and thus fail to embody the culturally coded definition of a man."[116] In the case of John Grady, his failure to live up to his own definition of manhood proves ironically heroic. Had he achieved what he set out to do, his heroism would further perpetuate destructive notions of hypermasculinity dangerous to men all over the world.

John Grady himself seems aware that his return to the United States smacks of failure. Racked with guilt over his inaction during Blevins's murder, killing the prison assassin, betraying Rocha, and nearly killing the captain, he realizes that what he has done has left him feeling cold and lost, not heroic. The destructiveness of his cowboy identity eludes him, which explains his aimlessness. Spurgeon notes, "Upon his return to Texas, John Grady is caught between two visions of the world, unable to return to the safe confines of the mythic past and as yet equally incapable of seeing how he must live his life in the future. He exists in a liminal space beyond myth, but not yet within history."[117] Like the hero who creates his own demise by rendering himself unnecessary by his heroic acts, once John Grady unwittingly proves the corrosive nature of cowboy hypermasculinity nothing else remains for him to do. He senses the anachronistic nature of his identity and appears unwilling to assimilate into modern culture, fulfilling Alfonsa's notion that "in the end we all come to be cured of our sentiments. Those whom life does not cure death will. The world is quite ruthless in selecting between the dream and the reality, even where we will not."[118] John Grady chooses a liminal space between the dream and the reality because while he seems to regret many of his decisions in Mexico he appears unwilling to give up his cowboy sentiments completely. Alfonsa, on the other hand, though wise, has given up completely the idealism that compelled her to fight for equality in Mexico when young. As a result, she both admires and ridicules the idealism in John Grady.

By the end of the novel John Grady has evolved from a boy who feels entitled to the family farm, judgmental of his mother and father, and capable of embodying all the cowboy heroes of his dreams into a humble man who understands the limits of self. After he details his story to the judge in order to prove the origins of Blevins's horse and the judge treats him like a hero, he tells the judge, "It just bothered me that you might think I was somethin special. I aint."[119] The John Grady at the beginning of the novel might have reveled in the showering of praise by the judge, but by the end he no longer requires the same sort of validation. Spurgeon points out, "the most important part of the Duena Alfonsa's lesson for John Grady—that to distinguish what is true from what is useful to believe means to discard all the myths one's culture holds dear and make one's way in the world alone, with nothing but one's own courage to call upon, and all without ever falling into hopeless bitterness."[120] John Grady has not learned Alfonsa's lesson in full. He has altered his view of himself and perhaps his notions of what it means to be a cowboy, but he has not given up his desire to live a rural life. Lydia R. Cooper agrees: "If his [John Grady's] actions depict him as a failed hero, his internal responses indicate a quite different trajectory: as John Grady's external failures increase, his internal recognition of those failures suggests that he may mature from a callow boy to a morally responsible man."[121] John Grady makes no excuses for his actions and accepts his guilt, perhaps finally intuiting the destructiveness of his cowboy dream.

There exists a tragic aura around him at the end, a sense of doom, a feeling that he cannot give up certain aspects of his hypermasculinity, such as his predilection for solitude and the selfish way he treats women. He has illustrated a lesson about hypermasculinities, but at the expense of himself as a character. If he refuses to finally give up those last strands of the unviable masculine hero, then he will fade into the past, an anachronism like the dime novels and old Hollywood Westerns. The final passage of the novel presents John Grady as just that, an image in a Hollywood film replayed for nostalgic purposes: "He rode with the sun coppering his face and the red wind blowing out of the west across the evening land and the small desert birds flew chittering among the dry bracken and horse and rider and horse passed on and their long shadows passed in tandem like the shadow of a single being. Passed and paled into the darkening land, the world to come."[122] He has evolved into a simulacrum with a blurred, distorted referential, doomed to fizzle out for no one's benefit, heroic if only because of the palpable doom that surrounds him. The lyricism of the language and the staginess of the light only further cast him as an actor in an anachronistic drama, illustrating the inviability of his cowboy identity.

Like the kid in *Blood Meridian*, John Grady Cole's failure to perpetuate a destructive hypermasculinity renders him ironically heroic. That he appears somewhat aware of his circumstances suggests redemption, even though he fades into the distance alone and a failure. Cooper further notes,

> In McCarthy's novels, the flawed moral characters often face defeat, their attempts at morality fall short of any effective outcome, and they typically die in the end without any external evidence that their actions have a quantifiable merit . . . [All] these characters who demonstrate acts of kindness or ethical awareness are heroes *because* they undergo epistemological crisis and fail to act out the good they know they ought to do.[123]

His understanding that his actions in Mexico, stereotypically those of a cowboy hero, have left him feeling empty presents a positive alternative to the status quo. Even though he appears unwilling or unable to relinquish all the reckless, oppressive traits of his rural cowboy hypermasculinity, it appears clear that he has come to an existential crisis, intuiting that he has been on a doomed destructive path all this time. He likely does not understand the origin of the cowboy myth and that his identity in large part stems from the cultural master narratives of cheap fiction and Hollywood films; yet he must face the fact that his ever more industrialized country has little room for a cowboy relentlessly in conflict with consumerism and the social gains of women and other marginalized people. While in Mexico John Grady attempts to embody a hypermasculine hero by masochistically redoubling his efforts to prove his manhood, culminating in symbolic masturbatory self-penetration. Though Mexico initially represents to him the untamed West of his dreams, he soon realizes the implications of a nation that has embraced a hyper-patriarchy predicated on violence and the oppression of women. If being a cowboy means he must witness and enact violence, betray his benefactors, and compromise the reputation of women, perhaps being a cowboy is not what he thought it was. In Mexico, Rawlins, Blevins, and very nearly John Grady play the role of the chingado perhaps because of their inability to act upon their gay desire at home and their subsequent need to prove themselves real hypermasculine cowboys. Well before John Grady, Rawlins, while in prison, admits he has been living a lie: "We think we're a couple of pretty tough cowboys . . . They could kill us any time."[124] For John Grady, giving up his hypermasculinity is not so easy. Only after he has confronted the captain, failed to win the heart of Alejandra, and retrieved Blevins's horse does he realize that what should make him feel like a cowboy who has had an adventure leaves him feeling empty and brokenhearted. He cannot forgive himself for killing the prison assassin, something a Hollywood cowboy would surely be proud of. His heroism relies mostly on the fact that he does not accept himself as a hero. His realization that he has acted destructively renders him *ironically* heroic in his failure. *All the Pretty Horses* falls short of a bildungsroman precisely because John Grady fails to fully accept Alfonsa's lesson and give up the myth of the hypermasculine cowboy; and yet the novel, if read closely, can be a coming-of-age tale for readers still clinging to outmoded definitions of masculinity.

NOTES

1. Merle Haggard, "I Wish Things Were Simple Again," *Live from Austin, TX* (New West, 2006), CD.

2. In chapter one I argue that the hypermasculinity of the American Southwest frontier during the middle of the nineteenth century stemmed in large part from "the deep-seated racial divide among the Apaches, Comanches, Mexicans, and Americans, as well as other American Indian tribes, [creating] a hotbed of violence where competing ethnicities fought unrelentingly for land, respect, and wealth." In *Blood Meridian*, "power," I argue further, "mostly held by the roving male gangs, evolves into the ability and willingness to wage war against anyone not male, white, and willing to worship war. This power develops into a . . . definition of hypermasculinity, resulting in warfare marked by culturally contrived symbols of emasculation, such as the sodomizing of corpses and the wounded and the cutting away of genitalia." The popular culture Hollywood cowboy appropriated and commodified this hypermasculine figure, projecting an antiseptic version without all the especially gruesome violence. John Grady is a boy who has read *The Horse of America* and seems well versed in the genealogies of horses in general, and yet cannot differentiate between real horses and "picturebook horses." Cormac McCarthy, *All the Pretty Horses* (New York: Vintage, 1993), 16, 116. Likely he has consumed mass quantities of popular culture and, like the rest of America, cannot differentiate between the real frontiersman and the Hollywood cowboy. Consequently, his notions of the hypermasculine

cowboy likely stem from popular culture and not from the actual brutal frontiersmen themselves.

3. One could argue that *All the Pretty Horses* parodies these early cowboy manifestations and in this way functions as a postmodern text. Linda Hutcheon in part defines a parodic postmodern text as one that "through a double process of installing and ironizing . . . signals how present representations come from past ones and what ideological consequences derive from both continuity and difference." Linda Hutcheon, *The Politics of Postmodernism* (Routledge: London, 1989), 93. In utilizing conventions from these early narratives, such as comedic twists and curt, tough dialogue, McCarthy in effect affirms these early genres. What makes *All the Pretty Horses* a parodic text and therefore postmodern pivots on the notion that the novel undermines the genre by presenting a cowboy who self-consciously fails to enact the stereotypical hero. John Grady's failures cast a destructive light on the early manifestations of the Western, drawing attention to their destructive emphasis on hypermasculinity.

4. When referring to John Grady Cole, I will often use his first and middle names in order to draw attention to his mother's maiden name, Grady. Although John Grady resents his mother for her strong-willed independence, much of his identity as a cowboy stems from her side of the family. John Grady grew up on his maternal grandfather's ranch, a setting that helped spawn and cultivate his cowboy identity.

5. I am referring to Freud's notion of moral masochism, which he defines as "the third form of masochism, the moral type . . . chiefly remarkable for having loosened its connection with what we recognize to be sexuality." John Grady engages in masochistic behavior because of the guilt he feels for not attempting to save Blevins; for insulting Rocha, his boss, by having sex with his daughter; for killing the prison assassin; and for his revenge on the captain. Freud points out that in moral masochism, "it is the suffering itself that matters." Sigmund Freud, "The Economic Problem of Masochism," in *Collected Papers of Sigmund Freud*, vol. 2, trans. Joan Riviere (New York: Basic Books, 1959), 262. John Grady's most prominent masochistic act occurs when he cauterizes a bullet wound in his leg with the red-hot barrel of his pistol. This act anticipates his admission to the judge that he "didn't feel justified." McCarthy, *All the Pretty Horses*, 290. Further, through the masochistic act John Grady satiates feelings of white male victimhood by proving his manhood and simultaneously punishing himself for desiring to prove his manhood.

6. Josef Früchtl, *The Impertinent Self: A Heroic History of Modernity*, trans. Sarah L. Kirkby (Stanford: Stanford University Press, 2009), 41.

7. Früchtl, *The Impertinent Self*, 41.

8. Sara Spurgeon, "Pledged in Blood: Truth and Redemption in Cormac McCarthy's *All the Pretty Horses*," in *Cormac McCarthy*, ed. Harold Bloom (Philadelphia: Chelsea House, 2002), 79.

9. Hugh Campbell, "Masculinity and Rural Life, An Introduction" in *Country Boys: Masculinity and Rural Life*, ed. Hugh Campbell, Michael Mayersfeld Bell, and Margaret Finney (University Park: Pennsylvania State University Press, 2006), 19.

10. McCarthy, *All the Pretty Horses*, 4.

11. McCarthy, *All the Pretty Horses*, 5.

12. Molly McBride, "From Mutilation to Penetration: Cycles of Conquest in *Blood Meridian* and *All the Pretty Horses*," *Southwestern American Literature* 25, no. 1 (Fall 1999): 24.

13. Campbell, "Masculinity and Rural Life," 167.

14. Campbell, "Masculinity and Rural Life," 7.

15. McCarthy, *All the Pretty Horses*, 7.

16. McCarthy, *All the Pretty Horses*, 12.

17. Campbell, "Masculinity and Rural Life," 159.

18. Sarah Gleeson-White, "Playing Cowboys: Genre, Myth, and Cormac McCarthy's *All the Pretty Horses*," *Southwestern American Literature* 33, no. 1 (Fall 2007): 27.

19. By contrast, Kaja Silverman in *Male Subjectivity at the Margins* highlights films that underscore the emasculating effects of World War II on men, such as *The Best Years of Our Lives* (1946), *It's a Wonderful Life* (1946), and *The Guilt of Janet Ames* (1947). She argues that these films are "characterized by a loss of faith in the familiar and self-evident. The hero no longer feels 'at home' in the house or town where he grew up, and resists cultural

(re)assimilation; he has been dislodged from the narratives and subject-positions which make up the dominant fiction, and he returns to them only under duress." Kaja Silverman, *Male Subjectivity at the Margins* (New York: Routledge, 1992), 53. The Western provided an alternative narrative to these films, which were released and took place just after World War II, in which the hero could take his rightful place in the subject-position of the dominant fiction of patriarchal masculinity.

20. John Cant, *Cormac McCarthy and the Myth of American Exceptionalism* (New York: Routledge, 2008), 180. Some of these early series and novels and their writers, according to Richard Slotkin, were the James Boys series (ca. 1883) by Frank Tousey, Deadwood Dick (ca. 1878) by Edward Wheeler, and *The Swamp Outlaws, or, The North Carolina Bandits* (1874) by George Alfred Townsed. Further, "some fiction factories like Beadle & Adams and Street and Smith" employed many writers for their titles. Richard Slotkin, *Gunfighter Nation* (New York: Atheneum, 1992), 128, 143, 684–85. Donald K. Meisenheimer Jr. contends that the early Western genre was "spawned in its modern guise by Owen Wister," most notably in his novel *The Virginian* (1902). Donald K. Meisenheimer Jr., "Machining the Man: From Neurasthenia to Psychasthenia in SF and the Genre Western," *Science Fiction Studies* 24, no. 3 (1997): 441. From these early novels Hollywood appropriated the genre and the stock images and figures in movies like *The Great Train Robbery* (1903) and, later, *Shane* (1953), *The Searchers* (1956), and *The Man Who Shot Liberty Valance* (1962). Gleeson-White, "Playing Cowboys," 24–26.

21. Edwin T. Arnold and Dianne C. Luce, "Introduction," in *A Cormac McCarthy Companion: The Border Trilogy*, ed. Edwin T. Arnold and Dianne C. Luce (Jackson: University Press of Mississippi, 2001), vii.

22. Gleeson-White, "Playing Cowboys," 31.

23. McCarthy, *All the Pretty Horses*, 177.

24. McCarthy, *All the Pretty Horses*, 178.

25. McCarthy, *All the Pretty Horses*, 16.

26. Gleeson-White, "Playing Cowboys," 28.

27. Jean Baudrillard, *Simulacra and Simulation*, trans. Sheila Faria Glaser (Michigan: University of Michigan Press, 2010), 2.

28. Früchtl, *The Impertinent Self*, 94.

29. McCarthy, *All the Pretty Horses*, 53.

30. McCarthy, *All the Pretty Horses*, 68.

31. Wade Hall, "The Human Comedy of Cormac McCarthy," in *Cormac McCarthy*, ed. Harold Bloom (Philadelphia: Chelsea House, 2002), 59.

32. Cant, *Cormac McCarthy and the Myth of American Exceptionalism*, 193.

33. Philip A. Snyder, "Cowboy Codes in Cormac McCarthy's Border Trilogy," in *A Cormac McCarthy Companion: The Border Trilogy*, ed. Edwin T. Arnold and Dianne C. Luce (Jackson: University Press of Mississippi, 2001), 223.

34. Früchtl, *The Impertinent Self*, 95.

35. McCarthy, *All the Pretty Horses*, 291.

36. Barcley Owens, *Cormac McCarthy's Western Novels* (Tucson: University of Arizona Press, 2000), 64.

37. McCarthy, *All the Pretty Horses*, 19.

38. McCarthy, *All the Pretty Horses*, 28.

39. Meisenheimer, "Machining the Man," 451.

40. Andrew Blair Spencer, "A Cowboy Looks at Reality: The Death of the American Frontier and the Illumination of the Cowboy Myth in Cormac McCarthy's *All the Pretty Horses*," in *Western Futures: Perspectives on the Humanities at the Millennium*, ed. Stephen Tchudi (Reno: Halcyon Press, 1999), 144–45.

41. Gleeson-White, "Playing Cowboys," 28.

42. James Bell, *Cormac McCarthy's West: The Border Trilogy Annotations* (El Paso: Texas Western Press, 2002), 43.

43. James Bell points out that in the novel during the year 1950, "between September 25 and November 30—[a]n inconsistency in the chronology occurs at this point. Though the text indicates that John Grady is in the mountains of northern Mexico for only a few days after the release of the captain, his arrival in Langtry, Texas, occurs more than two months after he parts

with the captain." Bell, *Cormac McCarthy's West*, 5. McCarthy may have intended this inconsistency to demonstrate the point at which John Grady emerges from his timeless fantasy world
in Mexico. Considering McCarthy's attention to detail and the verisimilitude of his fictive
worlds, the intention of this error seems likely.

44. Linda Townley Woodson, "Deceiving the Will to Truth: The Semiotic Foundation of *All
the Pretty Horses*," in *Sacred Violence: Cormac McCarthy's Western Novels*, ed. Wade Hall
and Rick Wallach (El Paso: Texas Western Press, 2002), 52.

45. McCarthy, *All the Pretty Horses*, 44.

46. Cant, *Cormac McCarthy and the Myth of American Exceptionalism*, 192.

47. McCarthy, *All the Pretty Horses*, 168.

48. McCarthy, *All the Pretty Horses*, 180.

49. McCarthy, *All the Pretty Horses*, 193.

50. Gleeson-White, "Playing Cowboys," 27.

51. McCarthy, *All the Pretty Horses*, 10.

52. McCarthy, *All the Pretty Horses*, 10.

53. Cant, *Cormac McCarthy and the Myth of American Exceptionalism*, 179.

54. McCarthy, *All the Pretty Horses*, 31.

55. Jay Ellis, *No Place for Home: Spatial Constraint and Character Flight in the Novels of
Cormac McCarthy* (New York: Routledge, 2006), 200.

56. McCarthy, *All the Pretty Horses*, 17.

57. McCarthy, *All the Pretty Horses*, 15.

58. Nell Sullivan, "Boys Will Be Boys and Girls Will Be Gone: The Circuit of Male Desire
in Cormac McCarthy's Border Trilogy," in *A Cormac McCarthy Companion: The Border
Trilogy*, ed. Edwin T. Arnold and Dianne C. Luce (Jackson: University Press of Mississippi,
2001), 230.

59. Sullivan, "Boys Will Be Boys," 230.

60. McCarthy, *All the Pretty Horses*, 22.

61. McCarthy, *All the Pretty Horses*, 22.

62. McCarthy, *All the Pretty Horses*, 24.

63. McCarthy, *All the Pretty Horses*, 28.

64. McCarthy, *All the Pretty Horses*, 29.

65. David Savran, "The Sadomasochist in the Closet: White Masculinity and the Culture of
Victimization," *Differences: A Journal of Feminist Cultural Studies* 8, no. 2 (Summer 1996):
138.

66. Savran, "The Sadomasochist in the Closet," 146.

67. McCarthy, *All the Pretty Horses*, 274.

68. McCarthy, *All the Pretty Horses*, 51.

69. McCarthy, *All the Pretty Horses*, 231.

70. Spurgeon, "Pledged in Blood," 84.

71. Martha I. Chew Sanchez, "El Diablo en una Botella Nortena: Music and the Construction of Mexican Masculinity," *Third Text* 18, no. 5 (Sept. 2004): 486.

72. McCarthy, *All the Pretty Horses*, 97.

73. Bell, *Cormac McCarthy's West*, 24.

74. Sanchez, "El Diablo en una Botella Nortena," 488.

75. McCarthy, *All the Pretty Horses*, 123.

76. McCarthy, *All the Pretty Horses*, 136–37.

77. McBride, "From Mutilation to Penetration," 31.

78. After Alfonsa warns John Grady about his relationship with Alejandra, Rawlins says to
John Grady, "You got eyes for the spread?" John Grady responds, "I don't know . . . I aint
thought about it." Rawlins then says, "Sure you aint." McCarthy, *All the Pretty Horses*, 138.
Rawlins, John Grady's longtime best friend, believes John Grady has imagined replacing
Rocha as the patriarch of the ranch and senses danger.

79. McBride, "From Mutilation to Penetration," 31.

80. McCarthy, *All the Pretty Horses*, 123.

81. The *coleadero*, a Mexican dance and rodeo festival where men prove their masculinity
by illustrating their prowess over farm animals, offers an insight into the strict gender codes

and the oppression of women in Mexico. Sanchez reports, "In the *coleaderos* women occupy a socially and symbolically monitored secondary status. Women are informally but firmly assigned to a designated space and are not supposed to move away from it. If a woman needs to talk to her brother, husband, father, or son, she must either wait until he comes over or send him a message by way of child, preferably a young boy. A woman who does approach men must make sure her interaction is short, that she does not interrupt their conversation or look 'too bossy' so as to denigrate his power over her in front of other men. Women have to avoid verbally and non-verbally being the centre of the male gaze." Sanchez, "El Diablo en una Botella Nortena," 486. Much of Mexican gender codes happen in public where homosocially men grant other men their masculinity. Once other men see John Grady with Alejandra, he gains masculinity in their eyes, but simultaneously Rocha loses it, ultimately causing Rocha to have John Grady arrested.

82. Gloria Anzaldua, "Borderlands/La Frontera," in *Literary Theory: An Anthology*, ed. Julie Rivkin and Michael Ryan (Malden: Blackwell, 2004), 1018.

83. Anzaldua, "Borderlands/La Frontera," 1022.

84. Robert McKee Irwin, *Mexican Masculinities* (Minneapolis: University of Minnesota Press, 2003), xvii.

85. Irwin, *Mexican Masculinities*, xxi.

86. McCarthy, *All the Pretty Horses*, 182.

87. McCarthy, *All the Pretty Horses*, 193.

88. John Wegner, "Whose Story Is It?: History and Fiction in Cormac McCarthy's *All the Pretty Horses*," *Southern Quarterly: A Journal of the Arts in the South* 36, no. 2 (Winter 1998): 107.

89. *Sexual Behavior in the Human Male*, first published in 1948 and written by Alfred Kinsey, Wardell Pomeroy, Clyde Martin, and Paul Gebhard, detailed the contemporary sexual behavior of men based on thousands of interviews.

90. Campbell, "Masculinity and Rural Life," 167.

91. Campbell, "Masculinity and Rural Life," 167.

92. Campbell, "Masculinity and Rural Life," 167.

93. Sullivan, "Boys Will Be Boys," 229.

94. McCarthy, *All the Pretty Horses*, 10.

95. McCarthy, *All the Pretty Horses*, 118.

96. McCarthy, *All the Pretty Horses*, 59.

97. Sullivan, "Boys Will Be Boys," 249.

98. McCarthy, *All the Pretty Horses*, 6.

99. McCarthy, *All the Pretty Horses*, 45.

100. McCarthy, *All the Pretty Horses*, 57–58.

101. Perhaps the most famous narrative about homosexual cowboys, the short story "Brokeback Mountain," by Annie Proulx, which appeared in *The New Yorker* four years after the publication of *All the Pretty Horses*, bears a noteworthy resemblance to the novel. At one point, made famous in part by the film of the same name released in 2005 and directed by Ang Lee, Jack tells his clandestine lover, Ennis, "You're too much for me, Ennis, you son of a whoreson bitch. I wish I knew how to quit you." Annie Proulx, "Brokeback Mountain," in *Close Range* (New York: Scribner, 1999), 276. Similarly, in the text of *All the Pretty Horses*, after Blevins steals back his horse and gun, Rawlins expresses his fear and foreboding that trouble might be lurking ahead. John Grady then says to Rawlins, "You aint fixin to quit me are you?" Rawlins replies, "I said I wouldnt." After the Mexican authorities arrest the boys, Rawlins again expresses his anger, and John Grady responds, "You either stick or you quit and I wouldnt quit you I dont care what you done . . . I never quit you." McCarthy, *All the Pretty Horses*, 91, 156. The tone of these endearments evince a deeper, perhaps romantic connection. The boys harbor a loyalty to one another not unlike a husband and wife.

102. Irwin, *Mexican Masculinities*, xxxiv.

103. "Playing the dozens" refers to "verbal sparring," usually among African American males. The recriminations, or back-and-forth baiting, typically take on a jocular feel, but sometimes can lead to violence. Neal A. Lester, *Understanding Zora Neale Hurston's Their Eyes Were Watching God: A Student Casebook to Issues, Sources, and Historical Documents*

(Westport: Greenwood Press, 1999), 23. For African American males, whose masculinity has long been a point of sensitivity because of their inability to protect themselves or their wives and children during slavery, the dozens can reflect a dynamic similar to Mexican male culture. The loser of the dozens may be referred to as the "bitch" or the one with less masculinity as a result of the loss of face, while the winner tacitly gains in masculine stature.

104. Irwin, *Mexican Masculinities*, xxiii.

105. Irwin, *Mexican Masculinities*, xxiii.

106. McCarthy, *All the Pretty Horses*, 74.

107. McCarthy, *All the Pretty Horses*, 76.

108. Jay Ellis, "The Rape of Rawlins: A Note on All the Pretty Horses," *The Cormac McCarthy Journal* 1, no. 1 (Spring 2001): 68.

109. McCarthy, *All the Pretty Horses*, 163.

110. McCarthy, *All the Pretty Horses*, 165.

111. McCarthy, *All the Pretty Horses*, 169.

112. His tenuous acceptance of this fate suggests that McCarthy may have been undermining the cowboy myth all along. In any event, John Grady is still an ironic failed hero for illustrating the damaging effects of frontier/cowboy hypermasculinities.

113. Kevin Alexander Boon, "Heroes, Metanarratives, and the Paradox of Masculinity in Contemporary Western Culture," *Journal of Men's Studies: A Scholarly Journal about Men and Masculinities* 13, no. 3 (Spring 2005): 303.

114. Boon, "Heroes, Metanarratives, and the Paradox of Masculinity," 304.

115. Boon, "Heroes, Metanarratives, and the Paradox of Masculinity," 309.

116. Boon, "Heroes, Metanarratives, and the Paradox of Masculinity," 310.

117. Spurgeon, "Pledged in Blood," 88.

118. McCarthy, *All the Pretty Horses*, 238.

119. McCarthy, *All the Pretty Horses*, 293.

120. Spurgeon, "Pledged in Blood," 87.

121. Lydia R. Cooper, *No More Heroes: Narrative Perspective and Morality in Cormac McCarthy* (Baton Rouge: Louisiana State University Press), 2011.

122. McCarthy, *All the Pretty Horses*, 302.

123. Cooper, *No More Heroes*, 176

124. McCarthy, *All the Pretty Horses*, 186.

Chapter Three

Black Masculinities and Cultural Incest in *Song of Solomon*

Toni Morrison's *Song of Solomon* highlights two defining eras in African American history: Reconstruction, ending in the onset of the Jim Crow South (1869–1907), and the Civil Rights Movement (1955–1965). These eras, vital in understanding the plight of African Americans, provide loci for destructive definitions of various black masculinities. After Macon Dead I receives his free papers in 1869, he initiates a definition of black masculinity based on materialism by developing property and amassing the material wealth his son, Macon II, later thinks defines successful white masculinity. After Macon Dead's murder, signaling the brutal end of Reconstruction and the onset of the Jim Crow South, Macon Dead II, as a way to honor his father and avenge his murder, adopts the philosophy that material wealth *alone* determines manhood and worth. Macon Dead II's faith that material wealth by itself determines manhood vitiates his character and all of his relationships throughout the rest of the novel. The African American Black Power Movement, the strong arm of the Black Liberation Movement of the 1950s and 1960s, paved the way for two notions of black masculinity, one predicated on violence and the other on the disempowerment of women. The novel's character Guitar, Milkman's best friend, adopts the Black Power Movement's philosophy of violence, resulting in a black masculinity predicated on violence. Historically, this philosophy affirmed hypermasculine black male stereotypes created by whites after Reconstruction in order to justify mass lynching[1] and the activities of white terrorist groups like the Ku Klux Klan. Further, Guitar and, to a degree, Milkman and Solomon, Milkman's great-grandfather, symbolize the ethos of the Black Power Movement by attempting to relegate women to the home, or disavow them altogether. Black masculinity then evolves into a construction defined by the absence of women,

55

sexism, or flight from the potential feminist/womanist[2] within black male subjectivity. Black manhood based on feminine negation echoes a black male trope stemming from slavery whereby black men gained freedom by symbolically or literally flying away from slavery and their families and communities. Consequently, black male flight ambiguously represents both freedom from slavery and abandonment of family, community, and the possibility of a feminine masculinity. Thematically, *Song of Solomon* critiques black masculinity by presenting symbols and tropes of masculine flight in a negative light in favor of the feminine salve of orality. The novel privileges the oral dissemination of black history and culture, mostly by women, over the cold, analytical, white masculine written word and disavowal of black history and culture. The implied critique of black masculinity positions the female character Pilate Dead as a failed and ironic hero,[3] in that her death allows Milkman Dead and the reader to realize that Pilate, though not the novel's central protagonist, represents the strongest, most complete character in a novel ostensibly about black men. Her death at the end of the novel transfers the focus from the Dead men to the black women who exist bound and limited by kinship systems and the incest taboo. Ruth and Hagar function as commodities exchanged by men in order to homosocially enact their masculinity and to negotiate their way up the American *white* class structure. Ruth's and Hagar's incestuous relationships with the men of the novel, such as Dr. Foster and Milkman Dead, show their limited opportunities for love within their own families, as well as their disillusionment with patriarchal social structures. Further, their incestuous acts and desires function as metaphors for alternative constructions of blackness based on black culture, history, and experience. Morrison shows men basing their masculinities on existing kinship systems and the incest taboo, while the women, through their incestuous desires, construct blackness based on black experience. The images of literal incest in *Song of Solomon* operate as metaphor for black identity arrived at via black experience, a notion I call *cultural incest*.

In league with the notion of black identity stemming from alternative sexualities based on black experience, writers such as bell hooks and Darieck Scott argue that black men must quit trying to compete with white males for hypermasculine supremacy and embrace a politics of failure marked by new constructions of sexuality and identity less destructive and less threatening, including symbolic and literal incest. Only by disavowing white definitions of success, family, and blackness stemming from slavery and beyond can black men and women create a solidarity strong enough to confront and conquer American racism.

AMERICAN CONTEXT

Morrison creates a black family history of the Deads, starting with Macon Dead I, in order to trace the development of black masculinities among the Dead men. Macon Dead I, also known as Jake, son of Solomon, symbolizes the precarious situation of a newly freed African American male in the post-bellum South. Rolland Murray notes, "The period between 1869, when the teenage Macon Dead I first receives his free papers, and his murder in 1907, straddles both the First Southern Reconstruction and what has been called the Nadir of black American history . . . [when] blacks saw the decimation of their right to participate in American democracy."[4] The entrenchment of white power effectively washed away the political gains African Americans acquired from the Emancipation Proclamation. When the North removed troops from the South in 1877, allowing white southerners to "reclaim their land and political power," African Americans once again fell into the vulnerable and deadly position of a people preyed upon.

Macon Dead I purchases and cultivates land, creating a definition of black manhood based on materialism that later generations of Dead men co-opt and falsely assume as an identity. Murray asserts, "What distinguishes Macon Dead I from the black men who became political representatives during Reconstruction is that he views the accumulation of individual land ownership rather than political and legal enfranchisement as a central category of black liberation."[5] Macon Dead ultimately defines himself, and later is defined by his son, as a man who bought and cultivated a stretch of land called "Lincoln's Heaven . . . a hundred and fifty acres. We tilled fifty. About eighty of it was woods. Must have been a fortune in oak and pine; maybe that's what they wanted—the lumber, the oak and the pine. We had a pond that was four acres. And a stream, full of fish. Right down in the heart of a valley."[6] Macon Dead I's successful cultivation of land in the American South after the Civil War reflects an admirable heroic courage. The reason Macon Dead I's actions launch a definition of black masculinity based on materialism centers on *Macon Dead II's* belief that all that mattered about Macon Dead I depended on the land that he owned. Macon Dead II boasts, "I worked right alongside my father. Right alongside him. From the time I was four or five we worked together."[7] Macon Dead II's early exposure to luxury and wealth leaves him with a sense of entitlement, resulting in his own Lincoln's Heaven in the black slum district of the Blood Bank where he presides as landlord. Even Macon Dead I's contemporaries view his aggregate wealth not as a means to develop a sense of family or cultivate and carry on black culture but rather as a testimonial to what *black men* and black men only could achieve: "You see, the farm said to them . . . See what you can do? Never mind you can't tell one letter from another, never mind you born a slave, never mind you lose your name, never mind your daddy dead, never mind nothing. Here . . . is what *a man can do* if he puts his mind to it and his back in it" (emphasis mine).[8] For these men, and later for Macon Dead II, Macon Dead I's sole achievement is his accumulation of wealth. Nevertheless, as Murray points out, African American disenfranchisement limits Macon Dead I's ability to maintain his Moses-like status: "Macon Dead I cannot possibly fulfill the promise of his patriarchal status because disenfranchisement leaves him as vulnerable to white aggression as the most dispossessed black citizen."[9] Pilate, Macon Dead II's sister, explains to Milkman, Macon Dead II's son, "Our papa was dead, you see. They blew him five feet up into the air. He was sitting on his fence waiting for 'em, and they snuck up from behind and blew him five feet into the air."[10] Macon Dead II later reflects, "His father had sat for five nights on a split-rail fence cradling a shotgun and in the end died protecting his property."[11] The difference between Pilate's version and Macon Dead II's version of the events surrounding their father's death pivots on the latter's emphasis on the lost property that he equates with his father's manhood. Murray notes, "Through the figure of Macon Dead I, a former Virginian slave, the novel demonstrates that the limbo that black Americans find themselves in after the 1863 emancipation facilitates the emergence of a myth that a black patriarch would lead them out of the wilderness."[12] Macon Dead II seizes the myth his father failed to realize and attempts to fulfill it by mimicking the baser qualities of white capitalists and exploiting poor blacks whose choices of housing prove limited to what Macon Dead II offers. Instead of using his power and financial wherewithal to help the community, he attempts to distance himself from the black community while simultaneously and unyieldingly demanding his rents on time.

Most of the novel takes place during what Philip Page describes as "the most violent years" of the tumultuous American Black Liberation Movement, between 1955 and 1964, providing the ethos for two additional versions of black masculinity, violence and androcentrism, or outright misogyny.[13] Guitar Bains represents the idea that inflicting revolutionary violence on whites is the duty of all black males. Further, black males must dutifully and simultaneously protect and preside over black females. Though Guitar's violent philosophy results in bloodshed, he insists the impetus centers on a love for all black people. Ralph Story contends, "For black folk 'to love so much they would kill' is a profoundly radical idea yet one which can be clearly discerned in the poetical works of the Black Arts Movement of the late 1960s."[14] Guitar's philosophy degenerates into simply a love for violence that ultimately ruins his relationship with Milkman. Guitar represents the baser aspects of the Black Arts Movement and the Black Power Movement, which contended that "if more than just a handful of courageous, righteous, and sacrificial black men and women had been willing to 'love' enough to avenge the murders of their people, virtually giving up their lives, then the overt and covert oppression of black folk might have ended long ago."[15] The methodology of the Seven Days develops into the credo "an eye for an eye," literally copying the violence of their white oppressors. bell hooks describes the historical analogue of the Seven Days: the Black Panther Party:

> The images that everyone remembered were of beautiful black men wearing leather jackets and berets, armed with machine guns, poised and ready to strike. The message that lingered was that black men were able to do violence, that they had stood up to the white man, faced him down. No matter that they lost in the armed struggle; they had proven they were men by their willingness to die.[16]

hooks's evocation suggests that a philosophy of violence suffers from a limited purview and a romantic fatalism. Instead of death, the message should focus on healing. If the ultimate gain costs one his or her life, then no real gain takes place. hooks further writes, "After the black power militants lost their armed resistance struggle to the white male patriarchal state, they were left without a platform. Since their platforms . . . had been given them by the very imperialist capitalist patriarchal state they were claiming to want to overthrow, they were easy to silence."[17] The message of the Black Power Movement unraveled due to its reliance and emphasis on the very violence of which their white oppressors were guilty. Once the ability to wage violence was silenced the movement sputtered.

The other definition of black masculinity that emerges from the Black Power Movement and Guitar's revolutionary philosophies depends on the disempowerment of women, or the absence of women. In *Song of Solomon*, this aspect of the movement is reflected in Guitar's desire to define himself without women. Guitar feels as though black women "want your whole self" and call it "Love."[18] When asked by Milkman "if a colored woman is raped and killed, why do the Seven Days rape and kill a white woman," Guitar answers, "Because she's *mine*."[19] By raping white women, Guitar not only contributes to the culture of violence toward all women but also perpetuates the white myth of the black rapist. Paradoxically, Guitar argues that the impetus for the violence of the Seven Days relies on their love of black people, especially black women, a love predicated on the oppression of black women by black men. Calvin Hernton notes that in "the 1960s . . . the legacy of male chauvinism in the black . . . world continued to predominate. In fact, during the Black Power/Black Arts Movement of the 1960s the unequal recognition and treatment of women . . . was enunciated more bigotedly than perhaps ever before."[20] Stokely Carmichael, a Black Panther member, once said, "The only position in the revolution for women is the prone position."[21] Meanwhile, members of the Seven Days cannot "marry" or "have children";[22] contradictorily, Guitar's masculinity depends not only on protecting and harboring black women but on the literal absence of black women.

Similar to how white males use the disempowerment of black males to define their masculinity, so too does Guitar use the domination of women, especially black women, to define his.

Manhood based on the absence of women, sexism, or flight from a possible feminine masculinity echoes the legend of the flying African. Gay Wilentz asserts, "evidenced by slavers' reports, many slaves committed suicide by jumping overboard during the Middle Passage. Yet in the southern United States and throughout the Caribbean, legends abound which tell us that the slaves flew back to Africa."[23] In most versions of the story, the slave, always male, leaves behind the rest of his family. Awkward suggests, "*Song of Solomon*, then, is a record both of transcendent (male) flight and of the immeasurable pain that results for the female who, because of her lack of access to knowledge, cannot participate in this flight."[24] Black masculinity evolves by responding to whiteness, by emulating whiteness, or by being defined by whites. *Song of Solomon* critiques all of these black hypermasculinities derived from whiteness, offering up through Pilate an alternative of black identity derived from black experience.

BLACKNESS AS AN INVENTION OF WHITES

Those who embrace black hypermasculinities solely based on materialism, violence, and/or the disempowerment of women fail to recognize the flaws in white patriarchy that rigs the system to serve those in power. By trying to out "man" the "man," black men only succeed in perpetuating already entrenched stereotypes that reduce them to a blackness defined by whites. Darieck Scott argues, "to 'be' black is to have been black*ened*."[25] In the contemporary United States, blackness has come to signify the hyperbolic attempt of black men to parody white masculinity. Scott further points out, "blackness is an invention that accomplishes the domination of those who bear it as an identity."[26] Blackness in this sense, albeit a process of copying white patriarchy, evolves into a marker of degradation: "One becomes black in order to be subjugated by a conqueror who in creating you as black becomes white; blackness is both the mark and the means of subjugation."[27] There exists little chance for a black man to become a powerful patriarch in a system of white patriarchy where one's blackness automatically disqualifies one from positions of power. A black man's very attempt at patriarchal domination becomes blackness itself. Scott points out further,

> Superior masculinity to black men is rooted in racist conceptions of the inherent savagery, the supposed authenticity and rapacious sexuality of black(male)ness. But that supposed authenticity, the vitality which racist discourse often projects onto the black male body, has also been used as a source of political strength, as a strategic essentialism of sorts; this was especially true

in the late-1960s brand of black nationalism and its cultural arm, the Black Arts Movement.[28]

Sexual prowess and violent power are seductive stereotypes appropriated by much of the Black Liberation Movement of the 1950s and 1960s to gain political advantage over white men. Kobena Mercer asserts, "a central strand in history is the way black men have incorporated a code of 'macho' behavior in order to recuperate some degree of power over the condition of powerlessness and dependency in relation to the white male slave master."[29] Some black hypermasculinities evolve into a form of blackness itself, defined or put in motion by the abominations of slavery. As Arthur Flannigan Saint-Aubin insists, "There is no 'true' black masculinity that existed prior to the black man's contact with enslavers."[30] Saint-Aubin is correct in noting the influence of slavery on African American masculinities, for as hooks notes, black men "had to be taught to equate their higher status as men with the right to dominate women, they had to be taught patriarchal masculinity. They had to be taught that it was acceptable to use violence to establish patriarchal power."[31] According to hooks, while in some cases African men originated from communities where sex roles shaped the division of labor and men enjoyed a higher social status than women, men did not equate this elevated status with the right to violently dominate women.[32] Guitar's violence toward women, for instance, results from the eye-for-an-eye philosophy of the Seven Days, predicated on white acts of violence enacted on black bodies. In *Song of Solomon*, particular black masculinities manifest *almost always* as a parody of white maleness. As Susan Neal Mayberry states, "Having married his wife to co-opt her physician father's social position and pursuit of light skin color, Macon goes about undoing her lovely, complicated undergarments . . . as methodically as he attempts to unlock the most intimate secrets of white male dominance."[33] Alternatively, *Song of Solomon*, as well as theorists like Darieck Scott, bell hooks, and Riki Wilchins, argues that blackness, rather than existing as a pastiche of white hypermasculinities, should be forged anew as a completely new construction predicated on white hypermasculine failure, a symbolically incestuous state of living passed down solely within the black community.

BLACK MASCULINITIES

In *Song of Solomon*, Milkman must negotiate his way through competing constructions of masculinity embodied by the men in his life. Mayberry notes, "Guitar and Macon represent two of the relatively static models of black manhood that Milkman incorporates into what will become his own flexible masculinity by the conclusion of the novel."[34] These two models can be called masculinity as violence and masculinity as materialism. A possible third definition of blackness, and arguably the one Milkman chooses by novel's end, is black masculinity defined by male flight, which also entails flight from women, community, and the potential for feminine masculinity. Milkman's central conflict grows into "his alienation . . . his doubled fragmentation—cut off from the community and internally divided between loyalties to his competing mentors."[35] For Milkman, and for black men in general, the central paradox rests on the notion that male blackness, while existing as a parody of whiteness, functions as the very pinnacle of masculinity. As a response to white oppression, blackness develops into a paragon of hypermasculinity to be admired and emulated. The inauthenticity and danger stem from the reality that this hypermasculinity depends on the generally baser qualities of the human condition: violence, materialism, and oppression. Nevertheless, Milkman feels pressure to live up to this inauthentic and contrived definition of manhood, all the while feeling unfulfilled and intuiting the thin nature of the definition. Saint-Aubin notes, "In a white supremacist, patriarchal culture, the black man is thought to embody the essence of masculinity—masculinity in its purest . . . and therefore [most] dangerous form. Although he is not considered to be a 'man' . . . he is the masculine icon."[36] Blackness, while operating as a form of masculinity, also functions as a process of othering. Black men are expected to live up to a definition of blackness that denotes a quality to be feared and reviled. Milkman's desire to affect black hypermasculinities explains his deformed leg. Morrison writes, "By the time Milkman was fourteen he had noticed that one of his legs was shorter than the other . . . It wasn't a limp—not at all—just the suggestion of one, but it looked like an affected walk, the strut of a very young man trying to appear more sophisticated than he was . . . The deformity was mostly in his mind."[37] Milkman's leg symbolizes the expectations of swagger that white and black society impose on young black men. Milkman feels insecure as a result of the pressure to live up to black hypermasculinities. In turn, he thinks one leg is shorter than the other (possibly a phallic metaphor) and responds by inadvertently affecting a strut, or hypermasculine performance. Others begin to mimic his walk, misreading it as evidence of hypermasculinity rather than insecurity.

Milkman's father, Macon Dead II, attempts to recruit Milkman into the family business and into his dreams of wealth and status derived from a misapprehension of his own father's life. The novel's narrator states,

> And his father. An old man now, who acquired things and used people to acquire more things. As the son of Macon Dead the first, he paid homage to his own father's life and death by loving what that father had loved: property, good solid property, the bountifulness of life. He loved these things to excess because he loved his father to excess. Owning, building, acquiring—that was his life, his future, his present, and all the history he knew. That he distorted

life, bent it, for the sake of gain, was a measure of his loss at his father's death.[38]

For Macon Dead II, ownership, wealth, and middle-class membership are the Dead men's legacy. Catherine Carr Lee agrees: "The drive to own property that meant liberation to the first Macon Dead has been perverted into selfishness and endless acquisition by the second."[39] Indeed, Macon Dead II evolves into an Andersonian grotesque,[40] living by one truth, which he attempts to pass on to Milkman: "Own things. And let the things you own own other things. Then you'll own yourself and other people too."[41] Macon distorts the concept of personal agency—a positive, empowering notion—into a twisted parody of masculinity based on the enslavement of blacks by whites. Macon entreats Milkman to own other people in order to gain power. He further admonishes Milkman, "Own it all. All of it. You'll be free. Money is freedom . . . The only real freedom there is."[42] After taking a job working for his father, Milkman ultimately rejects the materialism that nearly overwhelms his father, a character Wilentz describes as a "black white man."[43] Instead, Milkman, with the help of Pilate, realizes that understanding his own history might fulfill him more than material wealth. Story asserts, "Milkman . . . ends up rejecting his background and the world his father has created for him by setting out to rediscover his racial past—a noble quest but one which is only individually rewarding."[44] He must travel south to Shalimar, Virginia, where Macon Dead I's murder took place and the source of his father's grotesque materialism. He arrives in Shalimar, a town named after his great-grandfather Solomon, where "the people he meets . . . force him to throw off his pretenses before they offer him the help and information he needs. Only when he ceases to flaunt his wealth and refer to their women casually do they admit him into their community."[45] Once in the South, Milkman succeeds in ingratiating himself with the people and tracing the roots of his existence only after realizing "there was nothing [there] to help him—not his money, his car, his father's reputation, his suit, or his shoes. In fact they hampered him."[46] He begins to understand that his father's materialism and wealth obstruct his connections with his culture, his family, and his past rather than bridge them. Only by adopting alternative definitions of black masculinity as embodied in Pilate will Milkman survive and flourish.

Guitar Bains represents political violence, the second model of black masculinity vying for Milkman's acceptance. Guitar boasts, "I was never afraid to kill. Anything. Rabbit, bird, snakes, squirrels, deer . . . It never bothered me. I'd take a shot at anything. The grown men used to laugh about it. Said I was a natural-born hunter."[47] Guitar, a man seemingly born with a taste for violence, develops a hatred toward everyone who is not black and male: "Everybody wants the life of a black man. Everybody. White men want us dead or quiet—which is the same thing as dead. White women, same

thing. They want us, you know 'universal,' human, no 'race consciousness.'
Tame, except in bed . . . And black women, they want your whole self."[48]
Eventually, his taste for violence and his bitterness find an outlet in the secret
gang the Seven Days:

> There is a society. It's made up of a few men who are willing to take some
> risks. They don't initiate anything; they don't even choose. They are as indif-
> ferent as rain. But when a Negro child, Negro woman, or a Negro man is killed
> by whites and nothing is done about it by *their* law and *their* courts, this
> society selects a similar victim at random, and they execute him or her in a
> similar manner if they can. If a Negro was hanged, they hang; if a Negro was
> burnt, they burn; raped and murdered, they rape and murder . . . They call
> themselves the Seven Days.[49]

The obvious paradox centers on the fact that the Seven Days, rather than
healing the wounds of black Americans, imitates the violence of the dominant oppressor, thereby compounding the problem of violence and furthering
already entrenched stereotypes of black men. Furthering this idea, John N.
Duvall comments, "African American male violence does not simply imitate
white male violence; the former *self-consciously* imitates the latter."[50] Guitar
and the Seven Days knowingly and purposefully copy the violence of the
oppressor and consequently warrant little sympathy. Further, as Mayberry
notes, "the Seven Days' brand of violence . . . counters white madness with
the like-minded indifference, determination, and cold-blooded logic."[51] The
white victims Guitar and the Seven Days choose have nothing directly to do
with the violence enacted on black Americans other than their membership in
the dominant and racist white society. The Seven Days do not attempt to find
the guilty ones; they simply prey on white people by virtue of their whiteness, perpetuating racial violence and furthering the racial divide. Milkman
rejects Guitar's philosophy of violence and his work with the Seven Days, at
various times telling Guitar, "I'm not understanding you";[52] "You're con-
fused";[53] and "I can't see how it helps anybody."[54] Milkman's refusal to
adopt or even understand Guitar's philosophies rents their relationship and
inadvertently causes Pilate's death. Further, Milkman's rejection of Guitar's
construction of masculinity based on violence positions him better to adopt
alternative definitions of black masculinity espoused by Pilate, even though
he fails to ultimately do so.

The third and final definition of black masculinity that presents itself as
an option for Milkman Dead revolves around the issue of black male flight.
The notion of flight in *Song of Solomon* originates with the flight of Solomon, Milkman's great-grandfather, a man "who escaped slavery by flying
back to Africa. Legends abound throughout the new world about Africans
who either flew or jumped off slave ships as well as those who saw the
horrors of slavery when they landed in the Americas and in their anguish,

sought to fly back to Africa."[55] The core issue of Solomon's flight, and what Milkman fails to see, is that while Solomon's flight from slavery is heroic, his abandonment of his family is villainous. Awkward suggests,

> in *Song of Solomon,* the empowered Afro-American's flight . . . is a solitary one . . . [His] discovery of the means of transcendence—the liberating black word—is not shared with the tribe. He leaves his loved ones, including his infant son Jake, whom he tries unsuccessfully to carry with him, with the task of attempting to learn for themselves the secrets of transcendence. The failure of Solomon's efforts to transport Jake along with him, in fact, serves to emphasize the ultimately individualistic nature of the mythic figure's flight.[56]

Black masculinity as flight evolves into the definition of manhood Milkman *does* embrace. For him, Solomon's flight confirms Milkman's entitled status and emboldens him to take flight himself. After learning of his family history, Milkman tells Sweet, seemingly a sort of local prostitute, "Oh, man! He didn't need no airplane. He just took off; got fed up. *All the way up!* No more cotton! No more bales! No more orders! No more shit! He flew, baby. Lifted his beautiful black ass up in the sky and flew on home."[57] Milkman says this to Sweet, who critics such as Catherine Carr Lee mistakenly think represents a healing rebirth for Milkman but in actuality only confirms Milkman's incapacity to have a positive relationship with anyone he cannot leave whenever he wishes. While Milkman's journey to the South superficially releases him from his father's and Guitar's destructive influences, he leaves behind Hagar, who, because of his lack of concern and irresponsible treatment, commits suicide.

Ultimately, Milkman succumbs to the destructive definition of masculinity based on flight. Milkman does acknowledge his mistreatment of Hagar, "whom he'd thrown away like a wad of chewing gum after the flavor was gone,"[58] but he does not change based on his realization. Morrison writes, "Without wiping away the tears, taking a deep breath, or even bending his knees—he leaped. As fleet and bright as a lodestar he wheeled toward Guitar and it did not matter which one of them would give up the ghost in the killing arms of his brother. For now he knew what Shalimar knew: If you surrendered to the air, you could *ride* it."[59] Milkman merely succeeds in realizing an ability he already had. Nonetheless, like his male ancestors before him, he leaves behind his family and the opportunity to carry forth Pilate's message of cultural incest. As Gerry Brenner points out,

> Likewise did Jake Solomon desert his adoptive mother, Heddy Byrd, whom he left to go north with Sing, as did Macon Dead desert both his sister in the cave and his wife to her own bed; Milkman's desertion . . . then, honors the tradition of the man's prerogative—to escape domestication, to fly from responsibilities, in the name of self-fulfillment or self-discovery or self-indulgence.[60]

Milkman's flight at the end of the novel proves anything but heroic. The novel closes ambiguously, as the point has already been made: male flight in all its manifestations, while heroic for men, proves damaging to the families and communities left behind. Critics such as Melvin Dixon who believe that "Milkman's leap at the novel's close is a redeeming flight"[61] seem to have taken the author by her word,[62] always a treacherous decision. Awkward concludes,

> Analyses of Morrison's novel must be attentive both to the transcendent joy of knowledge-informed male flight and to the immeasurable pain of desertion felt by females like Hagar and Ryna . . . Future readings must . . . acknowledge that the blues lyrics and the novel encode *both* an afrocentric appreciation of the power and importance of transcendence, and a convincing critique of the fact that, in the updated version of the myth, that power is essentially denied to Afro-American women.[63]

Awkward emphasizes the duality of male flight in the novel but seems to fail to realize that male flight from women is also flight from family, community, and one's potential feminist/womanist self within, resulting in a critically dangerous version of black hypermasculinity.

AESTHETICS: FLIGHT TOWARD ORALITY

Flight and orality in *Song of Solomon* reflect the general focal movement in the novel from the men to the women. Milkman's discovery of Solomon's "heroic" flight emerges as a critique of the male penchant for escaping responsibility through selfish notions of freedom. By contrast, Pilate Dead represents an alternative construction of freedom predicated on cultural healing and communal storytelling—an identity arrived at through black experience, history, and culture, which I call cultural incest—which by novel's end Milkman regards as Pilate's way of flying without ever leaving the ground. Elemental to Pilate's being and philosophy of life, the spoken word replaces the written word as the healthier means of cultural sharing and healing. Orality, or communal storytelling of a shared cultural history, replaces flight and the written word as a positive vehicle for blackness, including notions of black masculinity.

Notions of flight, nearly always projected in a negative light, permeate the novel. For instance, the novel begins and ends with two flights, the first a suicide. Cedric Gael Bryant writes, "These two expressions of flight . . . are, in a sense, bookends that buttress the material in the middle of the novel. They are also reciprocally clarifying commentaries because without Milkman Dead's . . . gesture at the *end*, Robert Smith's at the *beginning* would be the only context for the idea of flying, one of the novel's central myths."[64]

Both flights stem from male pressure to live up to fraudulent definitions of black masculinity, and neither seems necessary. Though Solomon's flight from slavery is heroic in the sense that he escaped slavery, utilizing this act as a definition of black masculinity proves fatal for black families and communities. The myth of the flying African exists as the primary cultural myth that informs the entire novel. According to Julius Lester,

> Some [African American slaves] would run away and try to go back home, back to Africa where there were no white people, where they worked their own land for the good of each other, not for the good of white men. Some of those who tried to go back to Africa would walk until they came to the ocean, and then they would walk into the water, and no one knows if they did walk to Africa through the water or if they drowned. It didn't matter. At least they were no longer slaves.[65]

Lester goes on to say that Africans reportedly may have actually flown back to Africa. One such man, a sort of shaman back in his tribe in Africa, while working in the fields announced, "'Now! Now! Everyone!' He uttered the strange word, and all of the Africans dropped their hoes, stretched out their arms, and flew away, back to their home, back to Africa."[66] In this myth, unlike *Song of Solomon*'s depiction of Solomon, the shaman flies back to Africa with the rest of the community, including, one may assume, his family.

Even before Milkman finds out about his flying ancestor, he pines for flight, symbolized by the recurrent image of a peacock. Morrison writes, "Mr. Smith's blue silk wings must have left their mark, because when the little boy discovered, at four, the same thing Mr. Smith had learned earlier—that only birds and airplanes could fly—he lost all interest in himself. To have to live without that single gift saddened him and left his imagination so bereft that he appeared dull."[67] Ironically, this passage suggests that a man's suicide left an inspiring mark on Milkman, as though Robert Smith's *suicide* implanted in him the desire to fly his whole life. Milkman never realizes that the flight he pines for may destroy those who love him. It takes him a long time to figure out that flying may not have anything at all to do with leaving the ground. Linda Krumholz notes, "The rooster and the peacock, two flightless and domesticated male birds, represent masculine pride, vanity, and the desire for domination and material wealth."[68] Essentially, Krumholz argues, the very qualities that establish the rooster and the peacock as dynamic animals impede their ability to fly. In chapter eight, Guitar explains to Milkman that a peacock cannot fly because he has "too much tail. All that jewelry weighs it down. Like vanity. Can't nobody fly with all that shit. Wanna fly, you got to give up the shit that weighs you down."[69] Even though Guitar and Milkman note the aerodynamic failures of the peacock, they fail to see the similarities in themselves, such as their male vanity.

Orality in *Song of Solomon* forecasts the overall point of the novel, that Milkman and black men in general ought to look to their own culture and to women to learn how to "fly." Orality appears as a viable alternative to the written language southern whites used to swindle Macon Dead I. Both Macon Dead II's and Milkman's use of the written word reflect their isolation from their family and the community. Page says of the oral quality of the novel, "Its dominant feature is the dozens of flashbacks in which almost a third of the text is narrated. Almost all of these flashbacks are either told or remembered by the characters, not simply by the narrator, which suggests that the characters are endeavoring to regain contact with their pasts."[70] Milkman learns about his past primarily through Pilate, who "is unmistakably Morrison's preferred storyteller,"[71] or narrative *pilot*. Pilate's introduction to Milkman's past leads him to the South, where he learns about his kinship with Solomon, the flying African. Through four women—Pilate, Circe, Susan, and Sweet—Milkman learns of his past. Mayberry argues, "The female songs and the male stories of his people cultivate in Milkman what might be called feminine masculinity, a maleness connected to women, anchored by delicately balanced dualities, and based on flying without ever leaving the ground."[72] Up to this point, Milkman has basically ignored the women in his life, but now he depends on women to understand his culture, his past, and himself. Wilentz points out, "It is this apprehension of the possible loss of the orature and cultural history which informs this novel."[73] While Milkman depends on women to connect with his past, he never really learns the difference between cultural flying and actual flying. Rather than internalizing Pilate's lesson of flight through cultural incest, Milkman embraces Solomon's flight as the definition of his being and thus perpetuates the black male penchant for selfish escape.

In *Song of Solomon*, the written word undermines cultural literacy, paving the way for the novel's shift from hypermasculinities to cultural healing via storytelling. Joyce Irene Middleton asserts, "Morrison's readers observe how alphabetic literacy, a means to success and power in the external, material, and racist world—as Macon Dead's family achieves it—alienates these characters from their rituals, their inner lives, and their oral memories."[74] For instance, the novel's narrator states,

> Some of the city legislators, whose concern for appropriate names and the maintenance of the city's landmarks was the principal part of their political life, saw to it that "Doctor Street" was never used in any official capacity . . . they had notices posted in the stores, barbershops, and restaurants . . . saying that the avenue running northerly and southerly from shore road . . . had always been and would always be known as Mains Avenue and not Doctor Street.[75]

By systematically disavowing the organic naming of a street honoring the community's first black doctor, the white power structure diminishes the power of the black community to recognize one of its own. Moreover, the white power structure attempts to trump the oral designation of Doctor Street with the officially written and recognized Mains Avenue, further affirming the dangerous nature of the written word controlled by an oppressive and dominant society.

Macon Dead II believes that the chief reason his father lost Lincoln's Heaven lay in his illiteracy: "They tricked him. He signed something, I don't know what, and they told him they owned his property . . . Everything bad that ever happened to him happened because he couldn't read."[76] Consequently, Macon Dead II imbues the written word with a great deal of meaning, ignoring the fact that even with literacy, print culture poses a threat to the black community. Morrison writes, "He [Macon Dead II] even painted the word office on the door. But the plate glass window contradicted him. In peeling gold letters arranged in a semicircle, his business establishment was declared Sonny's Shop . . . His storefront office was never called anything but Sonny's Shop."[77] The more successful Macon Dead II grows, the further away he gets from the black community that ignores his signifiers of wealth and power. Milkman, before he travels to the South, makes the same mistake with Hagar, when he attempts to break up with her in a letter, instead of face-to-face: "And he did sign it with love, but it was the word 'gratitude' and the flat-out coldness of 'thank you' that sent Hagar spinning into a bright blue place where the air was thin and it was silent all the time."[78] Unlike his father, Milkman ultimately learns to function without the written word, realizing the importance of oral communication, even though eventually this realization translates into no real change. In order to fully understand his roots, he must remember and interpret a children's game, verbally documenting his family's history and the history of the town Shalimar: "Milkman took out his wallet and pulled from it his airplane ticket stub, but he had no pencil to write with, and his pen was in his suit. He would just have to listen and memorize it."[79] The significance of this moment lies in his ability to internalize the words of the children, so that perhaps later he can pass the game on *verbally*, thus taking part in the oral culture he has disavowed until now. Middleton concludes, "Morrison privileges orality so that her readers can hear and feel the unique oral character of the African-American community and see how it preserves cultural consciousness."[80] The movement in the novel from flight and the written word toward orality, understanding, and cultural enlightenment suggests a paradigm shift away from the hypermasculinities of Milkman and Macon Dead II to the children and Pilate. Mayberry notes, "That is one of the points of 'Song': all the men have left someone, and it is the children who remember it, sing about it, mythologize it, make it a part of their family history."[81] Morrison signals the thematic movement from flight toward orality and away from hypermasculinities in her epigraph heralding the beginning of *Song of Solomon*: "The fathers may soar / And the children may know their names." Indeed, the children may know their names but not the men themselves.

PILATE AS FAILED HERO

While critics such as Brenner anoint Milkman as "the hero of [the] much-admired *Song of Solomon*,"[82] perhaps only because of his abundance of "lines," the true hero of the novel is Pilate, a character whom Morrison herself had to mute because she had the potential to "overwhelm everybody."[83] Page writes, "As Milkman's spiritual guide, his *griot*, she [Pilate] models for Milkman the creation of self that is both within and without the community, she precedes him in her physical journey and her symbolic journey toward love and harmony, and she teaches him the values of a spiritual Afrocentric, nature-centered, nonlinear perspective as opposed to Macon's material one."[84] Pilate represents a life-affirming alternative to Macon Dead II, Guitar, and Solomon, predicated on cultural awareness and love. Brenner notes, "Her mission is exemplary, because it is nothing less than to live her life in manifest repudiation of the grasping ambitiousness and obsessive desires of those around her, who end up as grotesques, fanatics, neurotics, or fantasists."[85] Her lack of navel marks her as grotesque in the eyes of the various communities she enters, but the men and their hypermasculinities represent the real grotesques of the novel. As Wilfred D. Samuels suggests, her role "is guardian of cultural and familial lore,"[86] as well as foil for the men in the novel. Morrison writes, "Her stomach was as smooth and sturdy as her back, at no place interrupted by a navel. It was the absence of a navel that convinced people that she had not come into this world through normal channels; had never lain, floated, or grown in some warm and liquid place connected by a tissue-thin tube to a reliable source of human nourishment."[87] Pilate's uniqueness and position as misfit have more to do with her disavowal of gender expectations and white notions of success than with her navel.

Macon Dead II loathes Pilate primarily because she represents a successful human being outside of white definitions of success and gender expectations. Smith contends, "like Macon, she is self-made, but her self-creation departs from, instead of coinciding with, the American myth."[88] Unlike Macon, and most of white America, Pilate privileges humanity over wealth and status. Morrison writes, "She gave up . . . all interest in table manners or hygiene, but acquired a deep concern for and about human relationships."[89] Further, Pilate, unlike her brother, does not exploit the community in order to separate herself from it: "Along with winemaking, cooking whiskey became the way Pilate began to make her steady living. That skill allowed her more freedom hour by hour and day by day than any other work a woman of no means whatsoever and no inclination to make love for money could choose."[90] Macon II responds to her as an ignorant white man might: "To him . . . she was odd, murky, and worst of all, unkempt. A regular source of embarrassment . . . Why can't you dress like a woman?"[91] Pilate threatens his place in white society as a trusted liaison to the black community, able to collect funds where white men cannot. He ignores and perhaps feels jealous that "she was a natural healer, and among quarreling drunks and fighting women she could hold her own, and sometimes mediated a peace that lasted a good bit longer than it should have because it was administered by someone not like them."[92] Pilate is of the community, while Macon exploits the community.

Pilate's death at the end of the novel is heroic because it sheds a negative light on the men of the novel, including Milkman, Macon Dead II, and Solomon. Though Milkman succeeds in learning to fly, he once again jeopardizes the life of a woman who cares for him. Brenner argues,

> Beneath the positive thrust of her imaginative prose and the seemingly upbeat ending of her novel lies Morrison's disdain for Milkman because of what he fails to learn on his journey—that in his gene pool also swims the congenital habit of desertion. The nursery rhyme changed by the Shalimar schoolchildren indicts Solomon as a feckless father for abandoning the woman from whose womb he has fathered twenty-one children, Ryna.[93]

Pilate must die in order to illuminate the fact that Milkman's flight at the end of the novel proves tragic, not heroic. His flight is tragic not because, like Solomon, Milkman abandons his role as patriarch but because he abandons the women in his life who care for him and his community in general. The reader ought to take away from the novel the same notion that Milkman does: "Now he knew why he loved her [Pilate] so. Without ever leaving the ground, she could fly."[94] Pilate not only saves Milkman's life in taking a bullet meant for him, but perhaps she also saves the life of the male reader who might see in her a construction of *masculinity* able to take flight without self-destructing or destroying others. Her words prove prophetic when she tells Milkman's mother, "Won't no woman ever kill him. What's likelier is that it'll be a woman save his life."[95] Pilate's heroic, sacrificial act indicts Milkman and the other men in the novel as hypermasculine destroyers of community.[96]

THE TRAFFICKING OF WOMEN AND THE INCEST TABOO

Pilate's heroic death casts a negative light on the men in the novel, positioning the women as the retrospective focus. The women of the novel, especially Ruth and Hagar, suffer as a result of kinship systems and the incest taboo, practices adopted by the black men in their family. Black men adopting these cultural practices represent black identity stemming from existing institutions that cater to definitions of masculinity based on materialism and the disempowerment of women. Kinship systems and the incest taboo represent aspects of existing social institutions blacks have adopted at the expense of black culture. Incest in the novel, therefore, functions as an act that undermines black patriarchy based on the exchange of women. Further, the actual incest in *Song of Solomon* provides a literal corollary to cultural incest, which like literal incest disrupts established social norms that unfairly empower black men and disempower women.

I will give an overview of kinship systems predicated on the exchange of women and the incest taboo in order to show how the systems cater to materialism and the disempowerment of women. As Gayle Rubin points out, "Kinship systems vary wildly from one culture to the next. They contain all sorts of bewildering rules which govern whom one may or may not marry."[97] Kinship systems govern specifically whom *women* may or may not marry. Rubin further explains, "Kinship systems do not merely exchange women. They exchange sexual access, genealogical statuses, lineage names and ancestors, rights and people—men and women, and children—in concrete systems of social relationships."[98] Women function as the gifts men exchange in order to increase their status and social position. In order for women to function as gifts, they must be available to other families and not paired within their own family. Rubin asserts, "marriages are a most basic form of gift exchange, in which it is women who are the most precious of gifts . . . the incest taboo should best be understood as a mechanism to insure that such exchanges take place between families and between groups."[99] One of the main reasons for incest's stigma centers on ensuring female availability for the aggrandizement of men. As Jeffrey Weeks notes, "The sociobiological stress on the rituals of incest avoidance as a 'largely unconscious and irrational' 'gut feeling,' by emphasizing the limitations of close biological ties ignores the social reasons for exogamy, marriage outside the kin (the circulation of people and the cementing of social ties), and conflates them with the biological."[100] While some studies show[101] that offspring from close incestual ties often have genetic defects, the chief impetus for the incest taboo lies in the controlled exchange of women among men. Further, family members need not reproduce at all. The possibility of birth defects offers a flimsy argument against incestuous relationships. The ability to reproduce or the desire to reproduce need not enter into the equation at all when it comes to whether two people ought to engage in a relationship. Kaja Silverman writes, "a group within which marriage is forbidden implies another group, with which marriage is allowable or even obligatory. The incest taboo consequently serves to incorporate individual families into larger social units"[102] further up the economic social ladder. The incest taboo then serves men of wealthy families and "is a short-hand for expressing that the social relations of a kinship system specify that men have certain rights in their female kin, and that women do not have the same rights either to themselves or to their male kin."[103] The idea that not enough women exist to go around, a notion necessary to kinship systems and the incest taboo, stems from a male point of view, or what Luce Irigaray calls "the 'deep' polygamous tendency, which exists among all men, always [making] the number of available women seem insufficient . . . [E]ven if there were as many women as men, these women would not all be equally desirable . . . [The] most desirable women must form a minority."[104] White standards of beauty inform kinship systems by marking some women as desirable, usually women with light skin and straight hair, and others as undesirable, including those with marked African features. Through the male white gaze, men objectify women as gifts that can produce familial ties that translate into wealth.[105]

For men, women represent the very signifiers of masculinity by which other men judge them. As Michael Kimmel notes, "[Men] are under the constant careful scrutiny of other men. Other men watch us, rank us, grant our acceptance into the realm of manhood. Manhood is demonstrated for other men's approval."[106] Kinship systems and the incest taboo ensure men their masculinity through a homosocial enactment of masculinity. Kimmel further attests, "masculinity is a *homosocial* enactment. We test ourselves, perform heroic feats, take enormous risks all because we want other men to grant us our manhood."[107] Masculinity through kinship systems depends on the systematic oppression of women. Silverman argues, "The circulation of women can thus be seen to represent the most . . . basic mechanism for defining men, in contradistinction to women, as the producers and representatives of the social field."[108] Men define themselves as the owners of women and masculinity depends on this ownership, much the same way a rich man is defined by his bank account.

Ruth's incestuous impulses function as a way for her to undermine Macon Dead II's patriarchal stranglehold, and as a metaphorical possibility of black identity constructed from black culture, black history, and the black community. She is a product of exchange between Dr. Foster and Macon Dead II. Their involvement in kinship systems based on the incest taboo parallels their hypermasculinities based on white definitions of manhood. Macon Dead II attempts to marry Ruth "strictly for personal advancement rather than for love. She is no more than another piece of real estate to which he holds the keys."[109] Macon Dead II realizes that by winning the hand of the daughter of the only black doctor in the city, he will position himself that much closer to his dream of financial wealth. Macon Dead II explains to Milkman, "I married your mother in 1917. She was sixteen, living alone with her father. I can't tell you I was in love with her. People didn't require that as much as they do now."[110] Macon Dead II's claim to Ruth has more to do with the wealth he has already accumulated through real estate, which he feels places him at the top of any list of suitors. Morrison writes, "It was because of those keys that he could dare to walk over to that part of Not Doctor Street . . . and approach the most important Negro in the city. To lift the lion's paw knocker, to entertain thoughts of marrying the doctor's daughter was possible because each key represented a house which he owned at the time."[111] The problem with this arrangement lies in the fact that Ruth feels more for her own father, who she says is "the only person who ever really cared whether I lived or died,"[112] than she does for Macon Dead II. Ruth engages in the incest taboo set in place to ensure that women circulate, thereby disrupting the kinship system of exchanging women. The novel's narrator explains,

> In fact the doctor knew a good deal about him and was more grateful to this tall young man than he ever allowed himself to show. Fond as he was of his only child, useful as she was in his house since his wife had died, lately he had begun to chafe under her devotion. Her steady beam of love was unsettling, and she had never dropped those expressions of affection that had been so loveable in her childhood. The good-night kiss was itself a masterpiece of slow-wittedness on her part and discomfort on his. At sixteen, she still insisted on having him come to her at night, sit on her bed, exchange a few pleasantries, and plant a kiss on her lips. Perhaps it was the loud silence of his dead wife, perhaps it was Ruth's disturbing resemblance to her mother. More probably it was the ecstasy that always seemed to be shining in Ruth's face when he bent to kiss her—an ecstasy he felt inappropriate to the occasion.[113]

Once Ruth wears out her usefulness, Dr. Foster gladly transfers her services to Macon. Unfortunately for Macon, Ruth's incestuous feelings for her father never subside, causing the chief rift in their marriage. To Macon Dead II, marriage to Ruth equals access to her father's wealth. When this does not happen, he accuses the two of having an affair that compromises the tacit agreement. Macon tells Milkman,

> I tried to get him to spend some of that money out of those four banks once. Some track land was going for a lot of money—railroad money . . . I asked your mother to talk him into it. I told her exactly where the Erie was headed. She said it had to be *his* decision; she couldn't influence him. She told me, her husband, that. Then I began to wonder who she was married to—me or him.[114]

His accusation gains momentum when Ruth insists that her father deliver her children. Macon tells Milkman further, "I ended up telling him that nothing could be nastier than a father delivering his own daughter's baby . . . She had her legs wide open and he was there. I know he was a doctor and doctors not supposed to be bothered by things like that, but he was a man before he was a doctor."[115] After Dr. Foster's death, Macon Dead II thinks he finds evidence of incest when he walks in on his wife naked and sucking on the fingers of her father's dead body: "In the bed. That's where she was when I opened the door. Laying next to him. Naked as a yard dog, kissing him. Him dead and white and puffy and skinny, and she had his fingers in her mouth . . . I started thinking all sorts of things. If Lena and Corinthians were my children. I come to know pretty quickly they were, cause it was clear that bastard couldn't fuck nothing."[116] For Macon Dead II, Dr. Foster's perceived disavowal of the incest taboo is the central infraction. His relationship, as loving and harmless as it might have been, compromises Macon's power as a man over his wife. Macon further tells Milkman, "I'm not saying they had contact. But there's lots of things a man can do to please a woman, even if he can't fuck. Whether or not, the fact is she was in that bed sucking his fingers, and if she do that when he was dead, what'd she do when he was alive? Nothing to do but kill a woman like that."[117] Macon Dead II refuses to allow Ruth to express her love for her father without viewing it as a slight to his own power over her.

Ruth uses incest to undermine Macon Dead II's patriarchal privilege by breastfeeding Milkman until he "was old enough to talk, stand up, and wear knickers."[118] His name, Milkman, symbolizes Ruth's success in disconnecting her son from his father. By causing his new name she severs the nominal tie between the two men. Murray agrees: "Her rebellious behavior is successful in that her son is rechristened 'Milkman' (an act that completely undermines the patriarchal passing down of the father's name)."[119] Ruth's awareness of the impropriety of breastfeeding her child longer than necessary shows when, after Freddie the town gossip catches her in the act, she "jumped up as quickly as she could and covered her breast, dropping her son on the floor and confirming for him what he had begun to suspect—that these afternoons were strange and wrong."[120] Kinship systems and the incest taboo deny women certain rights over their own bodies. Ironically, young women must venture outside of the home for love and affection and then, once they grow older, must look only within the home for love and affection. As Murray writes, "Ruth's prolonged breast feeding serves as a ritual to create a space for her own autonomy within a domestic space that denies her self-hood."[121] Ruth's breastfeeding of Milkman succeeds in undermining the suffocating patriarchy of Macon and meets her need for human contact, a need all humans share.

While one can argue that Macon Dead II ultimately fails to bequeath to Milkman his sense of masculinity based on materialism, he succeeds in passing on his sense of male privilege. Milkman's rite of passage into patriarchy occurs when he punches his father, ostensibly in order to protect his mother. Duvall maintains, "the reproduction of the father function and the preservation of patriarchal privilege reside in Milkman's striking Macon. By hitting

his father, Milkman claims his privilege as an adult male to control and select
the sexuality of 'his' women."[122] Milkman's sister Corinthians realizes Milkman's violence toward their father, rather than changing anything, merely
perpetuates male privilege:

> Our girlhood was spent like a found nickel on you. When you slept, we were
> quiet; when you were hungry, we cooked; when you wanted to play, we
> entertained you . . . And to this day, you have never asked one of us if we were
> tired, or sad, or wanted a cup of coffee . . . Where do you get the *right* to
> decide our lives . . . I'll tell you where. From that hog's gut that hangs down
> between your legs . . . You are exactly like him . . . You think because you hit
> him once that we all believe you were protecting her. Taking her side. It's a
> lie. You were taking over, letting us know you had the right to tell her and all
> of us what to do.[123]

Despite Corinthians's critique, Milkman fails to see his own faults and sticks
to his delusion of heroism. Milkman's newfound confidence stems from his
sexual prowess, exercised mostly on his first cousin Hagar. Morrison writes,
"Milkman was twenty-two then and since he had been fucking for six years,
some of them with the same woman, he'd begun to see his mother in a new
light."[124] He has already begun to control the women in his family by sleeping with his first cousin, using the incest taboo to simultaneously keep Hagar
near him and away from him. Morrison writes, "Sleeping with Hagar had
made him generous. Or so he thought. Wide-spirited. Or so he imagined.
Wide-spirited and generous enough to defend his mother, whom he almost
never thought about, and to deck his father, whom he both feared and
loved."[125] Milkman's confidence stems from his realization that he has control over the women in his family, and this realization compels him to break
up with Hagar, since control also means adherence to kinship systems and
the incest taboo. Consequently, "he seldom took her anywhere except to the
movies and he never took her to parties where people of his own set danced
and laughed and developed intrigues among themselves. Everyone who
knew him knew about Hagar, but she was considered his private honey pot,
not a real or legitimate girl friend—not someone he might marry."[126] Kinship
systems create divisions among women and in the United States inculcate
white standards of beauty in order to create the impression of a limited pool
of females. Hagar, not realizing that the impetus for Milkman's lack of
seriousness stems from the incest taboo, believes it stems from her dark skin
and kinky hair. When she tells Pilate and her mother that Milkman only likes
"wavy, silky hair,"[127] they tell her, "How can he not love your hair? It's the
same hair that grows out of his own armpits. The same hair that crawls up out
his crotch on up his stomach. All over his chest. The very same. It grows out
of his nose, over his lips, and if he ever lost his razor it would grow all over
his face. It's all over his head, Hagar. It's his hair too. He got to love it."[128]

Kinship systems and the incest taboo not only ruin the marriage of Ruth and Macon II but in the end kill Hagar.

A POLITICS OF FAILURE

Sexual domination has been an effective tool in the oppression of African Americans since slavery. The rape of male and female slaves by both white males and white females occurred regularly during slavery and developed into a tool of dominance as important as whipping. While narratives such as Harriet Jacobs's *Incidents in the Life of a Slave Girl*[129] document the rape of female slaves by white male slave owners, the rape of slave men by these same white male slave owners has virtually gone undocumented. Scott notes,

> The emasculation trope's account of black male subjectivity tends toward a denial or erasure of part of the history of slavery: the sexual exploitation of enslaved black men by white men, the horror of male rape and of homosexuality—all of these memories are bundled together, each made equal to and synonymous with one another, and all are hidden behind the more abstract notion of lost or stolen manhood and are most readily figured by the castration which was so much a part of the practice of lynching.[130]

It is far easier for black men to acknowledge emasculation by beating or even the loss of power over one's wife and children; male-on-male rape, on the other hand, evokes something that cannot be overcome, as though once endured the invasion cannot be removed and one is forever and inextricably marked as homosexual. In many cases this history is either denied or overlooked and yet lives on in the psyche of black men and white men as well.

By contrast, in place of this history, sexual myths have continued about the hypersexuality of black men and women. Perhaps this is because of the inherently seductive nature of these myths—having others believe one has a supernatural capacity for sex. In order to justify the rampant raping of black female slaves, white slave owners argued that black women were inherently hypersexual and that slave owners had little choice but to indulge in their seductions. Further, in order to justify the sort of slave breeding that went on in various plantations, black males were marked as hypersexual studs. Finally, black men were drawn as rapacious beasts bent on raping white women in order to justify the mass lynchings that occurred after Reconstruction. Cornel West argues, "In fact, the dominant sexual myths of black women and men portray *whites* as being 'out of control'—seduced, tempted, overcome, overpowered by black bodies" (emphasis mine).[131] In this paradigm, whites are powerless under blacks. In other words, the dominant sexual myths took hold in part because African Americans, particularly men, embraced these myths as definitions of blackness. Regardless of whether or not black women em-

braced their self-definition as hypersexual, once the men did, the women had
no choice, for in the minds of whites, if one sex was hypersexual so must the
other be. Just as the Black Liberation Movement in general used popular and
mythical definitions of blackness as a political tool,[132] as embodied in a
character like Guitar Bains, Darieck Scott proposes to use the hidden definitions of blackness as a political tool, namely definitions of sexual domination: "Though sexuality is used against us, and sexual(ized) domination is in
part what makes us black . . . it is in and through that very domination and
defeat also a mapping of political potential, an access to freedom."[133] This
political, sexual, and cultural mapping involves using sexuality as a pathway
to relinquish the desire for normative patriarchal power. By embracing new
constructions of sexuality and culture not predicated on compulsory heterosexuality and hypermasculinity, black men can reject the losing fight for
sexual supremacy leading to their extinction. In *Song of Solomon*, Macon
Dead II and Guitar represent black hypermasculinities that threaten all black
men. Pilate, Hagar, and Ruth represent alternative definitions of black identity and black sexuality, including incest, stemming from black history and
culture. Scott further notes,

> Fanon observed that the depredations visited on the Algerians in internment
> camps that the French occupiers established to break the revolutionary will
> shattered traditional taboos governing proper sexual conduct in sexual matters
> and violated some of the basic predicates on which gender identities are
> founded—and in so doing, actually also created opportunities for wholly dif-
> ferent conceptions of gender and family relations.[134]

In a similar manner, Scott proposes that African Americans employ their
American history of oppression as a platform for a new vision of sexuality
and gender based in part on that very oppression. In this sense, blackness
signifies sexual and cultural rebirth rather than a parody of white domination,
similar to Pilate's philosophy of cultural incest promulgated in *Song of Solomon*.

This new politics does not position African Americans a priori at the
bottom of a social ladder with little opportunity for power but rather signals a
revolutionary sexuality and culture based on nonnormativity and hypermasculine failure. Scott suggests, "Here we have a black power that is queer,
powerful because it is queer, queer precisely because it insists on a confrontation with, a use of—a confrontation and use partly formulated as a surrender to—power."[135] As Scott further notes, "This is a politics of the bottom, a
desire to (a will to) love and live the bottom for its bottomness without
surrendering to or ceding the lion's share of the pleasure or power to the
top—indeed, in a way flamboyantly, exuberantly *ignoring* the top except
insofar as he dutifully presses on the levers of pleasure."[136] The literary trope
of failure as a response to hypermasculine dominance suggests revolutionary

possibilities for masculinity outside of the text. For example, black men, and the black community in general, might possibly embrace various nonnormative sexualities, including incest, as a way to disavow white patriarchal masculinity. This does not mean that all black men and women need to engage in homosexual activity or marry members of their own family; it simply demands a privileging of queerness,[137] a championing of nonnormative sexualities and hegemonic U.S. masculine failure. As Halberstam points out, "Under certain circumstances failing, losing, forgetting, unmaking, undoing, unbecoming, not knowing may in fact offer more creative, more cooperative, more surprising ways of being in the world."[138]

This politics of the bottom offers new definitions of black male humanity inspired by a history of sexual domination by whites. This new position subverts white definitions of manhood and sexual prowess based on abuse and oppression, offering up a viable alternative for black males. hooks quotes filmmaker Isaac Julien:

> It is important for black males to claim their failure as a way to resist the perfectionism patriarchal manhood demands . . . failure is something that should be celebrated. I don't want to buy into a formation of black male identity where one has to hold oneself in a rigid way—as in a march—even against how we might feel ourselves in terms of our pain, our skepticism, lack and self-doubt. All of these things are as much a part of black male identity as the things we might want to parade, like toughness and unity. We have to be willing to engage in a process of thinking through our failure as black men in this society . . . Black macho discourses of empowerment will never truly reach us where we live. There is something interesting we can learn from our so-called failure, because our failure also contains our resistance.[139]

This failure is based on white definitions of masculine success in a system rigged to exclude blacks and other marginalized human beings. If the only way to compete with white masculinity is to project hypermasculinities resulting in addiction, incarceration, and violence, the only answer is to create new forms of masculinity marked by a cultural queerness incestuously culled from black culture. hooks further argues, "To claim the space of healthy erotic agency black males . . . must envision together a new kind of sex, a non-patriarchal sexual identity. We must envision a liberatory sexuality that refuses to ground sexual acts in narratives of domination and submission, and lay claim to uninhibited erotic agency that prioritizes connection and mutuality."[140] This non-patriarchal sexual and cultural identity, while not necessarily a homosexuality or bisexual identity, or even incestuous, surely includes these identities, for extreme homophobia and sexism are at the root of the destructive hypermasculinities at play in much of the black community as a whole. As Wilchins notes,

A dozen years ago, a hate-based crime might have involved a white 30-year-old post-operative transsexual who had gone on the wrong date with the wrong guy. Today, it's more likely to be a teenager of color, often from an economically challenged home, who is gay, of indeterminate gender, experimenting with gender roles, or transgender—but not necessarily transsexual. The victim's assailant is likely to be another youth.[141]

Song of Solomon's critique of black masculinities based on materialism, violence, and sexism originating from particular historical periods in the United States, such as Reconstruction and the Civil Rights Movement, by the end shifts the focus to the women. Solomon, Macon Dead II, Milkman, and Guitar represent men who have adopted black masculinities in response to historical, racist, and naturalistic forces, resulting in the oppression of black women and men. Rather than looking to the black culture embodied in Pilate for positive identities, a sort of cultural incest, these characters adopt white masculinities that have prevailed since slavery, some created by whites in order to oppress black men. The privileging of black culture, mostly oral and mostly represented by Pilate, manifests in the thematic movement in the novel from flight to orality. The men, in adopting white notions of masculinity, fly away from black culture, leaving women and children to pick up the pieces. As the novel's epigraph suggests, "The fathers may soar / And the children may know their names." Pilate's death marks the moment at which the novel's focus shifts from black hypermasculinities to the plight of black women. Pilate's death proves heroic in that it causes Milkman and the reader to realize one can fly without ever leaving the ground (by accessing black history and black culture) and that Pilate represents the strongest character in the novel. Further, her death cements the critique of the black men in the novel and their destructive masculinities. Pilate's death and the shift in focus from the men to the women highlight the tragic plight of Ruth, Hagar, and Milkman's sisters, who exist as commodities limited by kinship systems and the incest taboo. Macon Dead II, Dr. Foster, and Milkman control these women by dictating whom they marry and whether or not they can marry. Ruth's and Hagar's incestuous desires function on two levels. Firstly, Ruth desires to subvert Macon Dead II's patriarchal privilege by engaging in the one act forbidden and necessary in furthering kinship systems. Secondly, Ruth's and Hagar's incestuous desires symbolize a rejection of blackness defined by existing social institutions in favor of an identity drawn from black experience. Darieck Scott, bell hooks, and Riki Wilchins argue for the need for new definitions of blackness and sexuality based on a failure to adopt standard institutional identities such as those derived from the incest taboo. This politics of failure includes favoring queer identities culled from black experience. *Song of Solomon* argues that black identity ought to come from black experience and this experience can be regarded as a form of cultural incest.

NOTES

1. Angela Davis argues that the myth of the black rapist developed in order to justify postbellum lynchings, which "were proving to be a valuable political weapon. Before lynching could be consolidated as a popular accepted institution . . . its savagery and its horrors had to be convincingly justified. These were the circumstances which spawned the myth of the Black rapist—for the rape charge turned out to be the most powerful of several attempts to justify lynching." Angela Y. Davis, *Women, Race and Class* (New York: Random House, 1981), 185.

2. "Womanist . . . A black feminist or feminist of color." Alice Walker, *In Search of Our Mothers' Gardens* (San Diego: Harcourt Brace Jovanovich, 1983), xi–xii.

3. In McCarthy's *Blood Meridian*, the kid's ironic failed heroism in chapter one stems from his ineffectual rebellion against the hypermasculine judge. John Grady Cole's ironic and heroic failure of chapter two sheds light on the destructiveness of cowboy hypermasculinity. Pilate's death proves ironically heroic partly because it shifts the focus of the novel from the men to the women. Her death compels Milkman, and subsequently the reader, to see that she could fly "without ever leaving the ground." Toni Morrison, *Song of Solomon* (New York: Vintage, 2004), 336. Had Pilate survived, Milkman's flight at the end of the book might appear even more falsely heroic, thus legitimizing his hypermasculine obsession with flight. Further, her heroism is ironic since she is a woman in a novel ostensibly about men.

4. Rolland Murray, "The Long Strut: *Song of Solomon* and the Emancipatory Limits of Black Patriarchy," *Callaloo* 22, no. 1 (Winter 1999): 126.

5. Murray, "The Long Strut," 125.

6. Morrison, *Song of Solomon*, 51.

7. Morrison, *Song of Solomon*, 5.

8. Morrison, *Song of Solomon*, 235.

9. Murray, "The Long Strut," 126.

10. Morrison, *Song of Solomon*, 40.

11. Morrison, *Song of Solomon*, 51.

12. Murray, "The Long Strut," 125.

13. Philip Page, "Putting It All Together: Attempted Unification in *Song of Solomon*," in *Toni Morrison*, ed. Harold Bloom (Philadelphia: Chelsea House, 2005), 119.

14. Ralph Story, "An Excursion into the Black World: The 'Seven Days' in Toni Morrison's *Song of Solomon*," *Black American Literature Forum* 23, no. 1 (Spring 1989): 150.

15. Story, "An Excursion into the Black World," 154.

16. bell hooks, *We Real Cool: Black Men and Masculinity* (New York: Routledge, 2004), 59.

17. hooks, *We Real Cool*, 58.

18. Morrison, *Song of Solomon*, 222.

19. Morrison, *Song of Solomon*, 223.

20. Calvin Hernton, "The Sexual Mountain and Black Women Writers," *Black American Literature Forum* 18, no. 4 (Winter 1984): 139.

21. Hernton, "The Sexual Mountain and Black Women Writers," 139.

22. Morrison, *Song of Solomon*, 159.

23. Gay Wilentz, "Civilizations Underneath: African Heritage as Cultural Discourse in Toni Morrison's *Song of Solomon*," *African American Review* 26, no. 1 (Spring 1992): 74.

24. Michael Awkward, "'Unruly and Let Loose': Myth, Ideology, and Gender in *Song of Solomon*," *Callaloo* 13, no. 3 (Summer 1990): 496.

25. Darieck Scott, *Extravagant Abjection: Blackness, Power, and Sexuality in the African American Literary Imagination* (New York: New York University Press, 2010), 38.

26. Scott, *Extravagant Abjection*, 4.

27. Scott, *Extravagant Abjection*, 38.

28. Scott, *Extravagant Abjection*, 134.

29. Kobena Mercer, "True Confessions," in *Black Male*, ed. Thelma Golden (New York: Whitney Museum of Modern Art, 1994), 196.

30. Arthur Flannigan Saint-Aubin, "Testeria: The Dis-ease of Black Men in White Supremacist, Patriarchal Culture," *Callaloo* 17, no. 4 (Autumn 1994): 1060.

31. hooks, *We Real Cool*, 3.

32. hooks, *We Real Cool*, 3–4.

33. Susan Neal Mayberry, *Can't I Love What I Criticize? The Masculine and Morrison* (Athens: University of Georgia Press, 2007), 82.

34. Mayberry, *Can't I Love What I Criticize?*, 101.

35. Page, "Putting It All Together," 109.

36. Saint-Aubin, "Testeria," 1058.

37. Morrison, *Song of Solomon*, 62.

38. Morrison, *Song of Solomon*, 300.

39. Catherine Carr Lee, "The South in Toni Morrison's *Song of Solomon*," in *Toni Morrison's* Song of Solomon: *A Casebook*, ed. Jan Furman (Oxford: Oxford University Press, 2003), 53.

40. In *Winesburg, Ohio* Sherwood Anderson writes, "The moment one of the people took one of the truths to himself, called it his truth, and tried to live his life by it, he became a grotesque and the truth he embraced became a falsehood." Sherwood Anderson, *Winesburg, Ohio* (1919; New York: Viking, 1958), 25. In *Song of Solomon*, Guitar and Macon Dead II represent grotesques since they live their lives by destructive personal truths such as violence and materialism. Even though some might consider Pilate's lack of navel grotesque, the men of the novel and their hypermasculinity are the real grotesques.

41. Morrison, *Song of Solomon*, 55.

42. Morrison, *Song of Solomon*, 163.

43. Wilentz, "Civilizations Underneath," 64.

44. Story, "An Excursion into the Black World," 156.

45. Valerie Smith, "The Quest for and Discovery of Identity in Toni Morrison's *Song of Solomon*," in *Toni Morrison's* Song of Solomon: *A Casebook*, ed. Jan Furman (Oxford: Oxford University Press, 2003), 38.

46. Morrison, *Song of Solomon*, 277.

47. Morrison, *Song of Solomon*, 85.

48. Morrison, *Song of Solomon*, 223.

49. Morrison, *Song of Solomon*, 154–55.

50. John N. Duvall, "Doe Hunting and Masculinity: *Song of Solomon* and *Go Down, Moses*," in *Toni Morrison's* Song of Solomon: *A Casebook*, ed. Jan Furman (Oxford: Oxford University Press, 2003), 122.

51. Mayberry, *Can't I Love What I Criticize?*, 101.

52. Morrison, *Song of Solomon*, 158.

53. Morrison, *Song of Solomon*, 159.

54. Morrison, *Song of Solomon*, 157.

55. Wilentz, "Civilizations Underneath," 63.

56. Awkward, "Unruly and Let Loose," 484.

57. Morrison, *Song of Solomon*, 328.

58. Morrison, *Song of Solomon*, 277.

59. Morrison, *Song of Solomon*, 337.

60. Gerry Brenner, "Rejecting Rank's Monomyth and Feminism," in *Toni Morrison's* Song of Solomon: *A Casebook*, ed. Jan Furman (Oxford: Oxford University Press, 2003), 101.

61. Melvin Dixon, "Like an Eagle in the Air: Toni Morrison," in *Toni Morrison*, ed. Harold Bloom (Philadelphia: Chelsea House, 2005), 40.

62. Toni Morrison, in the introduction to *Song of Solomon*, writes, "The challenge of *Song of Solomon* was to manage what was for me a radical shift in imagination from a female focus to a male one" (xii). She also states in an interview, "It was the first time that I had written about a man who was the central, the driving engine of the narrative." Quoted in Elissa Schappell, "Toni Morrison: The Art of Fiction," in *Toni Morrison's* Song of Solomon: *A*

Casebook, ed. Jan Furman (Oxford: Oxford University Press, 2003), 258. Mayberry writes, "Morrison finds flying 'one of the most attractive features about the black male life.'" Mayberry, *Can't I Love What I Criticize?*, 72. Simply because Morrison *says* these things does not mean they are true. The foremost black male criticism in the book centers on black male flight. Further, that Milkman is the protagonist of the novel does not mean he is its hero. Lastly, even though Morrison says the novel employs a male focus, by novel's end that focus is perhaps more androgynous based on its critique of male flight.

63. Awkward, "Unruly and Let Loose," 494.

64. Cedric Gael Bryant, "'Every Goodbye Ain't Gone': The Semiotics of Death, Mourning, and Closural Practice in Toni Morrison's *Song of Solomon*," *MELUS* 24, no. 3 (Autumn 1999): 103.

65. Julius Lester, "People Who Could Fly," in *Toni Morrison's* Song of Solomon*: A Casebook*, ed. Jan Furman (Oxford: Oxford University Press, 2003), 21.

66. Lester, "People Who Could Fly," 23.

67. Morrison, *Song of Solomon*, 9.

68. Linda Krumholz, "Dead Teachers: Rituals of Manhood and Rituals of Reading in *Song of Solomon*," in *Toni Morrison's* Song of Solomon*: A Casebook*, ed. Jan Furman (Oxford: Oxford University Press, 2003), 211.

69. Morrison, *Song of Solomon*, 179.

70. Page, "Putting It All Together," 102.

71. Wilentz, "Civilizations Underneath," 64.

72. Mayberry, *Can't I Love What I Criticize?*, 73.

73. Wilentz, "Civilizations Underneath," 64.

74. Joyce Irene Middleton, "Orality, Literacy, and Memory in Toni Morrison's *Song of Solomon*," *College English* 55, no. 1 (Jan. 1993): 65.

75. Morrison, *Song of Solomon*, 4.

76. Morrison, *Song of Solomon*, 53.

77. Morrison, *Song of Solomon*, 17.

78. Morrison, *Song of Solomon*, 99.

79. Morrison, *Song of Solomon*, 303.

80. Middleton, "Orality, Literacy, and Memory," 69.

81. Mayberry, *Can't I Love What I Criticize?*, 72.

82. Brenner, "Rejecting Rank's Monomyth and Feminism," 95.

83. Schappell, "Toni Morrison: The Art of Fiction," 83.

84. Page, "Putting It All Together," 106.

85. Brenner, "Rejecting Rank's Monomyth and Feminism," 107.

86. Wilfred D. Samuels and Clenora Hudson-Weems, *Toni Morrison* (Boston: Twayne, 1990), 64.

87. Morrison, *Song of Solomon*, 27.

88. Smith, "The Quest for and Discovery of Identity," 36.

89. Morrison, *Song of Solomon*, 149.

90. Morrison, *Song of Solomon*, 150.

91. Morrison, *Song of Solomon*, 20.

92. Morrison, *Song of Solomon*, 150.

93. Brenner, "Rejecting Rank's Monomyth and Feminism," 101.

94. Morrison, *Song of Solomon*, 336.

95. Morrison, *Song of Solomon*, 140.

96. Pilate's death also positions her as one of many, many female characters in novels from time immemorial who fail to live beyond death or marriage. As Rachel Blau Duplessis explains, "Once upon a time, the end, the rightful end, of women in novels was social—successful courtship, marriage—or judgmental of her sexual and social failure—death." Rachel Blau Duplessis, *Writing beyond the Ending: Narrative Strategies of Twentieth-Century Women Writers* (Bloomington: Indiana University Press, 1985), 2. In *Song of Solomon*, Pilate harbors no interest in marriage and attempts to construct a life outside of the kinship system of marriage. She sacrifices her life for a man undeserving of the gesture, proving herself heroic and allowing the reader to see Milkman's flight as destructive. Nonetheless, Morrison fails to execute "the

project of twentieth-century women writers to solve the contradiction between love and quest and to replace the alternate endings in marriage and death that are their cultural legacy from nineteenth-century life and letters by offering a different set of choices." Duplessis, *Writing beyond the Ending*, 4. Like the male and female writers who have gone before her, Morrison seems to care too much about the men of the novel, using the women as sacrificial lambs for the benefit of unworthy males.

97. Gayle Rubin, "The Traffic in Women," in *Literary Theory: An Anthology*, ed. Julie Rivkin and Michael Ryan (Malden: Blackwell, 2004), 776. Jeffrey Weeks reports, "In the Christian traditions of the Middle Ages, marriage to seventh degree of relationship was prohibited. Today, marriage to first cousins is allowed. In the Egypt of the Pharoahs, sibling marriages were permitted, and in some cases so were father-daughter marriages, in the interests of preserving the purity of the royal line . . . The existence of the incest taboo illustrates the need of all societies to regulate sex—but not how it is done. Even 'blood relationships' have to be interpreted through the grid of culture." Jeffrey Weeks, *Sexuality* (Chichester: Ellis Horwood, 1986), 27.

98. Rubin, "The Traffic in Women," 780.

99. Rubin, "The Traffic in Women," 778.

100. Jeffrey Weeks, *Sexuality and Its Discontents* (London: Routledge, 1985), 116.

101. For instance, David Lester states, "Recent reviews of studies of the effects of consanguinity on morbidity and mortality . . . have concluded that inbreeding does have deleterious effects on humans. Adams and Neel (1967) compared the offspring of brother-sister and father-daughter incest with control offspring and found a greater incidence of major defects and early death in the incestuous offspring." David Lester, "Incest," *The Journal of Sex Research* 8, no. 4 (Nov. 1972): 271.

102. Kaja Silverman, *Male Subjectivity at the Margins* (New York: Routledge, 1992), 36.

103. Rubin, "The Traffic in Women," 780.

104. Luce Irigaray, *This Sex Which Is Not One*, trans. Catherine Porter (Ithaca: Cornell University Press, 1977), 70.

105. Laura Mulvey writes, "In a world ordered by sexual imbalance, pleasure in looking has been split between active/male and passive/female. The determining male gaze projects its fantasy onto the female figure, which is styled accordingly. In their traditional exhibitionist role women are simultaneously looked at and displayed, with their appearance coded for a strong visual and erotic impact so that they can be said to connote *to-be-looked-at-ness*." Laura Mulvey, "Visual Pleasure and Narrative Cinema," in *The Norton Anthology of Theory and Criticism*, ed. Vincent B. Leitch (New York: Norton, 2001), 2186.

106. Michael Kimmel, "Masculinity as Homophobia: Fear, Shame, and Silence in the Construction of Gender Identity," in *Feminism and Masculinities*, ed. Peter F. Murphy (Oxford: Oxford University Press, 2004), 186.

107. Kimmel, "Masculinity as Homophobia," 187.

108. Silverman, *Male Subjectivity at the Margins*, 36.

109. Morrison, *Song of Solomon*, 60.

110. Morrison, *Song of Solomon*, 70.

111. Morrison, *Song of Solomon*, 22.

112. Morrison, *Song of Solomon*, 124.

113. Morrison, *Song of Solomon*, 23.

114. Morrison, *Song of Solomon*, 72.

115. Morrison, *Song of Solomon*, 71.

116. Morrison, *Song of Solomon*, 73.

117. Morrison, *Song of Solomon*, 74.

118. Morrison, *Song of Solomon*, 78.

119. Murray, "The Long Strut," 129.

120. Morrison, *Song of Solomon*, 14.

121. Murray, "The Long Strut," 125.

122. Duvall, "Doe Hunting and Masculinity," 119.

123. Morrison, *Song of Solomon*, 215–16.

124. Morrison, *Song of Solomon*, 64.

125. Morrison, *Song of Solomon*, 69.

126. Morrison, *Song of Solomon*, 91.

127. Morrison, *Song of Solomon*, 315.

128. Morrison, *Song of Solomon*, 315.

129. Harriet Jacobs unveils the brutal reality that for a slave woman "it is deemed a crime for her to wish to be virtuous." Harriet Jacobs, *Incidents in the Life of a Slave Girl, Narrative of the Life of Frederick Douglass, an American Slave and Incidents in the Life of a Slave Girl* (New York: The Modern Library, 2004), 162. Jacobs documents the insatiable desire of her married master Dr. Flint, one of the only town physicians, not only to rape Jacobs but that she *willingly* be his concubine. Jacobs vehemently argues that her experience was likely prevalent among African female slaves in America.

130. Scott, *Extravagant Abjection*, 150.

131. Cornel West, *The Cornel West Reader* (New York: Basic Books, 1999), 517.

132. Notable black thinkers such as Eldridge Cleaver "called rape an 'insurrectionary act' against 'white society.'" Davis, *Women, Race and Class*, 197. Cleaver and others erroneously used the myths of rapacious black men to implant fear into whites in order to combat the rampant violence of the Civil Rights Era and to undermine white masculinity while supposedly strengthening black masculinity.

133. Scott, *Extravagant Abjection*, 9.

134. Scott, *Extravagant Abjection*, 128.

135. Scott, *Extravagant Abjection*, 248.

136. Scott, *Extravagant Abjection*, 254.

137. I am using Wilchins's definition of "queerness," meaning "things like power and identity, language, and *difference*" (emphasis mine). Riki Wilchins, *Queer Theory, Gender Theory: An Instant Primer* (Los Angeles: Alyson, 2004), 5. In this sense any behavior that challenges white patriarchal heteronormativity is *queer* behavior.

138. Judith Halberstam, *The Queer Art of Failure* (Durham: Duke University Press, 2011), 3.

139. Quoted in hooks, *We Real Cool*, 244.

140. hooks, *We Real Cool*, 83.

141. Wilchins, *Queer Theory, Gender Theory*, 156.

Chapter Four

Staggerlee in the Closet

Rufus Scott as Failed Ironic Hero in Another Country

Another Country (1960), like *Song of Solomon* (1977), depicts an African American man entangled in the overwhelming and burgeoning forces fomenting in the United States during the 1960s, ranging from black armed militancy to sexual revolution. In *Another Country*, set primarily in New York City, Rufus Scott embodies the hypermasculine myths of Staggerlee and the black male rapist in an attempt to overcompensate for and conceal his homosexual desire. Rufus's desperate ambition to hide his same-sex desire resonates in Darieck Scott's call for the repudiation of white heteronormative patriarchy by African Americans. Scott argues for a politics of failure as a new definition of black power marked by an espousal of queerness and hypermasculine defection.[1] This politics of the bottom reclaims and re-envisions blackness not as a parody of whiteness but as a revolutionary queer black power capable of confronting the dominant fiction of white supremacy and possibly saving black men like Rufus Scott all over the world. James Baldwin's feud with Eldridge Cleaver and Norman Mailer between 1957 and 1965 over *Another Country* and Mailer's "The White Negro" (1957) exemplifies the volatile American context of *Another Country* in terms of the intersectionalities of black masculinities and black homosexuality. Cleaver and Mailer promulgate examples of the prevailing myths about black men that drive men like the closeted character Rufus Scott to his self-inflicted death. The novel implicates characters such as Vivaldo, Eric, Cass, Leona, Richard, and Ida as co-creators and curators of oppressive myths that lead to Rufus's suicide. *Another Country* utilizes images of sexual intercourse to highlight how intersectionalities of race and sexuality motivate and inform sexual behavior that in part contributes to Rufus's death. Perhaps the most salient aspect of the novel revolves around Rufus's abrupt and early suicide after his relationship with his white girlfriend, Leona, falls apart. The interracial complexity of their affair deeply affects Rufus, compelling him to enact a hypermasculine persona to justify in part his claim to white womanhood and punish Leona for her whiteness. Rufus proves ironically heroic in his failure to successfully assume a violent, hypersexual, and hypermasculine identity. His suicide is heroic since it sheds light on the vitiating forces behind black hypermasculinities and definitions of blackness created by whites. Once again, I am applying Linda Hutcheon's "concept of irony as 'counterdiscourse' . . . a 'mode of combat' . . . 'a *negative* passion, to displace and annihilate a dominant depiction of the world.'"[2] Deeming Rufus's suicide heroic, while unusual, illuminates the dangerous possibility of his succeeding in the overcompensating hypermasculinities that compel his violent and self-destructive behavior.

MORRISON, BALDWIN, AND FAMILY

While both authors were still alive (Baldwin died in 1987[3]), Toni Morrison and James Baldwin respected one another's work, warned readers about the dangers of black hypermasculinities, and emphasized the healing potential of black families in their novels. Lovalerie King reflects, "In the second half of the twentieth century, no two authors did more to shape an African American literary tradition and gain a broad national and international audience for that tradition than James Baldwin and Toni Morrison."[4] In part, what makes these two authors indispensable has to do with their critique of African American male hypermasculinities. Both *Song of Solomon* and *Another Country* employ black male protagonists who embody dangerous black hypermasculinities that arguably cause their destruction. The especially pernicious cowboy-derived black hypermasculinity embodied in a folkloric character like Staggerlee[5] provides a character type that reflects one of the more deadly aspects of some black male masculinities. Quentin D. Miller writes, "Baldwin and Morrison recognize the importance and power of Staggerlee within the context of black social protest of the 1960s but they refuse to glorify him. They interpret Staggerlee's story as a cautionary tale. His lawlessness, anger, and skewed sense of justice are options for Baldwin's and Morrison's protagonists, but not solutions."[6] Unlike many members of the Black Power Movement and white liberals such as Norman Mailer who embraced the myth of Staggerlee as a means to empower black men and define their existential condition, Baldwin and Morrison saw the glorification of violence endemic to the character for its dangerous seductiveness and potential for black male ruination.

In their respective novels, the two authors point to the black family as a potential locus of healing, particularly for their male protagonists. King argues, "Baldwin explores . . . the problem of racial self-hatred and the possibilities of the family as a place of resistance to white hegemony, through plot structures and devices that suggest an engagement with Morrison's family stories in . . . *Song of Solomon.*"[7] In *Song of Solomon*, Milkman refuses Pilate's offer of a black identity made up of black culture, black history, and the black family instead of a hypermasculine one based on materialism, violence, and flight. In Baldwin's novel, Rufus rejects his immediate black family, including his sister Ida, as a locus of healing and resistance to white racism. He also ignores his potential gay family because he fears the consequences of living his life as an openly gay black man. Ultimately, more than his repudiation of his black family, his abandonment of a possible homosexual family precipitates his demise. With some irony, Baldwin admits, "I think that Toni's very painful to read . . . because it's always, or most times, a horrifying allegory; but you recognize that it works. But you don't really want to march through it."[8] If *Song of Solomon* allegorizes Milkman as a black man in flight, then *Another Country* allegorizes Rufus Scott as a black man who cannot reconcile definitions of black masculinity imposed on him by both blacks and whites with his homosexual desire. Indeed, both male protagonists fly away in their respective novels as a response to the often painful and destructive societal pressure to embody rigid definitions of black masculinity.

STAGGERLEE AS HYPERMASCULINE FOLKLORIC REFERENT

Miller contends that Staggerlee, a salient example of hypermasculinity in American folklore, equates

> the familiar figure of the bad black man (also known as "baaadman," or "bad nigger") . . . and . . . is . . . its most enduring [incarnation]. Daryl Cumber Dance has defined the "bad nigger" as "tough and violent. He kills without blinking an eye. He courts death constantly and doesn't fear dying" . . . "Bad" can mean lawless, feared, or respected in this context. "Bad" can mean all three at the same time, and in the ultimate resistance to fixed meaning in language . . . it can even mean "good."[9]

For some African American men, embracing a figure such as Staggerlee compensates for feelings of insecurity about their manhood and operates as a response to emasculating white institutional racism. Miller further argues,

> At the same time, there is something seductive and powerful about Staggerlee; as Black Panther leader Bobby Seale said when his wife asked him why they should name their son Stagolee, "Stagolee was a bad nigger off the block[10]

and didn't take shit from nobody" . . . Such defiance and independence can
easily be associated with pure power. To regard [Staggerlee] as a hero is to
limit the choices that young black males have in contemporary America.[11]

The appeal of Staggerlee, who enjoys a reputation as a sexual dynamo and a
proud man willing to fight for his own dignity, proves powerful for African
American men. The problem, as Miller asserts, exists because "embracing
Staggerlee's rage and personal sense of justice would not protect young black
men from winding up in jail, or getting shot . . . Baldwin is cautious about
Staggerlee, entertaining the legendary figure's potential as a victim, a martyr,
or an inspiration, but never as an unmitigated hero."[12] In *Another Country*,
Rufus's desire to embody the bad black man as overcompensation for his
homosexual desire signifies the struggle between his two warring selves.

Toombs argues that the strong desire of African American men to project
a hypermasculine persona stems from slavery. He writes that due to "the
slave experience, many African American men have developed strange notions of what it means to be a man. For much of their history in America,
black men have had to prove that they were human, that they were not 'boys'
and 'uncles' and, after the Civil War, that they were entitled to full citizen-
ship rights."[13] In other words, black hypermasculinities often result from a
history of emasculating white oppression, transforming into a hypermasculine definition of blackness used to justify white racism toward African
American men. Toombs further contends,

> black men, because of the constant threats they faced—they could be lynched
> or beaten at any time in the post–Civil War South as well as much of the North
> and West by any white man or even white boy—assumed exaggerated notions
> of manhood in their own communities. They became, or tried to become,
> "super-masculine, super-men" . . . One consequence for black men of this
> "super-masculinity" was a lack of tolerance, respect, or acceptance of differ-
> ence whether that difference was because of one's gender or sexual orienta-
> tion. In addition to the tremendous suffering of black women because of this
> exaggerated masculinity . . . black-gay-men also were silenced and disre-
> garded . . . Rufus has accepted the dominant culture's superficial and inauthen-
> tic definitions of manhood and masculinity. In his fear of his homosexuality,
> he exhibits "super-masculinity," and in his encounters with women and gays,
> he berates, abuses, and tries to exert some nonexistent power over them.[14]

Rufus and other black men who embody a hypermasculine persona in order
to overcompensate for their feelings of emasculation due to systemic racism
or homosexual desire perpetuate the very stereotypes they feel they must live
up to. Arthur Flannigan Saint-Aubin states, "In a white supremacist, patriarchal culture, the black man is thought to embody the essence of masculinity—masculinity in its purest, most unadulterated and therefore dangerous
form. Although he is not considered to be a 'man,' he embodies a darker

shade of male; he is the masculine icon."[15] Along with the promulgation of the myth of the black rapist perpetuated after slavery to justify violence against black men, black men themselves aided in constructing themselves as paragons of masculinity at the expense of their intellectual capacity and their humanity in general. Subsequently, some black men strive to live up to the masculine icon used to oppress them.

For black homosexual men, the situation is worse; their very desire for same-sex partners unfairly marks them as emasculated. Because of their homosexuality, they are unjustly treated as inferior to hypermasculine black men, whom much of white society deems subhuman in the first place. Further, black homosexual men risk humiliation, alienation, and ridicule from many other blacks in their own community. Baldwin touches on the risks of black homosexual love when he notes, "Humiliation is the central danger of one's life. And since one cannot risk love without risking humiliation, love becomes impossible."[16] The closeted black homosexual man risks humiliation from other African Americans and further terror by white society. Paul Hoch notes, "In a white civilization which considers many forms of sexuality to be immoral and consigns them to the dark dungeons of the unconscious— the 'devil,' dark villain or black beast becomes the receptacle of all the tabooed desires, thereby embodying all the forbidden possibilities for ultimate sexual fulfillment and becoming the very apotheosis of masculine potency."[17] From the perspective of a racist white society, the black male homosexual exists as further evidence of the beastliness of African American men, who possibly possess the capacity to rape white women *and* white men. Hoch further concludes, "The conflict between hero and beast becomes a struggle between two understandings of manhood: human versus animal, white versus black, spiritual versus carnal, soul versus flesh, higher versus lower, noble versus base."[18] White society locates the pinnacle of hypermasculinity in the African American man and points to it as a reason for fear. Along with inciting fear of the African American man, this phenomenon also incites desire in white women and men. Americans, both black and white, begin to internalize the stereotypes created during and just after Reconstruction.[19] Frantz Fanon observes,

No longer do we see the black man; we see a penis: the black man has been occulted. He has been turned into a penis. He *is* a penis. We can easily imagine what such descriptions can arouse . . . Horror? Desire? Not indifference, in any case. So what is the truth? The average length of the African's penis, according to Dr. Palés, is seldom greater than 120 millimeters (4.68 inches). Testus in his *Traité d' anatomie humaine* gives the same figure for a European. But nobody is convinced by these facts. The white man is convinced the black man is an animal; if it is not the length of his penis, it's his sexual power that impresses the white man. Confronted with this alterity, the white man needs to

defend himself, i.e., to characterize "the Other," who will become the mainstay
of his preoccupations and his desires. [20]

White society seems oblivious to the reality that during Reconstruction *it*
created the myth of the black penis, which many both fear and desire, in
order to justify the activity of the Ku Klux Klan. Imbuing the black man with
hypersexuality in order to ensure white male domination elicits both desire
and fear in the white man: homosexual desire for the black male body oozing
sexuality, and fear that he might expose the white male as a homosexual.

In *Another Country*, Rufus embraces the myth of the black penis as a way
to ensure his own hypermasculinity, guard his closet, and combat the emasculating effects of white systemic racism. Rufus sees his best friend, Vivaldo,
as a competitor, as someone who may unmask him, and as a member of the
oppressive white society. Though he claims to love Vivaldo, his fear of
humiliation drives a wedge between them, provoking him to think, "To hell
with Vivaldo. He had something Vivaldo would never be able to touch."[21]
Rufus refers to his greater penis size, as well as suggests that Vivaldo actually wishes to *touch* his penis. Rufus emphasizes the difference between the
two men by continually referencing in his mind his exceedingly large penis
in comparison to Vivaldo's: "*You don't be careful, motherfucker, you going
to get a* black *hard on.*"[22] Rufus equates blackness with his penis, and suggests to Vivaldo that his whiteness more than anything else prevents him
from enjoying the kind of sexual prowess that Rufus enjoys.

The emphasis Rufus places on his penis and his fear and insecurity directed at white society destroy his relationship with Leona. Their volatile
romance ends up tainted by his insecurity that she will choose Vivaldo over
him because of Vivaldo's whiteness: "Go on, you slut . . . go on and make it
with your wop lover. He ain't going to be able to do you no good. Not now.
You be back. You can't do without me now."[23] Despite the fact that neither
Vivaldo nor Leona harbors any sort of desire for one another, Rufus insists
on defending his right to sleep with Leona to Vivaldo and then belittles her
for, in his opinion, only desiring him because of his penis: "'You know all
that chick knows about me? The *only* thing she knows?' He put his hand on
his sex, brutally, as though he would tear it out."[24] Rufus criticizes Leona for
what he thinks all white people feel about him. At the same time he suggests
a burden by violently drawing Vivaldo's attention to his own penis. Early in
the novel, the narration explores Rufus and Leona's relationship:

> They fought all the time. They fought each other with their hands and their
> voices and then with their bodies: and the one storm was like the other . . . he
> had, suddenly, without knowing that he was going to, thrown the whimpering,
> terrified Leona onto the bed, the floor, pinned her against a table or a wall; she
> beat at him, weakly, moaning, unutterably abject; he twisted his fingers in her
> long pale hair and used her in whatever way he felt would humiliate her the

most. It was not love he felt during these acts of love: drained and shaking, utterly unsatisfied, he fled from the raped white woman into the bars. In these bars no one applauded his triumph or condemned his guilt. He began to pick fights with white men. He was thrown out of bars. The eyes of his friends told him that he was failing. His own heart told him so. But the air through which he rushed was his prison and he could not even summon the breath to call for help.[25]

In this passage, Baldwin demonstrates Rufus's desire to prove his black hypermasculinity to other white men. After he sexually brutalizes Leona, he presents himself to white men not simply to gloat but to also witness their judgment of him as a man. His behavior stems not only from his desire to guard his black hypermasculine persona but also from a desire to punish, fuck, and own that which white men cherish, white women. Toombs holds, "part of this vengeance is the mere fact that the black man can sexually possess the white man's woman. This is especially important since so many black men have lost their lives or their sexual organs because white men assumed they desired their women, whether they did or not."[26] Rufus's constant thoughts of white men during sex with Leona and his penchant for picking fights with them after sex with her suggest that perhaps his sexual cathexis has more to do with white men than white women. Saint-Aubin writes, "One of the principal accusations against the black man is that he is preoccupied with sexual matters; in his case in particular he is, ostensibly, obsessed with the white (female) body . . . But, as some feminists have begun to suggest, the desire repressed reveals itself to be homosocial: a desire to possess, to appropriate by adjoining the white *male* body and therefore white male privilege."[27] In other words, perhaps Rufus's obsession with Leona's southern whiteness stems from his desire to touch the whiteness of southern men.

Rufus's desire to guard his masculinity, his desire to flout white southern racism, and possibly his desire for white men compel him to embody stereotypes used against black men since Reconstruction. He embraces the dehumanizing stereotypes as a defense against his homosexual desire. bell hooks makes an argument about some contemporary black males that one can connect with the character Rufus: "Yet what makes contemporary demonization of the black male different from that of the past is that many black males no longer challenge this dehumanizing stereotype, instead they claim it as a mark of distinction, as the edge that they have over white males."[28] While Rufus's hypermasculinity may in the short term serve his closeted homosexual desire, in the long run it causes his destruction. Toombs further points out, "Rufus's involvement with women also is noteworthy, as it reveals how well 'super-masculinity' serves the black man who has homosexual desires but cannot face them honestly. Rufus's first meeting with Leona and the night of partying and sex that follows captures the essence of straight and gay black men who acquiesce to 'super-masculinity.'"[29] In the novel, Baldwin indicts hypermasculinity as perhaps the greatest threat to all men, homosexual or heterosexual, since either way both parties often perpetuate a pernicious stereotype that has wreaked havoc on black men in particular since the Civil War. The narrative explores the character Eric's thoughts about New York City and hypermasculinity:

> [Eric] could not escape the feeling that a kind of plague was raging, though it was officially and publicly and privately denied. Even the young seemed blighted—seemed most blighted of all. The boys in their blue jeans ran together, scarcely daring to trust one another, but united, like their elders, in a boyish distrust of the girls. Their very walk, a kind of anti-erotic, knee-action lope, was a parody of locomotion and of manhood. They seemed to be shrinking away from any contact with their flamboyantly and paradoxically outlined private parts.[30]

The plague Eric notices in America centers on the hypermasculine socialization of American men. According to Eric, adults socialize young boys to distrust girls as the weaker, emasculating sex and to not look to one another for comfort. Further, the male children already practice walking "like a man," avoiding any sort of gait that may signify queerness. The boys, Eric notes, seem afraid of their privates, like Rufus, afraid that their genitalia may betray them. Baldwin writes of Rufus,

> He added his stream to the ocean, holding that most despised part of himself loosely between two fingers of one hand . . . He looked at the horrible history splashed furiously on the walls—telephone numbers, cock, breasts, balls, cunts, etched into these walls with hatred. *Suck my cock. I like to get whipped. I want a hot stiff prick up my ass. Down with Jews. Kill the niggers. Suck my cock.*[31]

Rufus despises his genitalia because he understands it as the locus of his homosexual desire. Adults, perhaps homosexual closeted adults, teach children to despise the phallus because of the same fear that grips Rufus; thus children grow up hypermasculine, sexist, cold to other men, and distrusting of women. Eric further thinks of all the hypermasculine men hiding their gayness:

> And he thought of these men, that ignorant army. They were husbands, they were fathers, gangsters, football players, rovers; and they were everywhere. Or they were, in any case, in all of the places he had been assured they could not be found and the need they brought to him was one they scarcely knew they had, which they spent their lives denying . . . The need seemed, indeed, to be precisely this passivity.[32]

The closeted hypermasculine men desire the very passivity they have been socialized to disavow.

The black community itself represents another force that exacerbates some African American men who feel they must live up to the rigid hypermasculine definitions of manhood placed upon them. Rufus must pass as heterosexual perhaps most of all under the eyes of other black men and women, including members of his own family. Rufus fears the black man who hosts the party where he and Leona first have sex because he fears the man may emasculate him or expose him as a homosexual. Baldwin writes,

> The host . . . was a big, handsome, expansive man, older and more ruthless than he looked, who had fought his way to the top in show business via several of the rougher professions, including boxing and pimping . . . Rufus liked him because he was rough and good-natured and generous. But Rufus was also a little afraid of him; there was that about him, in spite of his charm, which did not encourage intimacy. He was a great success with women, whom he treated with a large, affectionate contempt. [33]

The man's success with women automatically positions him in competition with Rufus and as a threat to Rufus's masculinity. Further, the host's black hypermasculinity symbolically confronts and exposes Rufus's hidden homosexual desire. Toombs notes, "It is not surprising that for Rufus, the party's host is both a model of the 'super-black man' and someone to fear. Black men like the host make it even more difficult for black-gay-men to emerge from the closet, for these men ridicule, humiliate, and figuratively and literally kill black-gay-men." [34] For Rufus and perhaps for Baldwin as well, men such as the host present a greater threat of bodily harm than even white men since other black men have putatively more to lose in the event of a black man living outwardly gay, namely the stability of the construction of black hypermasculinity.

Ida Scott, Rufus's sister, represents another member of the black community, this time his own blood, who impedes his ability to admit his same-sex desire. Ida seems to share the prevailing belief that homosexuality represents a disease, equates weakness, and hurts all black people. Not realizing that not only her brother but also her own boyfriend, Vivaldo, harbors homosexual desires, Ida says to Vivaldo, "I always feel so *sorry* for people like that . . . They're very sweet. And, of course, they make wonderful escorts. You haven't got to worry about them." [35] Rather than admit her brother's gayness, Ida would prefer to believe in not only the hypersexuality of black men but also the hypersexuality of black women. She equates gayness with whiteness and hypersexuality with blackness. She says to Vivaldo, "Every damn one of your sad-ass white chicks thinks they got a cunt for peeing through, and they don't piss nothing but the best ginger ale, and if it wasn't for the spooks wouldn't a damn one of you white cock suckers ever *get* laid." [36] For Ida, "spooks" represent bearers of sexuality and whites represent cock suckers. She later says of Eric, a man who Vivaldo hints to her had a sexual relationship with Rufus, "He wanted a roll in the hay with my brother, too . . . He wanted to make him as sick as he is."[37] Further, when she finds out about the affair between Eric and Cass, she says, "She's got a good man and he's really starting to get someplace, and she can't find anything *better* to do than start screwing some poor white faggot from Alabama. I swear, I don't understand white folks worth a damn."[38] For Ida, *white folks* engage in homosexuality and have the power to sexually recruit black people, but black men like her brother, whom she idolizes, could never harbor homosexual desire himself. Baldwin evokes Ida's investment in sexual, gender, and racial binaries. In her mind, inviolable boundaries exist between blacks and whites, men and women, and homosexuals and heterosexuals that come under attack by the rumored behavior of her brother and his white friends. Ida clings to these binaries because avowing obvious contradictions would necessitate a profound reevaluation of not only her brother, whom she feels she knows better than anyone else, but also her entire world view.

Ultimately, Rufus's black hypermasculinity imaged in *Another Country* signifies on white hypermasculinity in a counterproductive way if, as Gates maintains, "the nature and function of Signifyin(g) . . . *is* repetition and revision . . . with a signal difference."[39] The signal difference in Rufus's hypermasculinity compared to the dominant culture's definitions of manhood is one of exaggeration. Black hypermasculinities simply outdo already out-of-control hegemonic white hypermasculinities and thereby perpetuate already entrenched stereotypes that disempower black men.

POLITICS OF FAILURE

The character Rufus Scott's chief flaw centers on his acquiescence to white definitions of black masculinity. The primary flaw of Eldridge Cleaver, the minister of information for the Black Panther Party, and much of the Black Power Movement stems from the co-opting of white definitions of masculinity typically predicated on violence and sexism. Cleaver and Rufus fail to realize that by adopting canned identities as Staggerlees, they provide whites with ready justifications for further persecution based on the promulgation of fear. Like Milkman in Morrison's *Song of Solomon*, Rufus might have looked to his own history of oppression for identity. As Darieck Scott points out, "It is in and through that very domination and defeat also a mapping of political potential, an access to freedom."[40] In the case of *Another Country*, unlike *Song of Solomon*, this "black power that is queer,"[41] this "politics of the bottom,"[42] might politicize hypermasculine failure as a definition of blackness. This new and powerful definition confronts the dehumanizing erstwhile definitions created by whites to oppress blacks. Toombs argues,

> Instead of trying to be the big, bad, black, virile, promiscuous, vicious, cool (or down with it), I can do it all alone, "super-masculine" brother, Rufus should have taken the path followed by his forefathers, who did not acquiesce or succumb to white people's definitions of the world, who took what was here and made it their own, who said "oh, this is your religion, your philosophical ethos, your look at the world. Well, this is mine."[43]

African Americans might look to a recent past marked with degradations and depredations in order to locate a tool allowing them to confront destructive identities placed upon them by whites. Scott writes,

> African American critiques have long argued that any ascription of a kind of superior masculinity to black men is rooted in racist conceptions of the inherent savagery, the supposed authenticity and rapacious sexuality of black(male)ness. But that supposed authenticity, the vitality which racist discourse often projects onto the black male body, has also been used as a source of political strength, as a strategic essentialism of sorts; this was especially true in the late-1960s brand of black nationalism and its cultural arm, the Black Arts Movement.[44]

The political strength gleaned from these pernicious definitions of black maleness converts into white fear and hostility toward black men, resulting in further oppression. Scott writes, "Negrophobia is essentially a sexual phobia, because blackness is primarily associated in Western . . . cultures with perverse, [nonnormative] sexuality."[45] The association of blackness with queerness presents an opportunity to redefine blackness as hypermasculine failure. Scott further argues, "Blackness is constituted by a history of abjection, and *is* itself a form of abjection."[46] In this sense, the very failure of African Americans to measure up to destructive notions of hypermasculinity exists as new definitions of blackness. Indeed, "the break that is made by what conquest, enslavement, and domination has broken . . . of traditional life, and that is abjection—restarts sociogenic processes and makes possible new nations, different families, different gender positions and sexualities."[47] In *Another Country*, Baldwin clearly suggests that men like Rufus need new definitions of blackness in order to break free from the rigid definitions imposed on them by whites and embraced by blacks, definitions that secure his protagonist's ironically heroic death.

AMERICAN CONTEXT: BALDWIN, CLEAVER, AND MAILER

The textual feud among James Baldwin, Eldridge Cleaver, and Norman Mailer during the early 1960s and beyond provides an illuminating insight into the American context of *Another Country*. Kobena Mercer notes, "The origins of the modern gay liberation movement were closely intertwined with the black liberation movement of the 60s . . . the American gay community learned new tactics of protest through their participation in the civil rights struggles for equality, dignity and autonomy."[48] Nonetheless, these two movements proved volatile bedfellows, mostly because the Black Liberation Movement spearheaded by the Black Panther Party (BPP) espoused "sexist, misogynistic, and homophobic beliefs right at the historical moment when women's liberation and the movement for sexual liberation (with its focus on gay rights) were gaining momentum."[49] Cleaver[50] published his views in his book *Soul on Ice*, including an essay titled "Notes on a Native Son," in which, among many invectives, he accuses Baldwin of "[resorting] to a despicable underground guerrilla war, waged on paper, against black masculinity."[51] Cleaver rightly points out that Baldwin in *Another Country* does attack black hypermasculinities and in doing so implicates Cleaver himself and much of the BPP and the Black Liberation Movement on the whole. E. Frances White adds,

> Baldwin acknowledged that many of his new insights and attitudes came from younger men in the movement. Unfortunately, his bonds with these young black men were challenged by homophobia. Nowhere was this challenge more clear than in the famous confrontation between Baldwin and Eldridge Cleaver. In his celebrated essay entitled "Notes on a Native Son" (1968), Cleaver acknowledged that he initially found Baldwin's writings on race insightful but later began to think that Baldwin hated black masculinity. [52]

The character of Rufus Scott in *Another Country* seems to have infuriated Cleaver even more than Baldwin's own gayness. Cleaver writes, "Rufus Scott, a pathetic wretch who indulged in the white man's pastime of committing suicide, who let a white bisexual homosexual fuck him in the ass, and who took a Southern Jezebel for his woman, with all that these tortured relationships imply, was the epitome of a black eunuch who has completely submitted to the white man."[53] Perhaps Cleaver noticed qualities in Rufus Scott that reminded him of himself, to wit, Rufus's unabashed hypermasculinity. In the novel, Baldwin suggests that Rufus's hypermasculine self functions as a mask or overcompensation for his homosexual desire. If one takes this into consideration, one can better understand Cleaver's defensive position. Further, Cleaver may have felt threatened by the Gay Liberation Movement's power to indirectly subvert the Black Panther Party's hypermasculine pose:

After the clone look in which gay men adopted very "straight" signifiers of masculinity—mustache, short cropped hair, work clothes—in order to challenge stereotypes of limp-wristed "poofs," there developed a stylistic flirtation with S&M imagery, leather gear, [and] quasi-military uniforms . . . [T]hose who [embraced] the "threatening" symbolism of the tough-guy look were really only interested in the eroticization of masculinity.[54]

Considering that the uniform of the BPP consisted of "a black beret, black pants, powder blue shirt, black shoes, and black leather jackets,"[55] the Gay Liberation Movement's ability to eroticize exaggerated masculine signifiers may have helped spur Cleaver to level his considerable literary talents at queer men, including a fictional Rufus Scott and Rufus's creator, James Baldwin himself:

The black homosexual, when his twist has a racial nexus, is an extreme embodiment of this contradiction. The white man has deprived him of his masculinity, castrated him in the center of his burning skull, and when he submits to this change and takes the white man for his lover as well as Big Daddy, he focuses on "whiteness" all the love in his pent up soul and turns the razor edge of hatred against "blackness"—upon himself, what he is, and all those who look like him, remind him of himself.[56]

Cleaver attributes Rufus's black homosexuality to a direct response to white oppression. In Cleaver's narrative, Rufus has transformed into a homosexual because whites have emasculated him. As a result of the emasculation Rufus decides to submit sexually to men who oppress him, not only embracing them sexually but also assimilating their prejudice toward African Americans. Cleaver's principal charge centers on Baldwin's supposed self-hatred and hatred of blackness in general, which Cleaver associates with hypermasculinities: "There is in James Baldwin's work the most grueling, agonizing total hatred of the blacks, particularly himself, and the most shameful, fanatical, fawning, sycophantic love of the whites that one can find in the writings of any black American writer of note in our time."[57] For Cleaver, black hypermasculinities function as redress for the centuries of black emasculation by whites. Cleaver writes, "What has been happening for the past four hundred years is that the white man, through his access to black women, has been pumping his blood and genes into the blacks, has been diluting the blood and genes of the blacks."[58] If Baldwin then criticizes black hypermasculinities, which he most certainly does in *Another Country*, from Cleaver's vantage point he must also countenance the sexual violation of black women, the long systemic racist emasculation of black men, as well as sexually covet the white man:

The case of James Baldwin aside for a moment, it seems that many Negro homosexuals, acquiescing in this racial death-wish, are outraged and frustrated because in their sickness they are unable to have a baby by a white man. The cross they have to bear is that already bending over and touching their toes for the white man, the fruit of their miscegenation is not the little half-white offspring of their dreams but an increase in the unwinding of their nerves—though they redouble their efforts and intake of the white man's sperm.[59]

The fallacy of Cleaver's argument pivots on the idea that a homosexual black man cannot criticize black masculinities without coveting white men sexually. Marlon B. Ross argues, "According to Cleaver's racial logic—or more precisely, illogic—black homosexual desire is ultimately desire for whiteness, desire to vacate black manhood for an abject position appropriate only to the white female."[60] Cleaver's vilification of black homosexuality depends largely on his desire to maintain his vaunted sense of hypermasculine blackness. Stefanie Dunning suggests, "Cleaver's essay represents not only a castigation of homosexuality, but stages its rejection in the context of *interracial* homosexuality, because he conceptualizes it as a rejection of the worth and value of black masculinity."[61] Cleaver fails to understand the potential heterogeneity of masculinity—that one ought to be able to self-identify as homosexual *and* masculine.

Cleaver's defense of black hypermasculinities in his 1968 essay "Notes on a Native Son" compelled him to defend Norman Mailer's 1957 essay "The White Negro," about which Baldwin wrote in 1961, "I could not, with the best will in the world, make any sense out of *The White Negro* and, in fact, it was hard for me to imagine that this essay had been written by the same man who wrote the novels."[62] Cleaver responded to Baldwin's dismissive remarks by confessing, "I was therefore personally insulted by Baldwin's flippant, schoolmarmish dismissal of *The White Negro*. Baldwin committed a literary crime by his arrogant repudiation of one of the few gravely important expressions of our time."[63] Cleaver embraced the fact that Mailer locates the essence of "hip" in the African American man's desire to murder and rape, naming this hipness psychopathy. Mailer writes, "It is no accident that the source of Hip is the Negro for he had been living on the margin between totalitarianism and democracy for two centuries."[64] That Cleaver felt so strongly about Mailer's essay proves ironic in that Mailer writes, "It is . . . no accident that psychopathy is most prevalent with the Negro."[65] Mailer equates African Americans with psychopaths, asserting, "The psychopath, like the child, cannot delay the pleasures of gratification; and this trait is one of his underlying, universal characteristics. He cannot wait upon erotic gratification which convention demands should be preceded by the chase before the kill: he must rape."[66] Mailer further argues, "At bottom, the drama of the psychopath is that he seeks love. Not love as the search for a mate, but love as the search for an orgasm more apocalyptic than the one which preceded it. Orgasm is his therapy."[67] The very hypermasculinities that Baldwin decries, Mailer, and subsequently Cleaver, view as the locus of power for the African American male. Mailer further contends,

> the Negro (all exceptions admitted) could rarely afford the sophisticated inhibitions of civilization, and so he kept for his survival the art of the primitive, he lived in the enormous present, he subsisted for his Saturday night kicks, relinquishing the pleasures of the mind for the more obligatory pleasures of the body, and in his music he gave voice to the character and quality of his existence, to his rage and the infinite variations of joy, lust, languor, growl, cramp, pinch, scream and despair of his orgasm. For jazz is orgasm.[68]

Mailer peddles stereotypes of African Americans prevailing since slavery that dehumanize them and justify white oppression. Mailer, perhaps feeling insecure about his own masculinity in the face of black hypermasculinities, promulgates stereotypes that ensure the systematic oppression of African Americans; and Cleaver, who sees these stereotypes as seductive and empowering, embraces them seemingly without regard for their obvious dehumanizing result. Relaying Baldwin's feelings about Mailer, Magdalena J. Zaborowska reports,

> Baldwin's essay "The Black Boy Looks at the White Boy," published as Baldwin was struggling with *Another Country* and right before he went to Turkey, portrays Mailer and his posturing as the "White Negro" as having much to do with American racialized and heteronormative notions of masculinity: "that myth of the sexuality of Negroes which Norman, like so many others, refuses to give up."[69]

Mailer, in "The White Negro," perpetuates the myth of the black rapist as a locus of power for African American males, much like Cleaver did for the Black Panther Party, thereby alienating black homosexuals, and homosexuals in general, such as James Baldwin and his creation Rufus Scott. bell hooks writes,

> Therapist Donald Dutton, who has conducted research on violent men for more than twenty years, calls attention to studies that suggest that the brains of psychopaths do not work like those of mentally stable individuals. Dutton explains: "The psychological syndrome of psychopathy includes the loss of the ability to imagine another person's fear or pain or the dreadful consequences that might follow abuse. Other key signs include shallow emotional responses and an unrealistic future scenario . . . accompanied by an unwillingness to examine past problems."[70]

According to Mailer, the birth of cool stems from the psychopathy of the African American male, a man who cannot empathize with other human beings and does not possess the intellectual ability to examine his past.

Baldwin, unfortunately, never really responded to Cleaver's attacks as one might think he would have. Zaborowska attributes this relative silence on the part of Baldwin to perhaps

> a French kiss Cleaver shared with Baldwin at a party where Huey Newton saw them[71] . . . Rather than taking his revenge on Cleaver, Baldwin called him "valuable and rare," perhaps because he understood the contradictions and pain behind Cleaver's assault; Baldwin knew, perhaps, that in assaulting him, the older black male artist, the angry young man was also assaulting a part of himself.[72]

Like Rufus, then, perhaps Cleaver in his essays on Baldwin overcompensates for his homosexual panic by adopting a hypermasculine persona, and in this way attacks the black men who he feels may be eroticizing his black power theatrics, including his black leather Black Panther Party regalia. White offers another answer regarding Baldwin's refusal to counterattack Cleaver when she writes,

> When I was around "Jimmy," I sensed the reconstruction of an elaborate closet. We all knew that there were so many ways in which Baldwin was out: he was regularly surrounded by men who were interested in him, and his fiction clearly spoke for him. But his kind of open homosexuality threatened the terms of masculinity and the politics of respectability in which many in his following were invested; somehow he needed to find a way for homosexuality to be recognized but ignored.[73]

Perhaps Baldwin's silence had to do with his own reluctance to come out fully on a public stage and risk the alienation of a black lumpen proletariat that probably already knew about his sexual orientation. Maybe he simply did not wish to promote more infighting. Nevertheless, Baldwin, Cleaver, and perhaps Mailer's closeted homosexuality allowed the homophobic rhetoric of both Cleaver and Mailer to resonate nearly unmolested. For Mailer, Cleaver, and Baldwin, American male privilege and power are at stake. Cleaver's sense of black masculine power predicated on violence and sexual prowess is threatened by black homosexuality, which he finds counterrevolutionary. Mailer perpetuates dehumanizing myths about black masculinity in order to maintain white male dominance. Baldwin, finally, appears ultimately unwilling to invest in an alternative to white patriarchy, or surrender to a form of abjection that may have saved his life and the life of black men like his creation Rufus Scott.

CLOSETED SEXUALITIES

The Henry James epigraph Baldwin employs at the beginning of the novel references the various nonnormative sexualities in *Another Country*: "They strike one, above all, as giving no account of themselves in any terms already consecrated by human use; to this inarticulate state they probably form, collectively, the most unprecedented of monuments; abysmal the mystery of what they think, what they feel, what they want, what they suppose themselves to be saying." For Baldwin, "they" refers in all likelihood to the characters Rufus, Vivaldo, and Eric, and subsequently to many human beings whose sexuality has gone relatively undocumented in American literature. Indeed, these nonnormative sexualities remain far too marginalized, rendering these characters and their sexualities "inarticulate." Baldwin, in this sense, has monumentalized these sexualities, illuminating the complex humanity of these characters even if the characters themselves, especially Vivaldo and Rufus, have difficulty transcending their false normative identities. While James in this quote signals a new generation of nonconformists for whom "queerness . . . was exactly, after all, their most familiar note,"[74] *Another Country* is a novel about stifled queer identity.

Rufus and Vivaldo's inability to admit and possibly act on their homosexual desire for one another proves fatal for Rufus. His final attempt to make contact with another human being involves attempting to discuss his own homosexual desire with Vivaldo: "'Have you ever wished you were queer?' Rufus asked, suddenly. Vivaldo smiled, looking into his glass. 'I used to think maybe I was. Hell, I think I even *wished* I was.' He laughed. 'But I'm not. So I'm stuck.'"[75] Immediately after denying his same-sex desire to Rufus, Vivaldo admits his uncertainty. Yet this fails to console Rufus. After Rufus's suicide, Vivaldo admits to Cass,

> I had the weirdest feeling that he wanted me to take him in my arms. And not for sex, though maybe sex would have happened. I had the feeling that he wanted someone to hold him, to hold him, and that, that night, it had to be a man . . . I wondered . . . what would have happened if I'd taken him in my arms . . . I was afraid . . . I could have saved him if I'd just reached out that quarter of an inch between us on that bed, and held him.[76]

Like Rufus, Vivaldo clandestinely hides in the closet and experiences homosexual paranoia: "He had been one of them [blue-collar working men]. He had been proud of his skill and his muscles and happy to be accepted as a man among men. Only—it was they who saw something in him which they could not accept, which made them uneasy."[77] Vivaldo never explicitly states that any of these men ever intimated that they did not accept him; rather, their rejection of him exists in his head as insecurity for his own queer desire, perhaps for the men themselves.

Indeed, what Vivaldo and Rufus most have in common is their closeted homosexual desire. The narrator summarizes, "They had slept together, got drunk together, balled chicks together, cursed each other, and loaned each other money. And yet how much, as it turned out, had each kept hidden in his heart from the other! It had all been a game, a game in which Rufus had lost his life. All of the pressures that each had denied had gathered together and killed him."[78] Neither Rufus nor Vivaldo feels as though he can afford to let his secret out to the other even though he likely knows the other will admit the same. Always there remains the possibility that the other will continue to deny it, remain in the closet, thereby alienating the one who emerges. Vivaldo admits at one point that "he had never associated Rufus with violence, for his walk was always deliberate and slow, his tone mocking and gentle."[79] Perhaps these thoughts point to the contradictions in Rufus, signaling to Vivaldo Rufus's hidden sexuality.

Perhaps the most dangerous aspect of Rufus's and Vivaldo's closeted queerness centers on the homosexual panic each man evinces when confronted with another's gayness. Eve Kosofsky Sedgwick defines homosexual panic as a "defense for a person (typically a man) accused of antigay violence [that] implies that his responsibility for the crime was diminished by a pathological psychological condition, perhaps brought on by an unwanted sexual advance from the man whom he then attacked."[80] Both Rufus and Vivaldo prove guilty of homosexual panic as a defense for their own queer desire. After Rufus and Leona meet, he responds to a man staring at them with a homophobic slur: "'Cock sucker,' Rufus muttered."[81] Further, after he knowingly instigates a transaction with a man involving the exchange of his body for a sandwich, he thinks, "If you touch me . . . I'll beat the living shit out of you."[82] Similar to projecting sexual prowess as a means to mask one's same-sex desire, engaging in violence targeted at other homosexuals ensures the violent enactor a stable closet. Sedgwick further suggests, "It is all very well to insist, as I have done, that homosexual panic is necessarily a problem only . . . of nonhomosexual-identified men."[83] In other words, homosexual panic largely exists as a specious phenomenon unique not to heterosexual people but rather to people who do not *identify* as homosexual, or people in the closet. On the way to Rufus's funeral, Vivaldo confesses to Cass,

> You had to be a man where I come from, and you had to prove it, prove it all the time . . . One time . . . we got into a car and drove over to the village and we picked up this queer, a young guy, and we drove him back to Brooklyn. Poor guy, he was scared green before we got halfway there but he couldn't jump out of the car. We drove into this garage, there were seven of us, and we made him go down on all of us and then we beat the piss out of him and took all his money and took his clothes and left him lying on that cement floor. [84]

Readers unfamiliar with the closet and the phenomenon of homosexual panic endemic to nonhomosexual-identified men might find this passage confusing. Why would they mouth-rape this man first, before beating him nearly to death? The reason lies in *their* gay desire. By mouth-raping the boy and then beating him, the men engage in group rape in order to mask their queerness with violence.

Another Country presents the homosexual closet as a disempowering space for the characters who occupy it, such as Rufus and Vivaldo, who must carry on in the world in fear of being exposed. Baldwin represents closeted men, such as Vivaldo, as potentially homicidal men prone to homosexual panic. The violent act he confesses to Cass irrevocably taints him as a character, casting an ever more gloomy and foreboding pall over the entire novel. Further, the novel illuminates the link between homosexual panic and the fear of being exposed as a homosexual before a white patriarchal society that itself fears exposure. In this sense, both Vivaldo and Rufus aspire to a destructive normalcy. Michael Warner says of heteronormativity, "Why would anyone *want* to be normal. If normal just means within a common statistical range, then there is no reason to be normal or not. By that standard, we might say that it is normal to have health problems, bad breath, and outstanding debt."[85] It seems that Vivaldo and Rufus would rather be normal and immoral than accept their sexuality and help promulgate Warner's notion that "variations from the norm . . . are not necessarily signs of pathology. They can become new norms."[86] Further, embracing new norms of sexuality that question the standardization of patriarchal heteronormativity might contribute to a revolutionary politics of failure whereby one's nonnormativity would empower rather than marginalize.

BLACKNESS DEFINED BY WHITES

Rufus's death, occurring early in the action of the novel, casts a shadow on the rest of the characters, revealing in their attempt to make sense of his death their culpability in creating the very rigid definition of homophobic black hypermasculinity that contributes to Rufus's demise. Anna Kérchy notes, "In *Another Country* Rufus's friends and relatives try to re-member their beloved Rufus by recalling their memories of him, reconstructing from different perspectives the potential reasons for his suicide."[87] Indeed, the mostly white characters do "re-member" Rufus by attempting to reattach to him the black phallus that his suicide severs. His suicide points to his difficulty with his own identity, which the mostly white characters help create. Susan Feldman asserts, "Rufus's absence is used to signify this failure to provide a place for the black male in the United States. Rufus, Baldwin claims, is the black corpse floating in the national psyche—he and what he represents must be squarely faced if we are to find peace in our society."[88] Rufus's suicide destabilizes his identity as a hypermasculine, hypersexual black man, which his white friends help fashion. They refuse to recognize their guilt in enabling his closeted identity, preferring to remember the false projected identity instead. Feldman argues,

> The myth of a hyperbolic black male sexuality, as it has been constructed in the white imagination, not only is perceived as threatening in its own right, but his myth is itself a sign of the white male's libidinal investment in the black male body. When reflected back to the white male, the black male thus becomes the specter of the white male's repressed sexual desire for men, and the threat of emasculation that accompanies the expression of such desire in a society based on patriarchal heterosexuality . . . Vivaldo's refusal to acknowledge the significance of racial difference clearly stems from his inability to explore his own desire for men, [and] overcoming his fear of homosexuality becomes a necessary first step toward understanding and accepting his own complicity in Rufus's death.[89]

Vivaldo simultaneously denies his own same-sex desire and his white privilege because he refuses to acknowledge his complicity in creating the myth that informs Rufus's hypersexual identity. Only after Rufus's death does he avow Rufus's and his own homosexual desire, because at that point Rufus can neither expose his closet nor usurp his masculinity. Vivaldo fails to recognize his complicity in what Steve Martinot calls the "machine" of white supremacy, a system of racial ethics "that renders white supremacist actions permissible."[90] He refuses to acknowledge his membership in a white supremacist society that defines itself in contrast to the racial other; as a result, Vivaldo never really develops into an antiracist character in the novel.

Along with Vivaldo, Leona, Richard, and Eric, in remembering Rufus, recreate their own definition of blackness. For Leona, Rufus's blackness functions in part as a counterpoint to her southern upbringing and as vengeance against her abusive husband. Just before she and Rufus have sex for the first time, she comments, "'If my husband could see me now,' and she giggle[s], 'my, my, my!'"[91] Like Vivaldo, she denies her investment in whiteness as a contributing factor in constructing Rufus's blackness and yet relishes imagining her white southern husband seeing her with a black man. Both she and Vivaldo refuse to acknowledge their sexual attraction to a dehumanizing hypersexual *blackness* they assign to black men like Rufus for personal gain.

Richard, in refusing to take Rufus's absence seriously, betrays his own feelings about Rufus's blackness: "Bastard's probably found some other defenseless little girl to beat up."[92] Like the others, Richard does not imagine that his own whiteness and membership in the dominant race have anything to do with black despair. Richard comments, after hearing of Rufus's suicide, "There was nothing anyone could have done. It was too late. He wanted to die."[93] Further, Richard attributes Cass and Vivaldo's outpouring of emotion to white guilt or pity rather than true affection: "I couldn't help feeling, anyway, that one of the reasons all of you made such a kind of—*fuss*—over him was partly just because he was colored."[94] Richard represents the racist liberal who makes a show of knowing black people yet secretly guards his white privilege with a sword and shield. In this manner, faux-liberal "artists" can congratulate themselves for their progressive attitudes toward multiculturalism while secretly perpetuating white supremacy. While they might allow themselves to be seen in public with a black man such as Rufus, or even let him into their homes on occasion, they do nothing substantial to address racial inequality and will often be the first to ascribe one's behavior to one's race.

Even Eric, who critics such as Robert A. Bone, Donald B. Gibson, and John S. Lash feel resonates as the novel's most successful character and the liberating sexual and phallic key, questions whether or not his desire for Rufus centers on a mere desire for the exotic black body: "Was it the body of Rufus to which he had clung, or the bodies of dark men, seen briefly, somewhere, in a garden or a clearing, long ago."[95] Eric's investment in romanticized hypersexual blackness from his southern childhood makes it difficult for Rufus to exist outside of it. Eric employs the myth in order to rebel against the southern mores he so despises. His rebellion and subsequent flight from the American South free him up to embody his homosexual identity. Unfortunately, he leaves Rufus and Leroy, his first black male lover, to their masked identities as hypersexual black studs. As Leroy tells him, "'Ain't but so much they can do to you. But what they can do to *me*—!' And he spread his hands wide."[96] While Eric enjoys the ability to expatriate to France when things get tough, neither Leroy nor Rufus has that financial freedom. At this point in Eric's life, his white privilege and naïveté, instilled in him because of his family's money, endanger the black men whom he claims to love.

SEX, RACE, AND HEROIC FAILURE

The erotic scenes in *Another Country* reveal intersectionalities of race and sexuality that motivate the central characters. Bone argues to the contrary: "*Another Country* . . . is a failure on the grand scale . . . The plot consists of little more than a series of occasions for talk and fornication. Since the latter is a limited vehicle for the expression of complex ideas, talk takes over, and the novel drowns in a torrent of rhetoric."[97] Bone exposes his moral bias by referring to the sex between the characters as *fornication*, and blinded by his prudery fails to understand that some of these ideas can really *only* be expressed sexually. For instance, the scenes between Rufus and Leona, Vivaldo and Ida, and Vivaldo and Eric hold important keys to understanding these particular characters and how race informs their sexuality, as well as the power of sexuality to combat the homophobic, repressive forces at play in the novel. Feldman writes of Rufus and Leona, "His paranoia that Leona is sleeping with other men reflects his own fears of emasculation and feminization. Rather than confronting these fears . . . Rufus uses sex as a weapon to avenge racism and to reaffirm his masculinity . . . delivering himself more fully into the power of the forces that sought to control him."[98] The narrator conveys this information to the reader through depicting the actual sex act with Leona. Baldwin reveals Rufus's sense of his own penis as a weapon and his desire to confront racism by impregnating Leona. Baldwin writes,

> Under his breath he cursed the milk-white bitch and groaned and rode his weapon between her thighs. She began to cry. *I told you*, he moaned, *I'd give you something to cry about*, and, at once, he felt himself strangling, about to explode or die. A moan and a curse tore through him while he beat her with all the strength he had and felt the venom shoot out of him, enough for a hundred black-white babies.[99]

His violence proves ineffectual in that Leona *enjoys* the rough sex and has been left barren by her abusive husband. Rufus not only fails to *prove* his sexual dominance by viciously inflicting pain on Leona, but he also fails to impregnate her. Consequently, his fertility fantasy is degraded. Further, their first sexual encounter foreshadows a destructively sadomasochistic relationship informed by Rufus's blackness that leads to her mental breakdown and his suicide.

On the other hand, the erotic scenes involving Vivaldo and Ida reveal Vivaldo's feelings of imperial white supremacy. Though he claims he does not view Rufus or Ida any differently because of their blackness, his thoughts uncover a very different story. Zaborowska contends,

> the lovemaking between Ida and Vivaldo shows how love and its every possibility have been debased by racism and sexism that transcend the borders of the United States. By focusing on Vivaldo's observing consciousness in the scene, Baldwin is able to explore—at the risk of having Ida's consciousness made invisible—how a white American man might experience sex with a black woman and what he might be thinking in the process.[100]

During sex Vivaldo imagines himself at first as the groom in an arranged marriage on his wedding night, deflowering a young virgin, and then as some sort of white explorer conquering a savage, untouched land. Baldwin writes, "The way she then looked at him; looked at him as though she were, indeed, a virgin, promised at her birth to him, the bridegroom."[101]

Both Rufus and Vivaldo feel that sex with a woman of a different skin color might prove their sexual prowess and mask their homosexual desire. For Rufus, Leona represents that which white men most value sexually; by penetrating his vaunted trophy he gains revenge on white men and augments his masculinity. For Vivaldo, Ida represents "a savage, jungle river," and he the white explorer, "looking for the source that remained hidden just beyond the black, dangerous, dripping foliage."[102] For both men, these racialized conquests represent their desire to mask their queerness. Zaborowska further notes, "By juxtaposing these sex scenes between a black man and a white woman, and a white man and a black woman, Baldwin thus shows us that both men cannot help debasing the females they are having sex with, and that they both resort to fantasies that displace them from their American contexts."[103] Further, the counterpoint of the two sex scenes strengthens the idea that Vivaldo's interest in Ida stems mostly from his sexual interest in Rufus. By sleeping with Ida, Vivaldo attempts to consummate his relationship with Rufus because Rufus and Ida share the same blackness. The doubleness of Rufus and Ida underscores the linked stereotype of black hypersexual men and black hypersexual women. Angela Davis explains,

> The portrayal of Black men as rapists reinforces racism's open invitation to white men to avail themselves sexually of Black women's bodies. The fictional image of the Black man as rapist has always strengthened its inseparable companion: the image of the Black woman as chronically promiscuous. For once the notion is accepted that Black men harbor irresistible and animal-like sexual urges, the entire race is invested with bestiality. If Black men have their eyes on white women as sexual objects, then Black women must certainly welcome the sexual attention of white men.[104]

The novel's sex scenes emphasize how Vivaldo creates and perpetuates stereotypes about black men and women; unable to admit his investment in Rufus's hypersexuality, he cannot admit it in Ida either.

In the novel, Baldwin's fantasy narrative depicting Vivaldo's sexual experience with Eric confirms Vivaldo's desire for exotic black bodies and his unacknowledged investment in his own whiteness. Baldwin writes, "Then, to his delight and confusion, Rufus lay down beside him and opened his arms. And the moment he surrendered to this sweet and overwhelming embrace, his dream, like glass, shattered . . . and [he] found that it was Eric to whom he clung."[105] Vivaldo then knowingly submits to Eric as the passive partner, imagining it is Rufus who penetrates him: "He moaned and his thighs, like the thighs of a woman, loosened, he thrust upward as Eric thrust down . . . *Rufus. Rufus.*"[106] Vivaldo can only submit to Rufus vicariously after Rufus has died because he cannot give up his white masculine privilege. While his experience with Eric may represent a sexual breakthrough, racially he still clings to his investment in whiteness.

As a result of Eric's role as sexual liberator, Barry Gross contends, "in many important respects, Eric is the key to this novel: he is the link between Vivaldo and Rufus and, consequently, between Vivaldo and Ida. He is the common denominator."[107] Eric represents the one man in the novel who functions generally at ease with his nonnormative sexuality; he is the least American outsider. While Eric emancipates Vivaldo by anally penetrating him, just before Rufus commits suicide he thinks of Eric: "He thought of Eric. His straining arms threatened to break. *I can't make it this way.* He thought of Ida. He whispered, *I'm sorry, Leona*, and then the wind took him."[108] Eric's existence outside of the closet separates him from Vivaldo, rendering Eric as perhaps the most powerful character in the novel. Lash asserts, "Eric Jones is the actual hero of *Another Country*, the phallicist to whom men—and one woman—turn in their hours of bafflement and exalta- tion, the ministering angel, as it were, of the phallic god residual in the flesh of every man."[109] On the other hand, Bone questions Eric's designation as the hero of the novel:

> We must now ask of Baldwin's hero: does he face the void and emerge with a new sense of reality, or does he pitch his nomad's tent forever on the shores of the burning lake? The answer hinges . . . on the strength of Eric's commitment to Yves. Baldwin describes it as total, and yet, within a few weeks' span, while Yves remains behind in France, Eric betrays him with a woman and a man. How can we grant to this lost youth redemptive power?[110]

We cannot. The heroism in Eric ironically lies in his masculinity despite his homosexuality. In this sense, Eric signifies an answer to Rufus's belief that one cannot exist as masculine and homosexual. The difference lies in Eric's whiteness. Though still extremely difficult and perilous for white men, living openly gay can be harder for African American men because of the belief of some black men that black gay men pose a threat to revolutionary blackness.

There exists no sort of antiquated heroism in any of the characters in *Another Country*. Nevertheless, Baldwin describes Eric heroically: "His lips were swollen and very red, like those of heroes and gods of antiquity."[111] At this point in the novel, Eric does not reside on Mount Olympus; flushed from a hangover, he has just fucked another man's wife while awaiting the arrival of his lover Yves. The hero in the novel, ironic in his failure, is Rufus. Dunning maintains, "The title of the novel suggests the wish for 'another country,' another nation, in which our racial and sexual selves are imagined and defined differently or perhaps where they are not defined at all."[112] Rufus's decision to commit suicide signifies not only his desire for another country but also his view that his country is unlivable. His suicide exposes the miserable societal pressures imposed on homosexual men, especially black homosexual men. American society demands that he as a black man project a hypermasculine self inconsistent with what he feels. Rufus's failure to continue the hypermasculine charade heroically indicts the society that demands it as well as the cool pose itself.

In *Another Country*, Rufus Scott is a closeted African American male attempting to live up to a definition of blackness based on black cowboy–derived hypermasculinities embodied in the enduring myth of Staggerlee while struggling with his homosexual desire. One alternative possibility for African Americans and men like Rufus Scott exists in what Darieck Scott calls a "politics of the bottom."[113] Instead of adopting white notions of masculinity and power, African Americans might use their history of oppression as an opportunity to withdraw from the hypermasculine power-scramble, creating a queer black power marked by hegemonic masculine failure. Only by espousing new definitions of blackness can African Americans return men like Rufus Scott to the folds of political empowerment and dignity, while confronting white racism that capitalizes on the alienation blacks impose on other blacks. The primarily textual feud between Baldwin and Cleaver, and to a lesser degree Mailer, represents the larger and more important conflict of African American male identity that has the power to inform all African American identities. Cleaver, representing black militancy, embraces the figure of Staggerlee and co-opts the myth of the black rapist created by whites during Reconstruction as a means to black male empowerment, not realizing the long-term deadly repercussions of owning a myth created with the intent of exterminating the owner. The appropriation of the myth of the black male rapist, a hypermasculine, hypersexual myth, alienates many African Americans, creating a less empowered, closeted generation of men and women afraid of themselves and other people. Rufus's closeted guilt manifests in self-destructive, violent outbursts and eventually suicide. The remaining characters, mostly white, for the rest of the novel must deal with their own contributions in creating the fatal myth of the black male rapist. Thematically, Baldwin employs images of sexual intercourse to reveal the intersectionalities of race and sexuality. These images expose Rufus and Leona's racially charged sexual vengeance toward white men and Vivaldo's racist feelings toward Ida, as well as the consummation of his latent homosexuality when he allows Eric to penetrate him anally. Rufus Scott represents the ironic hero of the novel because Rufus's death implicates hypermasculinities and the desire to adhere to the myth of the black male rapist as the true villain of the novel. His heroism rings ironic since typically, and perhaps obviously, suicide does not constitute a heroic act. *Another Country* does not entertain its readers; it educates them about the horrors of racism and homophobia brought on by hypermasculinities. Scott's suicide exposes the bleakness of contemporary society, the inviability of conventional definitions of manhood for black men, and the need for a new vision of black masculinity predicated on the repudiation of white compulsory heteronormativity.

NOTES

1. In my chapter on *Song of Solomon*, I use Scott's call for a politics of the bottom as a means of cultural incest, or drawing from one's own ancestral past in order to create unique maps of cultural identity. In *Song of Solomon*, this includes literal incest, which I argue functions as a metaphor for cultural incest. In *Another Country*, Scott's directive functions much more literally. Scott's philosophy of surrendering to hypermasculine failure would grant men like the character Rufus Scott in contemporary society a new black power derived from nonnormative sexualities and based on cultural queerness.

2. Linda Hutcheon, *Irony's Edge: The Theory and Politics of Irony* (New York: Routledge, 1994), 30.

3. James Baldwin died on December 1, 1987, of cancer of the esophagus. W. J. Weatherby, *James Baldwin: Artist on Fire* (New York: Laurel, 1989), 419, 423.

4. Lovalerie King, "Introduction: Baldwin and Morrison in Dialogue," in *James Baldwin and Toni Morrison: Comparative Critical and Theoretical Essays*, ed. Lovalerie King and Lynn Orilla Scott (New York: Palgrave, 2006), 1.

5. "[Cecil] Brown's study traces the origins of the [Staggerlee] legend to 1895, when the historical event that spawned it took place: Lee Shelton (who becomes Stagolee, Stack Lee, or Staggerlee in various versions) shot one William Lyons (who becomes Billy Lyons, Billy DeLyon, Bully, or Lion). The dispute took place in a barroom and escalated to murder when Billy grabbed Lee's Stetson hat. This tragic but not monumental event grew into a full blown legend as it was passed along through oral narrative and blues songs. [Staggerlee] became an archetype of a man so powerful and fear-inspiring that he even conquers the devil and takes over hell in some versions of the tale." Quentin D. Miller, "Playing a Mean Guitar: The Legacy of Staggerlee in Baldwin and Morrison," in *James Baldwin and Toni Morrison: Comparative Critical and Theoretical Essays*, ed. Lovalerie King and Lynn Orilla Scott (New York: Palgrave, 2006), 121–22.

6. Miller, "Playing a Mean Guitar," 123.

7. King, "Introduction," 3.

8. King, "Introduction," 1.

9. Miller, "Playing a Mean Guitar," 121.

10. For the Black Panther Party (BPP), the import of the notion of a black man "off the block" stemmed from the idea that "the Black Panther Party was the self-described organization of brothers on the block—the disgruntled poor." Jeffrey O. G. Ogbar, *Black Power: Radical Politics and African American Identity* (Baltimore: The Johns Hopkins University Press, 2004), 94. Another name for the brothers off the block is "lumpen proletariat." Despite Marx's warning that this lowest class could not be trusted to be revolutionary, the BPP depended on them for better or worse.

11. Miller, "Playing a Mean Guitar," 126.

12. Miller, "Playing a Mean Guitar," 127.

13. Charles P. Toombs, "Black-Gay Man Chaos in *Another Country*," In *Re-viewing James Baldwin: Things Not Seen*, ed. D. Quentin Miller (Philadelphia: Temple University Press, 2000), 116.

14. Toombs, "Black-Gay Man Chaos in *Another Country*," 109–10.

15. Arthur Flannigan Saint-Aubin, "Testeria: The Dis-ease of Black Men in White Supremacist, Patriarchal Culture," *Callaloo* 17, no. 4 (Autumn 1994): 1058.

16. James Baldwin, "Here Be Dragons," in *Traps: African American Men on Gender and Sexuality*, ed. Rudolph P. Byrd and Beverly Guy-Sheftall (Bloomington: Indiana University Press, 2001), 209.

17. Paul Hoch, "White Hero Black Beast: Racism, Sexism and the Mask of Masculinity," in *Feminism and Masculinities*, ed. Peter F. Murphy (Oxford: Oxford University Press, 2004), 98.

18. Hoch, "White Hero Black Beast," 98.

19. Angela Davis notes, "lynchings, reserved during slavery for the white abolitionists, were proving to be a valuable political weapon. Before lynching could be consolidated as a popularly accepted institution, however, its savagery and its horrors had to be convincingly justified.

These were the circumstances which spawned the myth of the Black rapist." Angela Y. Davis, *Women, Race and Class* (New York: Random House, 1981), 185.

20. Frantz Fanon, *Black Skin, White Masks*, trans. Richard Philcox (New York: Grove, 2008), 147–48.

21. James Baldwin, *Another Country* (New York: Vintage, 1993), 26.

22. Baldwin, *Another Country*, 301.

23. Baldwin, *Another Country*, 58.

24. Baldwin, *Another Country*, 68.

25. Baldwin, *Another Country*, 53.

26. Toombs, "Black-Gay Man Chaos in *Another Country*," 112.

27. Saint-Aubin, "Testeria," 1067.

28. bell hooks, *We Real Cool: Black Men and Masculinity* (New York: Routledge, 2004), 48.

29. Toombs, "Black-Gay Man Chaos in *Another Country*," 110.

30. Baldwin, *Another Country*, 230–31.

31. Baldwin, *Another Country*, 83.

32. Baldwin, *Another Country*, 211.

33. Baldwin, *Another Country*, 15–16.

34. Toombs, "Black-Gay Man Chaos in *Another Country*," 113.

35. Baldwin, *Another Country*, 263.

36. Baldwin, *Another Country*, 280.

37. Baldwin, *Another Country*, 323.

38. Baldwin, *Another Country*, 323.

39. Henry Louis Gates Jr., *The Signifying Monkey: A Theory of African American Literary Criticism* (Oxford: Oxford University Press, 1988), xxiv.

40. Darieck Scott, *Extravagant Abjection: Blackness, Power, and Sexuality in the African American Literary Imagination* (New York: New York University Press, 2010), 9.

41. Scott, *Extravagant Abjection*, 248.

42. Scott, *Extravagant Abjection*, 254.

43. Toombs, "Black-Gay Man Chaos in *Another Country*," 117.

44. Scott, *Extravagant Abjection*, 134.

45. Scott, *Extravagant Abjection*, 6.

46. Scott, *Extravagant Abjection*, 5.

47. Scott, *Extravagant Abjection*, 129.

48. Kobena Mercer, "True Confessions," in *Black Male*, ed. Thelma Golden (New York: Whitney Museum of Modern Art, 1994), 192.

49. hooks, *We Real Cool*, 52.

50. Though Eldridge Cleaver functioned as the Black Panther Party's minister of information, he did not represent the views of the entire party. In fact, Charles E. Jones writes, "Another critical facet of the legacy of the BPP is linked to the organization's commitment to the virtue and dignity of individuals regardless of race, gender, or sexual orientation. Unlike many of the Black power organizations of the period, the BPP demonstrated a willingness to enter into functional alliances with White leftist groups. Moreover, Panthers were early advocates of the rights of women and homosexuals during the embryonic stage of each of these liberation movements." Charles E. Jones, "'Don't Believe the Hype': Debunking the Panther Mythology," in *The Black Panther Party Reconsidered*, ed. Charles E. Jones (Baltimore: Black Classic, 1998), 31. Former Panther member Jimmy Slater admits, "Eldridge Cleaver was one of the biggest contradictions in the Black Panther Party. When we were heading into the political arena, and he was out hollering and screaming these militaristic ideas, it was so counterrevolutionary until all it did was damage the Black Panther Party. The vast majority of the people in the community accepted what Eldridge Cleaver said, as though it represented the major body of the Black Panther Party, and it really didn't. It wasn't the idea of the vast majority of the Black Panther Party." Charles E. Jones, "'Talkin' the Talk and Walkin' the Walk': An Interview with Panther Jimmy Slater," in *The Black Panther Party Reconsidered*, ed. Charles E. Jones (Baltimore: Black Classic, 1998), 152.

51. Eldridge Cleaver, *Soul on Ice* (New York: Delta, 1968), 75.

52. E. Frances White, "The Evidence of Things Not Seen: The Alchemy of Race and Sexuality," in *James Baldwin and Toni Morrison: Comparative Critical and Theoretical Essays*, ed. Lovalerie King and Lynn Orilla Scott (New York: Palgrave, 2006), 253.

53. Cleaver, *Soul on Ice*, 73.

54. Mercer, "True Confessions," 191–92.

55. Charles E. Jones, "Introduction: Reconsidering Panther History: The Untold Story," in *The Black Panther Party Reconsidered*, ed. Charles E. Jones (Baltimore: Black Classic, 1998), 1.

56. Cleaver, *Soul on Ice*, 70.

57. Cleaver, *Soul on Ice*, 67.

58. Cleaver, *Soul on Ice*, 70.

59. Cleaver, *Soul on Ice*, 70.

60. Marlon B. Ross, "White Fantasies of Desire: Baldwin and the Racial Identities of Sexuality," in *James Baldwin Now*, ed. Dwight A. McBride (New York: New York University Press, 1999), 17.

61. Stefanie Dunning, "Parallel Perversions: Interracial and Same Sexuality in James Baldwin's *Another Country*," *MELUS* 26, no. 4 (Winter 2001): 103.

62. Quoted in Nick Aaron Ford, "The Evolution of James Baldwin as Essayist," in *James Baldwin: A Critical Evaluation*, ed. Therman B. O'Daniel (Washington: Howard University Press, 1977), 97.

63. Cleaver, *Soul on Ice*, 67.

64. Norman Mailer, "The White Negro: Superficial Reflections of the Hipster," in *The Portable Beat Reader*, ed. Ann Charters (New York: Penguin, 1992), 585.

65. Mailer, "The White Negro," 594.

66. Mailer, "The White Negro," 590.

67. Mailer, "The White Negro," 593.

68. Mailer, "The White Negro," 586.

69. Magdalena J. Zaborowska, *James Baldwin's Turkish Decade: Erotics of Exile* (Durham: Duke University Press, 2009), 299.

70. hooks, *We Real Cool*, 48.

71. Newton's claims ought to be viewed with a healthy dose of skepticism, considering the many rifts he and Cleaver experienced and the fact that "part of the effectiveness of COINTEL-PRO," J. Edgar Hoover's domestic counterintelligence program, "was its ability to make the most of larger societal contradictions that also existed within the liberation movement. An example of this was the FBI's ability to use the homophobia of many persons in and outside the Party to its own advantage. In September 1968, the Chicago FBI office included in its strategy a fraudulent letter written by 'a black friend' that was sent to a leader of a lumpen group called the *Maus Maus*. This letter insinuated that two members of the Panther leadership in Chicago were homosexual lovers." Winston A. Grady-Willis, "The Black Panther Party: State Repression and Political Prisoners," in *The Black Panther Party Reconsidered*, ed. Charles E Jones (Baltimore: Black Classic, 1998), 374. Perhaps Newton's claims were in fact claims made by the FBI.

72. Zaborowska, *James Baldwin's Turkish Decade*, 231–32.

73. White, "The Evidence of Things Not Seen," 256.

74. Henry James, *The Art of the Novel* (New York: Scribner: 1962), 208.

75. Baldwin, *Another Country*, 51.

76. Baldwin, *Another Country*, 342–43.

77. Baldwin, *Another Country*, 61.

78. Baldwin, *Another Country*, 133.

79. Baldwin, *Another Country*, 66.

80. Eve Kosofsky Sedgwick, *Epistemology of the Closet* (Berkeley: University of California Press, 1990), 19.

81. Baldwin, *Another Country*, 30.

82. Baldwin, *Another Country*, 43.

83. Sedgwick, *Epistemology of the Closet*, 201.

84. Baldwin, *Another Country*, 112.

85. Michael Warner, *The Trouble with Normal: Sex, Politics, and the Ethics of Queer Life* (New York: Free Press, 1999), 54.

86. Warner, *The Trouble with Normal*, 58.

87. Anna Kérchy, "Narrating the Beat of the Heart, Jazzing the Text of Desire: A Comparative Interface of James Baldwin's *Another Country* and Toni Morrison's *Jazz*," in *James Baldwin and Toni Morrison: Comparative Critical and Theoretical Essays*, ed. Lovalerie King and Lynn Orilla Scott (New York: Palgrave, 2006), 40.

88. Susan Feldman, "Another Look at *Another Country*: Reconciling Baldwin's Racial and Sexual Politics," in *Re-viewing James Baldwin: Things Not Seen*, ed. Quentin D. Miller (Philadelphia: Temple University Press, 2000), 91.

89. Feldman, "Another Look at *Another Country*," 95–96.

90. Steve Martinot, *Machinery of Whiteness: Studies in the Structure of Racialization* (Philadelphia: Temple University Press, 2010), 6.

91. Baldwin, *Another Country*, 18.

92. Baldwin, *Another Country*, 92.

93. Baldwin, *Another Country*, 105.

94. Baldwin, *Another Country*, 107.

95. Baldwin, *Another Country*, 194.

96. Baldwin, *Another Country*, 206.

97. Robert A. Bone, "James Baldwin," in *James Baldwin: A Collection of Critical Essays*, ed. Kenneth Kinnamon (Englewood: Spectrum, 1974), 41. Leslie Fiedler also criticized *Another Country*, calling it "shrill" and "inept." Leslie A. Fiedler, *Love and Death in the American Novel* (New York: Stein and Day, 1966), 366. While Fiedler recognized the centrality of gender, sexuality, and race in American literature early on and should be applauded for doing so, *Another Country* confronts Fiedler's idea that U.S. writers avoid heterosexual relationships. Rufus Scott does not avoid heterosexual relationships; he destructively forces one as overcompensation for his queerness.

98. Feldman, "Another Look at *Another Country*," 93.

99. Baldwin, *Another Country*, 22.

100. Zaborowska, *James Baldwin's Turkish Decade*, 129.

101. Baldwin, *Another Country*, 175.

102. Baldwin, *Another Country*, 177.

103. Zaborowska, *James Baldwin's Turkish Decade*, 130.

104. Davis, *Women, Race and Class*, 182.

105. Baldwin, *Another Country*, 382–83.

106. Baldwin, *Another Country*, 386.

107. Barry Gross, "The 'Uninhabitable Darkness' of Baldwin's *Another Country*: Image and Theme," *Negro American Literature Forum* 6, no. 4 (Winter 1972): 118.

108. Baldwin, *Another Country*, 87–88.

109. John S. Lash, "Baldwin beside Himself: A Study in Modern Phallicism," in *James Baldwin: A Critical Evaluation*, ed. Therman B. O'Daniel (Washington: Howard University Press, 1977), 50.

110. Bone, "James Baldwin," 46.

111. Baldwin, *Another Country*, 293.

112. Dunning, "Parallel Perversions," 105.

113. Scott, *Extravagant Abjection*, 254.

Conclusion

Masculinity as Hypermasculine Failure

In *Blood Meridian*, *All the Pretty Horses*, *Song of Solomon*, and *Another Country*, McCarthy, Morrison, and Baldwin challenge readers to reevaluate hegemonic American masculinities by presenting protagonists who embody putatively admirable male characteristics that contribute to their demise. By illustrating the factors that inform these hypermasculinities, such as nationalism, pop culture, and racism, the authors expose them as destructive forces. For the fictional protagonists, the stakes are nothing less than life and death.

At first glance one might mistake the rural white man and the black man as polar opposites, but their difficulties in constructing viable masculinities outside of hypermasculine expectations prove similar. Both groups of men experience external and internal pressures to resemble existing definitions of hypermasculinities. If rural white men and urban black men ceased attempting to live up to their own hypermasculine standards, which other men look to for guidance, hypermasculinities on the whole would lose their privileged multivalent stature. Consequently, men attempting to embody hypermasculine images would be exposed as destructive human beings.

American hypermasculinities, stemming in large part from a western frontier mythology, have grown into powerful reactionary forces that at best impede social change and at worst provoke global violence. Sarah Gleeson-White points out, "The Frontier—that appealingly and frighteningly vulnerable border between savagery and civilization—was the central process in the development of the American character, American democracy, in fine, American exceptionalism."[1] American entitlement to lands west of the Mississippi launched an American character predicated on violence and racism highlighted in Cormac McCarthy's *Blood Meridian*. Robert L. Jarrett suggests, "the rhetoric of Manifest Destiny justified territorial acquisition by combining racism with an appropriated version of the Puritan notion of pre-destination . . . [Justification] for the individual and the communal enterprise of expansion and settlement lay in the subjugation of nature, both within man and without."[2] For example, in *Blood Meridian* the judge is an earth scientist and murderer in hot pursuit, as he makes his way west, of the heart of darkness that lies in the earth's core as well as the human heart.

The twentieth-century hypermasculine cowboy then appropriated a set of behaviors and characteristics gleaned from dime novels and films that ro-manticized and distorted life on the frontier and the men who inhabited it. Donald K. Meisenheimer Jr. argues, "At the time . . . the frontier was closing; the cowboy hero . . . represents at his very inception an inherently nostalgic masculinity, one that is threatened by advancing (over)civilization."[3] The changing American cultural landscape of the 1950s into the 1960s threatened the racist, sexist, and violent values of the imagined frontiersman embodied in many American rural southerners, causing a nostalgic character like John Grady Cole in McCarthy's *All the Pretty Horses* to "[set] out . . . to find a place where he can run a ranch, where cowboys are the cowboys of the Western myth, and where the frontier really exists as it did in the days before modernization."[4] Long before John Grady treks to Mexico in search of a frontier where he can actualize his cowboy hypermasculinity, white societal apparatuses have already deemed the black man a beastly rapist bent on white women. As a result of this stereotype the hypermasculine, primarily urban, African American male exists as perhaps the only rival to the American cowboy as hypermasculine symbol.

The anti-heroes of this study are defined by their failure to perpetuate destructive and dehumanizing hypermasculinities, continuing what Jesse Matz describes as the modernist trend of the anti-hero. One might consider classic American modern characters such as Jake Barnes in Ernest Heming-way's *The Sun Also Rises* (1926) and Jay Gatsby in F. Scott Fitzgerald's *The Great Gatsby* (1925), characters possessing irrevocable chinks in their hyper-masculine armor that prevent them from *getting the girl*. To aid in designat-ing these characters as ironic heroes, we might once again employ Linda Hutcheon's definition of irony as a sort of rhetorical guerrilla warfare aimed at disrupting the dominant fiction of phallic power and privilege. As a result, these novels, perhaps inadvertently, might compel some readers to abandon hypermasculinities as manifestations of maleness. While the primarily south-ern rural white man and the African American, primarily urban, man share blame for perpetuating out-of-control American masculinities, the African American man seems to have emerged as *the* American icon of hypermascu-linities and so finds himself in a peculiar situation whereby both white and black men look to him for masculine guidance. As Riki Wilchins reveals, "White suburban boys call themselves 'wiggers,' and try to perform blackness, adopting the dress, masculinity, swagger, and style they see in urban black males. At the same time middle-class suburban black youth worry that they are not black enough."[5] Paradoxically, the despicable southern white creation of the myth of the black rapist has emerged as the very example of American male hypermasculinities white men increasingly emulate.

Unfortunately, from the mid-twentieth century to the present, many black men have welcomed these pernicious African American male stereotypes. As Darieck Scott contends, "The black man *is* his body, is *the* body, is the excess of meaning associated with the body, above all the sexuality of the body."[6] During the various Black Liberation Movements of the 1950s through the 1980s, the fervent welcoming of sexual stereotypes for some black men functioned as a way to best white men. Thus, as Scott reveals, "he [the black man] is powerful but restrained; he sings even though he is forced to perform body-breaking labor; he endures heroically, but there hangs about him the lingering question of criminality. He is thus a body invested, saturated, with pathos, with the nonintellectual, the emotive, which is also the province of blackness in the black/white binary."[7] The hypersexualization of black bodies, rather than a means to empowerment, signifies a sub-intellectual beast in need of control. As Arthur Flannigan Saint-Aubin suggests, "We might then characterize the impulse of white supremacist, patriarchal culture as the eroticizing othering of the black male subject."[8] Indeed, these novels provoke readers to confront white society's libidinal investment in black bodies. As Frantz Fanon might suggest, no longer do readers see Rufus; they see only a penis. Many black men, by adopting these stereotypes, reflect cowboy-derived black hypermasculinities that simultaneously represent ideal hypermasculinity and the central argument for white supremacy. As Henry Louis Gates Jr. argues, "Black formal repetition always repeats with a difference, a black difference."[9] In this sense, African Americans, especially men, remain in need of a redefinition of masculinity culled from black experience and black history, a sort of cultural incest, based on their painful history, rather than from definitions of black masculinity provided by and in imitation of white power structures. While some of the male characters in Toni Morrison's *Song of Solomon*, Macon Dead II and Guitar, pine for power commensurate with their white counterparts based on materialism and violence, Gerry Brenner notes, "[Pilate's] mission is exemplary, because it is nothing less than to live her life in manifest repudiation of the grasping ambitiousness and obsessive desires of those around her, who end up as grotesques, fanatics, neurotics, or fantasists."[10] Her reliance on her own culture for her identity is her way of "flying" without ever leaving the ground.

The images and tropes of failure in these novels point to opportunities outside of the text for utilizing failure as a strategic means to combat the scourge of U.S. hypermasculinities. In this vein, Darieck Scott argues that African Americans ought to break with white patriarchy as a means to black empowerment. With the repudiation of whiteness as a cultural goal, a new vision of blackness and masculinity may ensue. Scott emphasizes, "the break that is made by what conquest, enslavement, and domination has broken . . . of traditional life, and that is abjection—restarts sociogenic processes and makes possible new nations, different families, different gender positions and sexualities."[11] The repudiation of heteronormative patriarchal whiteness makes possible a new conception of blackness. This new blackness centers on a level of sexual openness previously denied African Americans. According to bell hooks,

> Early in the twentieth century, black males and females sought to create an alternative sexuality rooted in eros and sensual pleasure distinct from the repressed sexuality of white racists and the puritanism that had been embraced as a protective shield to ward off racist/sexist stereotypes about black sexuality. Black males, deemed hypersexual in a negative way in the eyes of whites, were in the subculture of blackness deemed sexually healthy. The black male body, deemed demonic in the eyes of white racist sexist stereotypes, was in the world of segregated black culture deemed erotic, sensual, capable of giving and receiving pleasure.[12]

Scott argues that African Americans extend this alternative sexuality delineated by hooks to include *all sexualities*, especially nonnormative sexualities that do not privilege heteronormativity to the exclusion of all others. In this manner, African Americans might capitalize on their history of oppression and profit by subverting their own definitions of normativity. hooks further argues, "Since whiteness had repressed black sexuality, in the subculture space of blackness, sexual desire was expressed with degrees of abandon unheard of in white society."[13] Unfortunately, this degree of abandon only applied to heterosexual couples, causing a character like Rufus Scott in James Baldwin's *Another Country* to commit suicide rather than address his same-sex desire. Since sexuality and sexual identity exist as loci for definitions of blackness, African Americans might use these identities as political tools completely separate from a whiteness that embraces patriarchal heteronormativity. Embracing all manner of queerness as a way of repudiating white notions of power and gender, black masculinity might undergo a radical change for the better. Further, since black hypermasculinities operate as paragons of American hypermasculinities that large numbers of American men emulate, redefining black masculinities might have a revolutionary effect on definitions of American masculinities for men of all colors, creeds, and sexualities. As Judith Halberstam notes, "Failing is something queers do and have always done exceptionally well; for queers *failure can be a style*" (emphasis mine).[14] It is difficult and perhaps fruitless to speculate as to what, for example, Rufus Scott might look like in a world where African Americans were revolutionizing masculinity toward a politics of the bottom, but I am reminded of Ras the Exhorter's words in Ralph Ellison's *Invisible Man* (1952): "Come in with us, mahn. We build a glorious movement . . . [This] mahn be a chief, a black king!"[15]

For African Americans hungry for a post-black[16] America, embracing all manner of queerness as a way of repudiating white notions of heteronormativity might appear limiting rather than empowering. Such a colossal undertaking for a generation of black people living in a post–Civil Rights America may seem essentialist, counterproductive, and restrictive. I have even heard a rattle that proper African American literature is no longer being written, since African Americans no longer face the issues out of which the literature sprang. To these optimists, I would urge caution. One need only look at current rates of incarceration, unemployment, drug use, and disease among African Americans, as well as education levels attained, to realize that pervasive racism still exists in the United States and the machinery of whiteness is well oiled. Now is not the time for antiracist Americans to claim victory in achieving the promises of the Declaration of Independence. On the contrary, now is the time when change is finally possible.

Sustainable change *is* possible when one considers that "a new generation of young *pro*womanist Black men have emerged, many of whom have read or studied with some of the most well-known Black feminists of the day."[17] Gary Lemons reports, "We speak in womanist terms, calling for Black male accountability on the issue of sexism."[18] This movement[19] is exciting because it focuses on the potential feminist self from whom Milkman is flying in *Song of Solomon*. In this sense, Milkman is not, as Leslie Fiedler might say, running from the possibility of heterosexual love, but rather he is "seeing the 'female' strictly as other for the Afro-American male . . . [instead of as] an important aspect of the repressed in the black male self."[20] Michael Awkward further says of the prowomanist movement, "From my perspective, what is potentially most valuable about the development of black male feminism . . . lies in the possibility that . . . black men can expand the range and utilization of feminist inquiry and explore other fruitful applications for feminist perspectives . . . and new figurations of . . . black male sexuality."[21] The prowomanist movement Lemons, Awkward, *et alii* describe images a positive feminist masculinity that is purposefully anti-patriarchal and in line with Scott, hooks, Halberstam, Wilchins, and myself in calling for new visions of American masculinity across racial, sexual, and gendered lines, defining itself not in terms of binaries but rather in terms of hypermasculine failure.

NOTES

1. Sarah Gleeson-White, "Playing Cowboys," *Southwestern American Literature* 33, no. 1 (Fall 2007): 24.

2. Robert L. Jarrett, *Cormac McCarthy* (New York: Twayne, 1997), 70.

3. Donald K. Meisenheimer Jr., "Machining the Man: From Neurasthenia to Psychasthenia in SF and the Genre Western," *Science Fiction Studies* 24, no. 3 (1997): 443.

4. Andrew Blair Spencer, "A Cowboy Looks at Reality," in *Western Futures*, ed. Stephen Tchudi (Reno: Halcyon Press, 1999), 147.

5. Riki Wilchins, *Queer Theory, Gender Theory: An Instant Primer* (Los Angeles: Alyson, 2004), 115–16.

6. Darieck Scott, *Extravagant Abjection* (New York: New York University Press, 2010), 142.

7. Scott, *Extravagant Abjection*, 142.

8. Arthur Flannigan Saint-Aubin, "Testeria: The Dis-ease of Black Men in White Supremacist, Patriarchal Culture," *Callaloo* 17, no. 4 (Autumn 1994): 1058.

9. Henry Louis Gates Jr., *The Signifying Monkey* (Oxford: Oxford University Press, 1988), xxiii.

10. Gerry Brenner, "Rejecting Rank's Monomyth and Feminism," in *Toni Morrison's Song of Solomon: A Casebook*, ed. Jan Furman (Oxford: Oxford University Press, 2003), 107.

11. Scott, *Extravagant Abjection*, 129.

12. bell hooks, *We Real Cool: Black Men and Masculinity* (New York: Routledge, 2004), 70.

13. hooks, *We Real Cool*, 71.

14. Judith Halberstam, *The Queer Art of Failure* (Durham: Duke University Press, 2011), 3.

15. Ralph Ellison, *Invisible Man* (New York: Vintage, 1980), 371–72.

16. "Post-blackness" refers to the notion that generations of African Americans growing up after the black liberation movements of the 1950s, 1960s, 1970s, and 1980s no longer face the challenges their predecessors faced and are now free to transcend blackness as an identity and an all-consuming preoccupation.

17. Gary Lemons, "'When and Where We Enter': In Search of a Feminist Forefather," in *Traps: African American Men on Gender and Sexuality*, ed. Rudolph P. Byrd and Beverly Guy-Sheftall (Bloomington: Indiana University Press, 2001), 83.

18. Lemons, "'When and Where We Enter,'" 83.

19. Lemons notes, "During the last weekend of September 1996, a historic event occurred at Morehouse College in Atlanta, Georgia. On those two days, a group of young Black men staged a conference entitled 'To Be Black, Male, and Feminist/Womanist.' As an invited speaker—with bell hooks, Beverly Guy-Sheftall, Rebecca Walker, and Robert Allen, among others—I witnessed the emergence of a new generation of Black men committed to the eradication of sexism. As the central tenet of their purpose statement, these men state: 'We believe that although we are oppressed because of our color, we are privileged because of our sex and must, therefore, take responsibility for ending that privilege.'" Lemons, "'When and Where We Enter,'" 85.

20. Michael Awkward, "A Black Man's Place in Black Feminist Criticism," in *Traps: African American Men on Gender and Sexuality*, ed. Rudolph P. Byrd and Beverly Guy-Sheftall (Bloomington: Indiana University Press, 2001), 185.

21. Awkward, "A Black Man's Place," 185.

References Cited

Anderson, Gary Clayton. *The Conquest of Texas: Ethnic Cleansing in the Promised Land, 1820–1875.* Norman: University of Oklahoma Press, 2005.

Anderson, Sherwood. *Winesburg, Ohio.* 1919. New York: Viking, 1958.

Anzaldua, Gloria. "Borderlands/La Frontera." In *Literary Theory: An Anthology,* 1017–30. Edited by Julie Rivkin and Michael Ryan. Malden: Blackwell, 2004.

Arnold, Edwin T., and Dianne C. Luce. "Introduction." In *A Cormac McCarthy Companion: The Border Trilogy,* vii–xi. Edited by Edwin T. Arnold and Dianne C. Luce. Jackson: University Press of Mississippi, 2001.

Awkward, Michael. "A Black Man's Place in Black Feminist Criticism." In *Traps: African American Men on Gender and Sexuality,* 177–93. Edited by Rudolph P. Byrd and Beverly Guy-Sheftall. Bloomington: Indiana University Press, 2001.

———. "'Unruly and Let Loose': Myth, Ideology, and Gender in *Song of Solomon.*" *Callaloo* 13, no. 3 (Summer 1990): 482–98. http://www.jstor.org/stable/2931332.

Bakhtin, Mikhail. "Discourse in the Novel." In *Literary Theory: An Anthology,* 674–85. Edited by Julie Rivkin and Michael Ryan. Malden: Blackwell, 2004.

Baldwin, James. *Another Country.* 1960. New York: Vintage, 1993.

———. "Here Be Dragons." In *Traps: African American Men on Gender and Sexuality,* 207–18. Edited by Rudolph P. Byrd and Beverly Guy-Sheftall. Bloomington: Indiana University Press, 2001.

Baudrillard, Jean. *Simulacra and Simulation.* Translated by Sheila Faria Glaser. Michigan: University of Michigan Press, 2010.

Bell, James. *Cormac McCarthy's West: The Border Trilogy Annotations.* El Paso: Texas Western Press, 2002.

Bone, Robert A. "James Baldwin." In *James Baldwin: A Collection of Critical Essays,* 28–51. Edited by Kenneth Kinnamon. Englewood: Spectrum, 1974.

Boon, Kevin Alexander. "Heroes, Metanarratives, and the Paradox of Masculinity in Contemporary Western Culture." *Journal of Men's Studies: A Scholarly Journal about Men and Masculinities* 13, no. 3 (Spring 2005): 301–12. doi:10.3149/jms.1303.301.

Brenner, Gerry. "Rejecting Rank's Monomyth and Feminism." In *Toni Morrison's Song of Solomon: A Casebook,* 95–109. Edited by Jan Furman. Oxford: Oxford University Press, 2003.

Brombert, Victor, ed. *The Hero in Literature.* Greenwich: Fawcett, 1969.

Bryant, Cedric Gael. "'Every Goodbye Ain't Gone': The Semiotics of Death, Mourning, and Closural Practice in Toni Morrison's *Song of Solomon.*" *MELUS* 24, no. 3 (Autumn 1999): 97–110.

Butler, Judith. "Performative Acts and Gender Constitution." In *Literary Theory: An Anthology*, 900–911. Edited by Julie Rivkin and Michael Ryan. Malden: Blackwell, 2004.

Campbell, Hugh. "Masculinity and Rural Life: An Introduction." In *Country Boys: Masculinity and Rural Life*, 1–22. Edited by Hugh Campbell, Michael Mayersfeld Bell, and Margaret Finney. University Park: Pennsylvania State University Press, 2006.

Cant, John. *Cormac McCarthy and the Myth of American Exceptionalism.* New York: Routledge, 2008.

Chamberlain, Samuel. *My Confession: Recollections of a Rogue.* Austin: Texas State Historical Association, 1996.

Chollier, Christine. "Autotextuality, or Dialogic Imagination in Cormac McCarthy's Border Trilogy." In *A Cormac McCarthy Companion: The Border Trilogy*, 3–36. Edited by Edwin T. Arnold and Dianne C. Luce. Jackson: University Press of Mississippi, 2001.

Cleaver, Eldridge. "Notes on a Native Son." In *James Baldwin: A Collection of Critical Essays*, 66–76. Edited by Kenneth Kinnamon. Englewood Cliffs: Spectrum, 1974.

———. *Soul on Ice.* New York: Delta, 1968.

Cooper, Lydia R. *No More Heroes: Narrative Perspective and Morality in Cormac McCarthy.* Baton Rouge: Louisiana State University Press, 2011.

Davis, Angela Y. *Women, Race and Class.* New York: Random House, 1981.

Derrida, Jacques. *Acts of Religion.* Edited by Gil Anidjar. New York: Routledge, 2002.

Dixon, Melvin. "Like an Eagle in the Air: Toni Morrison." In *Toni Morrison*, 23–49. Edited by Harold Bloom. Philadelphia: Chelsea House, 2005.

Dunning, Stefanie. "Parallel Perversions: Interracial and Same Sexuality in James Baldwin's *Another Country*." *MELUS* 26, no. 4 (Winter 2001): 95–112.

Duplessis, Rachel Blau. *Writing beyond the Ending: Narrative Strategies of Twentieth-Century Women Writers.* Bloomington: Indiana University Press, 1985.

Duvall, John N. "Doe Hunting and Masculinity: *Song of Solomon* and *Go Down, Moses*." In *Toni Morrison's Song of Solomon: A Casebook*, 113–36. Edited by Jan Furman. Oxford: Oxford University Press, 2003.

Ellis, Jay. *No Place for Home: Spatial Constraint and Character Flight in the Novels of Cormac McCarthy.* New York: Routledge, 2006.

———. "The Rape of Rawlins: A Note on *All the Pretty Horses*." *The Cormac McCarthy Journal* 1, no. 1 (Spring 2001): 66–68.

Ellison, Ralph. *Invisible Man.* 1952. New York: Vintage, 1980.

Fanon, Frantz. *Black Skin, White Masks.* Translated by Richard Philcox. New York: Grove, 2008.

Feldman, Susan. "Another Look at *Another Country*: Reconciling Baldwin's Racial and Sexual Politics." In *Re-viewing James Baldwin: Things Not Seen*, 88–104. Edited by Quentin D. Miller. Philadelphia: Temple University Press, 2000.

Fiedler, Leslie A. *Love and Death in the American Novel.* New York: Stein and Day, 1966.

Fischer, Carl. *The Myth and Legend of Greece.* Dayton: Pflaum, 1968.

Ford, Nick Aaron. "The Evolution of James Baldwin as Essayist." In *James Baldwin: A Critical Evaluation*, 85–104. Edited by Therman B. O'Daniel. Washington: Howard University Press, 1977.

Freud, Sigmund. "The Economic Problem of Masochism." In *Collected Papers of Sigmund Freud*, vol. 2, 255–68. Translated by Joan Riviere. New York: Basic Books, 1959.

Früchtl, Josef. *The Impertinent Self: A Heroic History of Modernity.* Translated by Sarah L. Kirkby. Stanford: Stanford University Press, 2009.

Gates, Henry Louis, Jr. *The Signifying Monkey: A Theory of African American Literary Criticism.* Oxford: Oxford University Press, 1988.

Gibson, Donald B. "James Baldwin: The Political Anatomy of Space." In *James Baldwin: A Critical Evaluation*, 3–18. Edited by Therman B. O'Daniel. Washington: Howard University Press, 1977.

Gleeson-White, Sarah. "Playing Cowboys: Genre, Myth, and Cormac McCarthy's *All the Pretty Horses*." *Southwestern American Literature* 33, no. 1 (Fall 2007): 23–38.

Gopnik, Adam. "The Caging of America." *The New Yorker*, Jan. 30, 2012, 72–77.

Grady-Willis, Winston A. "The Black Panther Party: State Repression and Political Prisoners." In *The Black Panther Party Reconsidered*, 363–89. Edited by Charles E. Jones. Baltimore: Black Classic, 1998.

Gross, Barry. "The 'Uninhabitable Darkness' of Baldwin's *Another Country*: Image and Theme." *Negro American Literature Forum* 6, no. 4 (Winter 1972): 113–21. http://www.jstor.org/stable/3041199.

Guillemin, George. "'See the Child': The Melancholy Subtext of *Blood Meridian*." In *Cormac McCarthy: New Directions*, 239–61. Edited by James D. Lilley. Albuquerque: University of New Mexico Press, 2002.

Haggard, Merle. "I Wish Things Were Simple Again." *Live from Austin, TX*. New West, 2006. CD.

Halberstam, Judith. *The Queer Art of Failure*. Durham: Duke University Press, 2011.

Hall, Wade. "The Human Comedy of Cormac McCarthy." In *Cormac McCarthy*, 53–64. Edited by Harold Bloom. Philadelphia: Chelsea House, 2002.

Halldorson, Stephanie S. *The Hero in Contemporary American Fiction*. New York: Palgrave, 2007.

Hernton, Calvin. "The Sexual Mountain and Black Women Writers." *Black American Literature Forum* 18, no. 4 (Winter 1984): 139–45. http://www.jstor.org/stable/2904288.

Hoch, Paul. "White Hero Black Beast: Racism, Sexism and the Mask of Masculinity." In *Feminism and Masculinities*, 93–107. Edited by Peter F. Murphy. Oxford: Oxford University Press, 2004.

hooks, bell. *We Real Cool: Black Men and Masculinity*. New York: Routledge, 2004.

Hutcheon, Linda. *Irony's Edge: The Theory and Politics of Irony*. New York: Routledge, 1994.

———. *The Politics of Postmodernism*. Routledge: London, 1989.

Irigaray, Luce. *This Sex Which Is Not One*. Translated by Catherine Porter. Ithaca: Cornell University Press, 1977.

Irwin, Robert McKee. *Mexican Masculinities*. Minneapolis: University of Minnesota Press, 2003.

Jacobs, Harriet. *Incidents in the Life of a Slave Girl. Narrative of the Life of Frederick Douglass, an American Slave and Incidents in the Life of a Slave Girl*. New York: The Modern Library, 2004.

James, Henry. *The Art of the Novel*. New York: Scribner, 1962.

Jarrett, Robert L. *Cormac McCarthy*. New York: Twayne, 1997.

Johnson, Michael K. *Black Masculinity and the Frontier Myth in American Literature*. Norman: University of Oklahoma Press, 2002.

Jones, Charles E. "Introduction: Reconsidering Panther History: The Untold Story." In *The Black Panther Party Reconsidered*, 1–21. Edited by Charles E. Jones. Baltimore: Black Classic, 1998.

———. "'Talkin' the Talk and Walkin' the Walk': An Interview with Panther Jimmy Slater." In *The Black Panther Party Reconsidered*, 147–53. Edited by Charles E. Jones. Baltimore: Black Classic, 1998.

Jones, Charles E., and Judson L. Jeffries. "'Don't Believe the Hype': Debunking the Panther Mythology." In *The Black Panther Party Reconsidered*, 25–55. Edited by Charles E. Jones. Baltimore: Black Classic, 1998.

Kérchy, Anna. "Narrating the Beat of the Heart, Jazzing the Text of Desire: A Comparative Interface of James Baldwin's *Another Country* and Toni Morrison's *Jazz*." In *James Baldwin and Toni Morrison: Comparative Critical and Theoretical Essays*, 37–62. Edited by Lovalerie King and Lynn Orilla Scott. New York: Palgrave, 2006.

Kimmel, Michael S. "Masculinity as Homophobia: Fear, Shame, and Silence in the Construction of Gender Identity." In *Feminism and Masculinities*, 182–99. Edited by Peter F. Murphy. Oxford: Oxford University Press, 2004.

King, Lovalerie. "Introduction: Baldwin and Morrison in Dialogue." In *James Baldwin and Toni Morrison: Comparative Critical and Theoretical Essays*, 1–9. Edited by Lovalerie King and Lynn Orilla Scott. New York: Palgrave, 2006.

Krumholz, Linda. "Dead Teachers: Rituals of Manhood and Rituals of Reading in *Song of Solomon*." In*Toni Morrison's* Song of Solomon*: A Casebook*, 201–29. Edited by Jan Furman. Oxford: Oxford University Press, 2003.

Lash, John S. "Baldwin beside Himself: A Study in Modern Phallicism." In *James Baldwin: A Critical Evaluation*, 47–55. Edited by Therman B. O'Daniel. Washington: Howard University Press, 1977.

Lee, Catherine Carr. "The South in Toni Morrison's *Song of Solomon*." In *Toni Morrison's* Song of Solomon*: A Casebook*, 43–64. Edited by Jan Furman. Oxford: Oxford University Press, 2003.

Lemons, Gary. "'When and Where We Enter': In Search of a Feminist Forefather—Reclaiming the Womanist Legacy of W. E. B. Du Bois." In *Traps: African American Men on Gender and Sexuality*, 71–89. Edited by Rudolph P. Byrd and Beverly Guy-Sheftall. Bloomington: Indiana University Press, 2001.

Lester, David. "Incest." *The Journal of Sex Research* 8, no. 4 (Nov. 1972): 268–85. http://www.jstor.org.ezproxy.lib.usf.edu/stable/3811760.

Lester, Julius. "People Who Could Fly." In *Toni Morrison's* Song of Solomon*: A Casebook*, 21–23. Edited by Jan Furman. Oxford: Oxford University Press, 2003.

Lester, Neal A. *Understanding Zora Neale Hurston's* Their Eyes Were Watching God: *A Student Casebook to Issues, Sources, and Historical Documents*. Westport: Greenwood Press, 1999.

Mailer, Norman. "The White Negro: Superficial Reflections of the Hipster." In *The Portable Beat Reader*, 582–605. Edited by Ann Charters. New York: Penguin, 1992.

Martinot, Steve. *Machinery of Whiteness: Studies in the Structure of Racialization*. Philadelphia: Temple University Press, 2010.

Masters, Joshua J. "'Witness to the Uttermost Edge of the World': Judge Holden's Textual Enterprise in Cormac McCarthy's *Blood Meridian*." *Critique: Studies in Contemporary Fiction* 40, no. 1 (Fall 1998): 25–37.

Matz, Jesse. *The Modern Novel: A Short Introduction*. Malden: Blackwell, 2004.

Mayberry, Susan Neal. *Can't I Love What I Criticize? The Masculine and Morrison*. Athens: University of Georgia Press, 2007.

McBride, Molly. "From Mutilation to Penetration: Cycles of Conquest in *Blood Meridian* and *All the Pretty Horses*." *Southwestern American Literature* 25, no. 1 (Fall 1999): 24–34.

McCarthy, Cormac. *All the Pretty Horses*. 1992. New York: Vintage, 1993.

———. *Blood Meridian*. 1985. New York: Vintage, 1992.

Meisenheimer, Donald K., Jr. "Machining the Man: From Neurasthenia to Psychasthenia in SF and the Genre Western." *Science Fiction Studies* 24, no. 3 (1997): 441–58. http://www.jstor.org.ezproxy.lib.usf.edu/stable/4240646.

Mercer, Kobena, and Isaac Julian. "True Confessions." In *Black Male*, 191–200. Edited by Thelma Golden. New York: Whitney Museum of Modern Art, 1994.

Middleton, Joyce Irene. "Orality, Literacy, and Memory in Toni Morrison's *Song of Solomon*." *College English* 55, no. 1 (Jan. 1993): 64–75. http://www.jstor.org.ezproxy.lib.usf.edu/stable/378365.

Miller, Quentin D. "Playing a Mean Guitar: The Legacy of Staggerlee in Baldwin and Morrison." In *James Baldwin and Toni Morrison: Comparative Critical and Theoretical Essays*, 121–48. Edited by Lovalerie King and Lynn Orilla Scott. New York: Palgrave, 2006.

Morrison, Toni. *Song of Solomon*. 1977. New York: Vintage, 2004.

Mulvey, Laura. "Visual Pleasure and Narrative Cinema." In *The Norton Anthology of Theory and Criticism*, 2181–92. Edited by Vincent B. Leitch. New York: Norton, 2001.

Murray, Rolland. "The Long Strut: *Song of Solomon* and the Emancipatory Limits of Black Patriarchy." *Callaloo* 22, no. 1 (Winter 1999): 121–33. http://www.jstor.org.ezproxy.lib.usf.edu/stable/3299957.

Nietzsche, Friedrich. *On the Genealogy of Morals*. Translated by Horace B. Samuel. New York: Barnes and Noble, 2006.

———. *Thus Spoke Zarathustra*. In *The Portable Nietzsche*, 112–439. Edited and translated by Walter Kaufman. New York: Penguin, 1982.

Ogbar, Jeffrey O. G. *Black Power: Radical Politics and African American Identity*. Baltimore: The Johns Hopkins University Press, 2004.

Owens, Barcley. *Cormac McCarthy's Western Novels*. Tucson: University of Arizona Press, 2000.

Page, Philip. "Putting It All Together: Attempted Unification in *Song of Solomon*." In *Toni Morrison*, 99–120. Edited by Harold Bloom. Philadelphia: Chelsea House, 2005.

Park, Joseph F. "The Apaches in Mexico-American Relations, 1848–1861." In *U.S.-Mexico Borderlands: Historical and Contemporary Perspectives*, 50–65. Edited by Oscar J. Martinez. Wilmington: Jaguar, 1996.

Parkes, Adam. "History, Bloodshed, and the Spectacle of American Identity in *Blood Meridian*." In *Cormac McCarthy: New Directions*, 126–39. Edited by James D. Lilley. Albuquerque: University of New Mexico Press, 2002.

Proulx, Annie. "Brokeback Mountain." In *Close Range*, 251–83. New York: Scribner, 1999.

Ross, Marlon B. "White Fantasies of Desire: Baldwin and the Racial Identities of Sexuality." In *James Baldwin Now*, 13–55. Edited by Dwight A. McBride. New York: New York University Press, 1999.

Rubin, Gayle. "The Traffic in Women." In *Literary Theory: An Anthology*, 770–94. Edited by Julie Rivkin and Michael Ryan. Malden: Blackwell, 2004.

Saint-Aubin, Arthur Flannigan. "Testeria: The Dis-ease of Black Men in White Supremacist, Patriarchal Culture." *Callaloo* 17, no. 4 (Autumn 1994): 1054–73. http://www.jstor.org.ezproxy.lib.usf.edu/stable/2932171.

Samuels, Wilfred D., and Clenora Hudson-Weems. *Toni Morrison*. Boston: Twayne, 1990.

Sanchez, Martha I. Chew. "El Diablo en una Botella Nortena: Music and the Construction of Mexican Masculinity." *Third Text* 18, no. 5 (Sept. 2004): 483–95. doi:10.1080/0952882042000251714.

Savran, David. "The Sadomasochist in the Closet: White Masculinity and the Culture of Victimization." *Differences: A Journal of Feminist Cultural Studies* 8, no. 2 (Summer 1996): 127–52.

Schappell, Elissa. "Toni Morrison: The Art of Fiction." In *Toni Morrison's* Song of Solomon: *A Casebook*, 233–66. Edited by Jan Furman. Oxford: Oxford University Press, 2003.

Scott, Darieck. *Extravagant Abjection: Blackness, Power, and Sexuality in the African American Literary Imagination*. New York: New York University Press, 2010.

Sedgwick, Eve Kosofsky. *Epistemology of the Closet*. Berkeley: University of California Press, 1990.

Shaw, Patrick W. "The Kid's Fate, the Judge's Guilt: Ramifications of Closure in Cormac McCarthy's *Blood Meridian*." *The Southern Literary Journal* 30, no. 1 (Fall 1997): 102–19.

Silverman, Kaja. *Male Subjectivity at the Margins*. New York: Routledge, 1992.

Slotkin, Richard. *Gunfighter Nation*. New York: Atheneum, 1992.

Smith, Valerie. "The Quest for and Discovery of Identity in Toni Morrison's *Song of Solomon*." In *Toni Morrison's* Song of Solomon: *A Casebook*, 27–41. Edited by Jan Furman. Oxford: Oxford University Press, 2003.

Snyder, Philip A. "Cowboy Codes in Cormac McCarthy's Border Trilogy." In *A Cormac McCarthy Companion: The Border Trilogy*, 198–227. Edited by Edwin T. Arnold and Dianne C. Luce. Jackson: University Press of Mississippi, 2001.

Spencer, Andrew Blair. "A Cowboy Looks at Reality: The Death of the American Frontier and the Illumination of the Cowboy Myth in Cormac McCarthy's *All the Pretty Horses*." In *Western Futures: Perspectives on the Humanities at the Millennium*, 143–57. Edited by Stephen Tchudi. Reno: Halcyon Press, 1999.

Spurgeon, Sara. "Pledged in Blood: Truth and Redemption in Cormac McCarthy's *All the Pretty Horses*." In *Cormac McCarthy*, 79–94. Edited by Harold Bloom. Philadelphia: Chelsea House, 2002.

———. "The Sacred Hunter and the Eucharist of the Wilderness: Mythic Reconstructions in *Blood Meridian*." In *Cormac McCarthy: New Directions*, 75–101. Edited by James D. Lilley. Albuquerque: University of New Mexico Press, 2002.

Stegner, Wallace. "Walter Clark's Frontier." In *Walter Van Tilburg Clark: Critiques*, 60–75. Edited by Charlton Laird. Reno: University of Nevada Press, 1983.

Story, Ralph. "An Excursion into the Black World: The 'Seven Days' in Toni Morrison's *Song of Solomon.*" *Black American Literature Forum* 23, no. 1 (Spring 1989): 149–58. http://www.jstor.org.ezproxy.lib.usf.edu/stable/2903998.

Sullivan, Nell. "Boys Will Be Boys and Girls Will Be Gone: The Circuit of Male Desire in Cormac McCarthy's Border Trilogy." In *A Cormac McCarthy Companion: The Border Trilogy,* 228–55. Edited by Edwin T. Arnold and Dianne C. Luce. Jackson: University Press of Mississippi, 2001.

Toombs, Charles P. "Black-Gay Man Chaos in *Another Country.*" In *Re-viewing James Baldwin: Things Not Seen,* 105–27. Edited by D. Quentin Miller. Philadelphia: Temple University Press, 2000.

Walker, Alice. *In Search of Our Mothers' Gardens.* San Diego: Harcourt Brace Jovanovich, 1983.

Wallach, Rick. "Twenty-Five Years of *Blood Meridian.*" *Southwestern American Literature* 36, no. 3 (Summer 2011): 5–7.

Warner, Michael. *The Trouble with Normal: Sex, Politics, and the Ethics of Queer Life.* New York: Free Press, 1999.

Weatherby, W. J. *James Baldwin: Artist on Fire.* New York: Laurel, 1989.

Weeks, Jeffrey. *Sexuality.* Chichester: Ellis Horwood, 1986.

———. *Sexuality and Its Discontents.* London: Routledge, 1985.

Wegner, John. "Whose Story Is It?: History and Fiction in Cormac McCarthy's *All the Pretty Horses.*" *Southern Quarterly: A Journal of the Arts in the South* 36, no. 2 (Winter 1998): 103–10.

Wesley, Marilyn C. *Violent Adventure.* Charlottesville: Virginia University Press, 2003.

West, Cornel. *The Cornel West Reader.* New York: Basic Books, 1999.

White, E. Frances. "The Evidence of Things Not Seen: The Alchemy of Race and Sexuality." In *James Baldwin and Toni Morrison: Comparative Critical and Theoretical Essays,* 239–60. Edited by Lovalerie King and Lynn Orilla Scott. New York: Palgrave, 2006.

Wilchins, Riki. *Queer Theory, Gender Theory: An Instant Primer.* Los Angeles: Alyson, 2004.

Wilentz, Gay. "Civilizations Underneath: African Heritage as Cultural Discourse in Toni Morrison's *Song of Solomon.*" *African American Review* 26, no. 1 (Spring 1992): 61–76.

Woodson, Linda Townley. "Deceiving the Will to Truth: The Semiotic Foundation of *All the Pretty Horses.*" In *Sacred Violence: Cormac McCarthy's Western Novels,* 51–56. Edited by Wade Hall and Rick Wallach. El Paso: Texas Western Press, 2002.

Woodward, Richard B. "Cormac McCarthy's Venomous Fiction." *The New York Times Magazine,* Apr. 19, 1992, 28–31.

Woolf, Virginia. *A Room of One's Own.* 1929. London: Harvest, 1989.

Zaborowska, Magdalena J. *James Baldwin's Turkish Decade: Erotics of Exile.* Durham: Duke University Press, 2009.

Index

About the Author

Josef Benson is an assistant professor of English at the University of Wisconsin–Parkside, where he offers courses in contemporary literature, African American literature, poetry writing, and fiction writing. Over the past seventeen years, Dr. Benson's cultural history, literary and theoretical criticism, fiction, poetry, and creative nonfiction have appeared in over twenty publications, including *Journal of Medical Humanities, Journal of Bisexuality, Southwestern American Literature, The Raymond Carver Review, Saw Palm, Moon City Review, The Adirondack Review,* and *Prick of the Spindle.* Dr. Benson holds creative writing degrees from Missouri State University and the University of South Florida, as well as a Ph.D. in literature with a heavy emphasis in gender theory, also from the University of South Florida, where he studied primarily with Susan Mooney, John Henry Fleming, and Jay Hopler.

CPSIA information can be obtained at www.ICGtesting.com
Printed in the USA
BVOW07*1325080714

358264BV00001B/3/P